GLOBAL HISTORY OF THE PRESENT

Series editor | Nicholas Guyatt

In the Global History of the Present series, historians address the upheavals in world history since 1989, as we have lurched from the Cold War to the War on Terror. Each book considers the unique story of an individual country or region, refuting grandiose claims of 'the end of history', and linking local narratives to international developments.

Lively and accessible, these books are ideal introductions to the contemporary politics and history of a diverse range of countries. By bringing a historical perspective to recent debates and events, from democracy and terrorism to nationalism and globalization, the series challenges assumptions about the past and the present.

Published

Thabit A. J. Abdullah, *Dictatorship, Imperialism and Chaos: Iraq since 1989*

Alejandra Bronfman, *On the Move: The Caribbean since 1989*

Timothy Cheek, *Living with Freedom: China since 1989*

Alexander Dawson, *First World Dreams: Mexico since 1989*

Padraic Kenney, *The Burdens of Freedom: Eastern Europe since 1989*

Stephen Lovell, *Destination in Doubt: Russia since 1989*

Hyung Gu Lynn, *Bipolar Orders: The Two Koreas since 1989*

Nivedita Menon and Aditya Nigam, *Power and Contestation: India since 1989*

Forthcoming

James D. Le Sueur, *Between Terror and Democracy: Algeria since 1989*

Mark LeVine, *Impossible Peace: Israel/Palestine since 1989*

Helena Pohlandt-McCormick, *What Have We Done? South Africa since 1989*

Bryan McCann, *The Throes of Democracy: Brazil since 1989*

Nicholas Guyatt is lecturer in history at the University of York.

About the author

Hyung Gu Lynn is the AECL/KECPO Chair in Korean Research at the University of British Columbia. He has researched and taught at universities in Canada, the USA, South Korea, and Japan. His current research projects range from economic history to contemporary popular culture, plastic surgery to epistemology.

Bipolar Orders: The Two Koreas since 1989

Hyung Gu Lynn

Fernwood Publishing
HALIFAX | WINNIPEG

Zed Books
LONDON | NEW YORK

Bipolar Orders: The Two Koreas since 1989 was first published in 2007 by

in Canada: Fernwood Publishing, 32 Oceanvista Lane, Site 2A, Box 5,
Black Point, NS B0J 1B0
www.fernwoodpublishing.ca

in the rest of the world: Zed Books Ltd., 7 Cynthia Street, London N1 9JF, UK
and Room 400, 175 Fifth Avenue, New York, NY 10010, USA
www.zedbooks.co.uk

Cover designed by Andrew Corbett
Set in Melior and Futura by Long House Publishing Services, Cumbria, UK
Printed and bound in Malta by Gutenberg Press Ltd

Distributed in the USA exclusively by Palgrave Macmillan, a division of
St Martin's Press, LLC, 175 Fifth Avenue, New York, NY 10010

A catalogue record for this book is available from the British Library
Library of Congress Cataloging-in-Publication Data available

ISBN 978-1-84277-742-8 Hb (Zed Books)
ISBN 978-1-84277-743-5 Pb (Zed Books)
ISBN 978-1-55266-241-0 Pb (Fernwood Publishing)

Library and Archives Canada Cataloguing in Publication
Lynn, Hyung Gu, 1965-
Bipolar orders : the two Koreas since 1989 / Hyung Gu Lynn.
Includes bibliographical references and index.
ISBN 978-1-55266-241-0
1. Korea (South)—History—1988-. 2. Korea (North)—History.
3. Korea (South)—Foreign relations—Korea (North). 4. Korea (North)—
Foreign relations—Korea (South). I. Title.
DS922.462.L95 2007   951.904'3   C2007-903402-0

Contents

Acknowledgments

I am very grateful to Nick Guyatt, the editor of the Global History of the Present series, for inviting me to contribute to the project and for his insightful comments on the manuscript. I would also like to express my gratitude to the entire staff at Zed Books for their flexibility and efficiency. In particular, I must thank Ellen McKinlay for her constant patience and sound suggestions. Pat Harper also provided a rigorous reading that helped me avoid various inconsistencies. The anonymous reader provided some useful comments as well.

This book would not have been possible without the unwavering support of my parents, C. W. and K. H. Lynn, and my brother A. K. Lynn. Relatives, friends and colleagues in South Korea, Japan, Canada, the US, the UK and other countries also directly or indirectly facilitated the completion of this book. And last but not least, thanks, S.F.T., for everything. The author is however, solely responsible for any errors in fact or interpretation.

Acronyms

APEC	Asia Pacific Economic Cooperation
CAP	Consolidated Appeals Program (United Nations)
CCEJ	Citizens' Coalition for Economic Justice
CUBS	Citizens United for Better Society
DCRK	Democratic Confederal Republic of Korea
DLP	Democratic Liberal Party
DMZ	Demilitarized Zone
DPRK	Democratic People's Republic of Korea (North Korea)
ELD	export-led development
FAO	Food and Agriculture Organization
FDI	foreign direct investment
FKTU	Federation of Korean Trade Unions
FTA	Free Trade Agreement
GNI	gross national income
GNP	Grand National Party
GNP	gross national product
HCI	Heavy and Chemical Industries initiative
HEU	highly enriched uranium
IAEA	International Atomic Energy Association
IFAD	International Fund for Agricultural Development
IMF	International Monetary Fund
INGO	international non-governmental organization
ISI	import substitution industrialization
JCMK	Joint Committee on Migrant Workers in Korea
JSA	Joint Security Area

KBS	Korean Broadcasting System
KCTU	Korean Confederation of Trade Unions
KFEM	Korean Federation for Environmental Movement
KFSB	Korean Federation of Small Businesses
KEDO	Korean Energy Development Organization
KPA	Korean People's Army (North Korea)
KPR	Korean People's Republic
KTU	Korean Teachers and Education Workers Union
KWAU	Korean Women's Association United
KWP	Korean Workers' Party (North Korea)
LWR	light-water reactor
MDL	Military Demarcation Line
MDP	Millennial Democratic Party
NGO	non-governmental organization
NPO	non-profit organization
NPT	Non-Proliferation Treaty
OECD	Organization for Economic Cooperation and Development
OOP	Our Open Party / Uri Party
PDS	Public Distribution System (North Korea)
ROK	Republic of Korea (South Korea)
SOFA	Status of Forces Agreement
SOFE	System of Optimally Functioning Socialist Economy
UNFPA	United Nations Population Fund
USAMGIK	United States Army Military Government in Korea
WFP	World Food Programme
WTO	World Trade Organization

Notes on Transliteration

I follow the McCune–Reischauer system of transliteration for most Korean personal and place names throughout this book. However, in cases where non-standard transliterations are widely used (for example, Syngman Rhee), I use the more common form followed by the McCune–Reischauer transliteration in parenthesis at the first appearance of the name or place.

In the text, most Korean names (with some exceptions, for example, Syngman Rhee) are listed with the family names first, followed by the given name. For authors of works cited in the notes, I have listed the family names first unless the author reverses the order in the transliterated version of their name. Also, I have taken the liberty of inserting hyphens between the two first-name syllables for all Korean names in the text for consistency and clarity (even though I do not use a hyphen for my own given name).

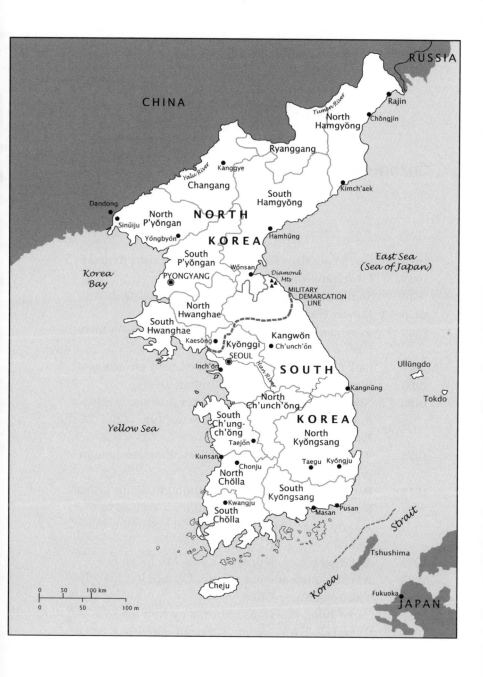

CHINA

RUSSIA

Rajin

Tumen River

North
Hamgyŏng

Chŏngjin

Ryanggang

Yalu River

Kanggye

Changang

Kimch'aek

South
Hamgyŏng

Dandong

North
P'yŏngan

NORTH

Sinŭiju

KOREA

Yŏngbyŏn

Hamhŭng

South
P'yŏngan

Wŏnsan

East Sea
(Sea of Japan)

Korea
Bay

PYONGYANG

Diamond
Mts

MILITARY
DEMARCATION
LINE

North
Hwanghae

South
Hwanghae

Kaesŏng

Kyŏnggi

SEOUL

Kangwŏn

Ch'unch'ŏn

Ullŭngdo

Inch'ŏn

Han River

SOUTH

Tokdo

North
Ch'unch'ŏng

Kangnŭng

Yellow Sea

South
Ch'ung-
ch'ŏng

KOREA

North
Kyŏngsang

Taejŏn

Kunsan

Taegu

Kyŏngju

Chonju

North
Chŏlla

Kwangju

South
Kyŏngsang

Masan

Pusan

Strait

South
Chŏlla

Tshushima

Korea

0   50   100 km

0   50   100 m

Cheju

Fukuoka

JAPAN

Map of the Korean Peninsula

Chronology

1910 Japan colonizes Korea; ending the Chosŏn dynasty
1945 Liberation from Japan
1948 South Korea and North Korea are established
1950–53 Korean War
1960 Syngman Rhee ousted in South Korea; Chang Myŏn
       takes over
1961 Park Chung-Hee overthrows the Chang government
1965 South Korea–Japan Normalization Treaty
1968 North Korean spies attack the presidential residence,
       the Blue House, in South Korea; capture of the US ship
       Pueblo by North Korea
1971 Park Chung-Hee narrowly defeats Kim Dae-Jung in
       presidential election
1972 Park announces Yusin Constitution in South Korea;
       North Korea's second constitution is revised to
       acknowledge Pyongyang rather than Seoul as the
       capital
1973 Kim Dae-Jung is kidnapped from his Tokyo hotel
1974 Assassination attempt on Park Chung-Hee; his wife,
       Yuk Yŏng-Su, is killed
1979 Park Chung-Hee is assassinated by Kim Jae-Kyu
1980 Chun Doo-Hwan's coup; Kwangju uprising; Kim Dae-
       Jung arrested
1981 Seoul is awarded the 1988 Summer Olympics
1983 Assassination attempt on Chun Doo-Hwan in Rangoon:
       17 South Korean and 3 Burmese officials die

1984	North Korea sends aid to South Korea after severe flooding in the South
1985	Opposition increases seats in National Assembly elections in South Korea; North Korea joins the Nuclear Non-Proliferation Treaty (NPT); first visits between families separated by the North–South division
1986	Seoul hosts the Asian Games
1987	Democratization Declaration in South Korea; Roh Tae-Woo is elected president of South Korea; KAL bombing incident
1988	"Anti-communist" education is replaced by "Unification Education" in South Korea; Seoul Olympics
1990	South Korea–Russia Normalization
1991	First North Korea–Japan Normalization talks; Kim Hak-Sun becomes the first "comfort women" survivor to testify publicly under her own name
1992	Kim Young-Sam is elected president of South Korea; South Korea–China Normalization
1993	North Korea nuclear crisis – threatens to withdraw from NPT
1994	Kim Il-Sung dies; Agreed Framework between US and North Korea; Kim Jong-Il succeeds his father to power; Sŏngsu Bridge collapses
1995	The Korean Energy Development Organization is established; the UN sends the first shipment of food aid to North Korea
1996	Hosting of 2002 soccer World Cup tournament awarded jointly to South Korea and Japan; South Korea joins the OECD
1997	Hanbo Bribery Scandal; Chun Doo-Hwan is sentenced to life imprisonment; financial crisis; Kim Dae-Jung is elected president of South Korea; Hwang Jang-Yop defects from North to South Korea; Kim Jong-Il consolidates his hold on power as the period of mourning of his father's death ends
1998	North Korea test launches missiles; Diamond Mountains Tours begin in North Korea

1999   Berlin Agreement between North and US

2000   Construction to reopen the Kyŏnggi rail line between South Korea and North Korea begins; second meeting of separated families; Madeleine Albright visits North Korea; South–North Summit in Pyongyang

2001   Kim Jong-Il visits China, Russia

2002   George W. Bush's "Axis of Evil" speech; South Korea and Japan host soccer World Cup; Japan–North Korea Summit in Pyongyang

2003   Roh Moo-Hyun is inaugurated as president of South Korea

2004   Impeachment of Roh fails; second Japan–North Korea summit

2006   North Korea conducts nuclear test; Roh Moo-Hyun's popularity at record low in South Korea

2007   US and South Korea agree to an FTA; first test run of passenger trains cross the DMZ; IAEA inspectors verify shutdown of the main North Korean nuclear reactor that had been agreed during the Six Party Talks meetings earlier in the year.

Introduction | Bipolar Orders

Korea.

For those who watch television news or glance through newspaper headlines on a regular basis, the word might invoke two starkly contrasting images. Satellite photographs of nighttime on the Korean peninsula show the Southern half below the 38th parallel densely packed with glittering lights, while the Northern half sits above, not a single light marring its darkness. This chiaroscuro is an apparent embodiment of Richard Rorty's observation that "the thesis will escape our notice ... unless it catches the reflection, the pale fire, of the ... antithesis."[1]

One Korea is incandescent with economic success, with names like Samsung, LG, and Hyundai having wended their way into the global consumer lexicon through their consumer electronics and automobiles. The population has seemingly been transformed overnight from the impoverished farmers who occasionally meandered into the backdrop for American doctors on the TV show *MASH* into successful businessmen garbed in fashionable suits, competing for dominance in the global market for semiconductors, mobile phones, steel, and behemoth tankers. The capital city of Seoul is bathed in neon and traffic, constantly abuzz with dreams wrought of capitalism and consumerism. South Korea (officially known as the Republic of Korea) appears to be a developmentalist dream brought to life, a capitalist success story polished to a poster-like sheen.

The other Korea is the "evil" doppelganger, an anachronism in the post-Perestroika world, often pejoratively described as a "rogue state" or the "Hermit Kingdom." Sharing essentially the same language, cuisine, and pre-1945 history as its capitalist sibling to the south, for all appearances it clings with desperate zeal to anachronistic, even alien doctrines and practices. At night, the boulevards of Pyongyang – its showcase capital – are empty and pitch black, as streetlights are often unlit because of energy shortages. Branded one of the three states comprising an "axis of evil" (along with Iraq and Iran) by US presidential pronouncement in 2002, North Korea (officially known as the Democratic People's Republic of Korea) remains a *bête noire de jour*, constant fodder for headline tickers and journalistic sensationalism around the world.

In between the polar opposite worlds, a four-kilometer-wide strip of sylvan land called the Demilitarized Zone (hereafter DMZ) winds along for some 250 kilometers, dividing the two Koreas roughly at the 38th parallel. Technically, the DMZ extends two kilometers on each side from the Military Demarcation Line (hereafter MDL) that marks the front line when the truce agreement was signed to end the Korean War in July 1953. High barbed wire, thick concrete barricades with grated metal gates, military vehicles, and uniformed soldiers bristle on either side of the DMZ.

Within the DMZ, hills looming above the valleys are dotted with guard posts, watchtowers, and bunkers. On some hilltops, the watchtowers on the far side of the MDL are close enough to spot with the naked eye. The muffled sound of an explosion occasionally drifts up to a watchtower from the valley below – the sound of an animal triggering one of the 1.2 million landmines planted within the DMZ. Surveys have confirmed that 146 species of rare animals and plants are the primary residents of the land, with two very small human villages on the southern and northern sides.[2] Small teams of troops that patrol either side of the DMZ within the fenced-off area are regular but temporary intruders onto the scene. The patrol teams are technically not allowed to cross the MDL, although there have been numerous violations over the years. The tension is palpable: newswires have been laden for decades now with dramatic descriptions of the DMZ, probably the most oft-cited quote being by US president Bill Clinton, who during a 2003 visit stated that the DMZ was "the scariest place on Earth."

Near the west coast of the DMZ lies a roughly circular area of land about 800 meters in diameter called the Joint Security Area (hereafter JSA), often referred to as "Panmunjom." Two three-floor concrete buildings mirror each other across an unfenced portion of the MDL, with soldiers from each side standing like menacing mannequins within close physical proximity, with only a 40-centimeter-wide piece of concrete marking the MDL separating them. In between the two concrete buildings, several smaller huts, powder blue on both the outside and the inside walls, straddle the MDL precisely half on one side, half on the other. These huts have served as meeting rooms for negotiations between the two sides, as temporary reunion spaces for families separated by the division, and as exchange points for prisoners. Fatal clashes have occurred here as well, such as the horrific so-called Axe Murders – an incident in 1976 where North Korean soldiers killed two US soldiers (one with axes) during a clash in the forests within the JSA – and a 1984 shoot-out during a Soviet defector's rush over the MDL that resulted in four deaths. Before the Axe Murders, soldiers had been allowed to cross the MDL under limited terms but this practice was ceased. After the 1984 incident, the North Koreans began posting guards that faced back or at least sideways towards their own side to prevent future dashes into the South.

As a site that distils international tensions into one riveting scene, the JSA is a popular destination for an estimated 100,000 or more tourists per year. It also remains a frequently invoked visual symbol of the polarities that divide the peninsula, especially after some incident or other triggers a media competition to portray North Korea as the oddest and the most menacing country in the world.

The Significance of the Two Koreas in Contemporary Global History

Even in the age of globalization, in which global information networks and free trade agreements abound, literal and figurative walls and boundaries exist between all nation-states. Nonetheless, the binary on the Korean peninsula is galvanizing for its appearance of being caught in a time warp in the post-Berlin Wall world – "the Cold War's last divide," according to Bill Clinton in his 1997 State of the Union address. The collapse of the Soviet bloc did have an undeniably major impact on both North and South Korea. This diptych of accelerated capitalism and intransigent communism packed onto a small peninsula seems inherently compelling, possibly triggering associations with Robert Louis Stevenson's Dr Jekyll and Mr Hyde, or perhaps the Chimera, the monster that pads around Greek mythology endowed with, in most accounts, the head of a lion, the body of a goat, and the tail of a serpent, a hybrid creature composed of oddly juxtaposed parts. The vividness of the literary associations notwithstanding, there are several more intellectually compelling reasons why the post-1989 histories of the two Koreas are important within the context of the global history of the present.

Against the 'end of history'

First, there is a very prevalent view of world history that sees 1989 as a watershed between outdated communism and a universal capitalism. While many countries challenge this teleology, few do so more starkly than the two Koreas. Given the contrasting political systems, the polar opposite economic situations, and the ostensibly ossified lines of engagement, the standard narrative of post-1989 millennial capitalism inexorably sweeping away the crumbling remnants of the old communist order does not seem to apply. If we take the collapse of the Berlin Wall as the dawn of a new era of capitalist globalization and liberal democratization, the logical expectation would be that North Korea, one of the smaller socialist states, would have evaporated from the unbearable lightness of its own irrelevance. The distant rumble of seismic changes in Eastern Europe in 1989 reached Pyongyang with clarity and force: ultimately, however, the disintegration of the former Soviet bloc only strengthened North Korea's resolve to stay the course.

Nevertheless, 1989 is not necessarily the year that stands out to most observers as the most prominent in the history of the two Koreas. In South Korea, the pros and cons of the "1987 system" or the long-term effects of the "1997 IMF Crisis" occupy academic attention; for North Korea, the dynastic succession of 1994 and the nuclear test of 2006 tend to attract as much analysis as the economic impact of the post-1989 changes in North Korea's relations with Russia and China. 1989 matters, but it is hardly the watershed we might have expected on this alleged front line of the Cold War.

Accelerated change

The second reason why the contemporary history of the two Koreas is significant is the pace of change, especially in the South.

The population has been aging, fertility dropping, divorce rates rising, and the population profile becoming more multicultural at an accelerated pace in South Korea. These demographic transformations have combined with epochal experiences such as the Korean War or the 1987 democracy movement that branded each cohort to exacerbate chasms in values and attitudes between various generational groups. Generational gaps exist in all societies, of course, and many of the intergenerational differences have been occasionally exaggerated in South Korea in an attempt to reduce the complex factors behind socio-political changes to a single cause. Nevertheless, the South Korean case is particularly salient in that the gaps and the changes have been greatly augmented by the speed and intensity of historical change.

As China, Russia, and other transitional economies navigate their way from socialism to more liberalized market economies, they have been experiencing similar, possibly even more pronounced, generational gaps and demographic problems. Thus, while the details will undoubtedly vary, the basic trajectories and social fissures that have arisen in South Korea may serve as usefully proximate templates for challenges awaiting other nation-states. Rather than view South Korea simply as a model of authoritarian development followed by democratization, one of the "third waves" of democracy, it is as interesting to frame South Korea as an experiment in "turbo-capitalism" – accelerated capitalist change with the button stuck on Fast Forward.[3]

Changes in North Korea have also been significant since 1989. The overall system has remained, but the ending of subsidies from the Soviet Union, large-scale famines, and economic malaise have forced experiments with profit incentives, markets, and new allocations of political power. If the South Korean government has been scurrying to keep up with accelerated social changes, the North Korean government has been facing the challenge of managing change while retaining political control and at the same time drastically reducing its obligations to its citizens.

Extreme polarization

The third reason why the Koreas matter to contemporary history is the extreme polarization that becomes evident when the recent shifts in the two Koreas are juxtaposed. Long-term domestic processes have been just as important as global trends in fueling this process of accelerating divergence. In South Korea, for example, the transition from decades of authoritarian dictatorships to a sustainable democracy began in 1987. The South Korean economy, despite several fluctuations in fortune, was ranked tenth in the world as of 2005 in terms of annual gross domestic product (GDP), the value of all final goods and services produced within a country in a given year.[4] The financial crisis of 1997 marked the beginning of the so-called IMF Period, but the last payment of South Korea's loan to the International Monetary Fund (IMF) was completed in the summer of 2001, nearly three years ahead of schedule. Since the late 1990s, South Korean films and television melodramas have been ubiquitous in many parts of Asia, while labyrinthine shopping malls and global brand names dot the streets of the ritzy neighborhoods in the capital, Seoul. South Korea has become first or second in the world for broadband penetration rates, and plastic surgery has become a widespread practice among young and old, male and female. In fact, the current president, Roh Moo-Hyun (No Mu-Hyôn), apparently concerned with his modest mien, underwent a surgical procedure that is the most popular in South Korea, the creation of a double eyelid fold (often called the Asian blepharoplasty), after becoming president.

In contrast, during the same period, in 1994 to be precise, North Korea's political system witnessed the first dynastic succession in a communist state after the death of Kim Il-Sung (Kim Il-Sŏng), who had ruled North Korea since its formation in 1948. Contrary to predictions by some outside observers of an imminent collapse, Kim Il-Sung's eldest son, Kim Jong-Il (Kim Chŏng-Il), who had been publicly introduced as the successor in 1980, inherited the reins of power, still garbed in his familiar custom-tailored grey work suit. Most signs indicate that despite the presence of various factions within the ruling elite, and the occasional wishful reporting by foreign presses, Kim Jong-Il still maintains a firm grip on power.

In foreign policy, since the spate of normalization agreements with several intermediary powers such as Italy, Canada, the Philippines, and the United Kingdom, and the realization of the historic Pyongyang summit meeting between Kim Jong-Il and South Korean president Kim Dae-Jung (Kim Tae-Chung) in 2000,

North Korea has become increasingly isolated from the rest of the world, especially after becoming the first country to withdraw from the Nuclear Non-Proliferation Treaty in early 2003 and after its nuclear weapons test in fall 2006. The economy experienced a steady decline from the early 1980s, and massive floods and famine in the early and mid-1990s exacerbated the downward trajectory. While the worst of the famines seem to be over, natural disasters still wreak havoc on the food supply, especially in the more remote provinces in the northeast. The general populace has extremely limited access to the outside world, with restrictions on travel and the use of cell phones, and no access to the Worldwide Web for the average citizen. Consequently, the polarization of the two Koreas spills over various areas and shows very few signs of change in trajectory.

Decussation effects

Fourth, what makes the contemporary history of the Korean peninsula even more compelling is that rather than the above polarizations bringing South Koreans closer to the US, these changes have been accompanied in South Korea by an apparent growth in anti-Americanism and in pro-North Korea sentiments. Standard variations of modernization theory would predict linear correlations between economic development, democracy, improved relations with the US, and harder stances against socialist countries. In South Korea, however, development and democracy have not necessarily resulted in increasing compliance or agreement with US politics or policies. Expectations of divergences notwithstanding, development, democratization, and consumerism appear to have improved South Korea's relations with North Korea. Opinions within South Korea towards the North are extremely polarized, with older generations and more conservative political parties in favor of a more hard-line policy towards their northern neighbor. Nevertheless, government policies have remained consistently conciliatory since Kim Dae-Jung introduced the Sunshine Policy in 1997.

Perhaps the most widely reported instance of anti-American sentiment in South Korea occurred when demonstrators gathered to protest in the winter of 2002 after a US military court found two American soldiers not guilty of negligent homicide in a case involving a military vehicle that crushed two fourteen-year-old South Korean girls to death. The incident, the verdict, and the demonstrations all highlighted the growing opposition to the presence of some 37,000 US troops stationed in South Korea. Various polls taken since 2000 have subsequently confirmed that there has been an increase in negative sentiments towards the US and its president, George W. Bush, especially among South Koreans under fifty.

As is the case in most industrialized countries, South Korea is frequently probed via public opinion polls, and these often portray a morass of contradictory and fleeting sentiments. Even with this caveat, it might come as a surprise to many readers to learn that a January 2004 poll indicated that 40% of South Koreans viewed the US as the primary security threat as compared with 32% who identified North Korea.[5] An April 2005 survey conducted by a different company indicated that 30% saw the US as the primary threat to South Korean security, followed by Japan at 29%, and North Korea at 18%.[6]

These developments appear to be counterintuitive. After all, North Korea and South Korea fought a prolonged, vicious, and traumatizing war from 1950 to 1953 that left an estimated 2.5 million North and South Koreans dead, and the economy of both sides in utter ruins. In fact, the two countries remain technically at war, since the Armistice Agreement of 1953 that brought an end to the war was a ceasefire agreement, a truce rather than a peace treaty.[7] Aside from its intensity, the war also brought in Chinese troops and Soviet advisors and equipment to the North, and a United Nations force, composed largely of US troops but also of soldiers from fifteen other member nations, to support the South.

This contradictory phenomenon of apparently improved relations despite polarization and the convergence of South Korea with the US is reminiscent of the "X-pattern" or crossover pattern of nerves in the human body, what is called "decussation." This crossover effect explains the triggering of a reaction in, say, the right foot when a nerve on the left hand is stimulated. As applied to changes on the Korean peninsula, the polarization of the Koreas and the South's convergence with the US are resulting in more criticisms of the US and more pro-North Korean sentiments in South Korea, what I call a "decussation effect." This book will examine whether this "decussation effect" is an optical illusion, a temporary aberration, or an indication of incremental progress toward reunification.

Bipolar order

Fifth, the contemporary histories of the two Koreas are important in that they encourage the questioning of what constitutes the "natural" boundaries of the nation-state, territorial and demographic. Many countries seek a return to a previous territorial configuration through reunification or irredentism. However, boundaries have been redrawn throughout history and need to be constantly maintained via border checks, armies, international law, and rhetoric. The historical contingencies driving the formation of nation-states and the clarification of national boundaries should provoke us to question how far back in history territorial claims should or can go, and what constitutes a legitimate boundary. Why is it that some nation-states must be "reunified," and others must be "liberated"? In December 2006, Roh Moo-Hyun, after posing the question of why unification was necessary, answered his own question by invoking the need to "ensure peace," and asserted that "those who share the same blood, language and culture should get together and live as one."[8]

If it is the destiny of peoples sharing a common history, language, and genetic pool to "live as one," why is it that there seems to be no public outcry calling for the restoration of the union of Finland with Sweden, which ruled Finland for nearly seven hundred years (1150–1809)? Where are the academic works generating "reunification" scenarios for Norwegian "reunification" with Denmark, since that union lasted for nearly three hundred years (1536–1814)? Why shouldn't India and Pakistan be "reunified," the UK, Canada, the US, New Zealand, and Australia be reconstituted into a new Commonwealth, or Hawai'i granted independence from the US?

Of course there are various differences and similarities in the various historical situations and geographic settings. But the variations should not deflect our attention from the fact that some unifications or irredentist aspirations are simply assumed to be normal or natural, while others simply trigger puzzlement. For example, some scholars assert that Korea did not undergo a process of decolonization, or experience complete state formation, because it was liberated not through a war of independence but via external intervention during World War Two. However, such statements merely reinforce the notion that the two Koreas somehow suffer from incomplete state formation without stopping to ask whether any process of liberation or decolonization is "natural." In fact, most decolonization processes in modern history have been achieved through external intervention and compromise. Any reasonably observant person who has seen the Canadian currency, adorned as it is with pictures of British royalty, or official Canadian government ceremonies dripping with colonial implications, might conclude that Canada suffers from a far more incomplete state formation than do the two Koreas. Yet there are no major scholarly subfields or political movements dedicated to making Canada a republic or abolishing such posts as the Governor General of Canada, the official representative of the monarch in the country.[9] Although the Quebec sovereignty issue and relations with the US understandably dominate public debate, the fact that the only formal republican organization in Canada, Citizens for a Canadian Republic, was not founded until 2002 should still cause some reflection about why some questions are seen as somehow self-evident, and others are not.[10]

The intention is not to mount a case against the "unification" of the Korean peninsula, but to question whether it is a necessary or inevitable process. Nor is it possible to overlook the incalculable personal tragedies that were created by the division of Korea. Anyone who has seen the tears of anguished joy flow when family members have been reunited for the first time in fifty years during one of the brief reunions negotiated by the two governments cannot help but feel that the contemporary history of the two Koreas has generated more human costs than any geopolitical calculations can ever hope to capture. While the actual number of first-generation family members currently affected by the division is hardly the "ten million" bandied about in many journalistic reports or used metaphorically in Korea, it is likely that there are around 750,000 people with immediate families that they cannot visit due to political conditions.[11]

The future of inter-Korean relations may involve close interactions, but as separate nation-states – as has been the case since 1948. The problem, it could be argued, is not the division itself, but the ways in which human mobility between the two countries is restricted. Willingness to question the boundaries that are being normalized requires challenging the preconceived notion that South Korea and North Korea somehow suffer from incomplete state formation or unnatural division.

In spite of the innumerable personal tragedies lodged between the lines of history textbooks, the recent history of the Korean peninsula has not just been a "history of the divided period,"[12] a figurative "bipolar disorder." Rather, it has been the development of two divergent systems and, within the single racial category of "Korean" over a long-term span, what might be termed a "bipolar order." In other words, a system that has been maintained, for better or for worse, over a sixty-year period should not be dismissed as a mere temporary aberration. In fact, the governments of both North and South Korea have recognized in *de facto* terms the existence of a "bipolar order" since the early 1970s. When South Korea explicitly announced in the early 1970s that the first goal would be to develop, then unify, the mathematical formula for the most expedient and low-cost method of maintaining stability came to the fore: 1 race = 2 systems. As Roh Moo-Hyun noted in a speech in May 2006, "The South Korean people do not want a collapse of the North Korean regime."[13]

It is also important to clarify that the bipolar order involves 1 race but 2 ethnicities. Definitions of the concept/term/category of "ethnicity" are often disputed. While "ethnicity" and "race" overlap, they are not synonymous. Ethnicity is generally viewed as a more general category that includes notions of race, cultural identity, and ancestry: in this sense of the term, North Koreans and South Koreans clearly can be seen to have distinct ethnic identities as they have each developed distinctive values and identities despite notions of common ancestry or racial identity.[14]

The very process of polarization, of developments propelling the two countries in opposite directions, is helping to maintain the current formula of 1 race (2 ethnicities) = 2 systems, rather than promoting a 1 race = 1 system outcome. The relative gap in economic performance allows South Korea to feel comfortable in its relations with North Korea, while nowadays democratization differentiates South Korea from North Korea far more than when military dictatorships were in place practicing the same kind of oppression on its citizens as did the government of the North. For North Korea as well, the policy priorities seem clear: stabilize North–South relations, implement economic reforms, normalize relations with potential sources of capital such as the US and Japan, and maintain nuclear capacity. Unification, at least as encapsulated in the 1 race = 1 system formula, is not actually high on the list of priorities for either government.

Objectives

The above discussion triggers a cascade of questions. How did the peninsula become divided in the first place? How did South Korea become democratic? What explains the long-term economic decline and political isolation of North Korea? Is North Korea a threat, and, if so, for whom? Why is the South Korean government "soft" towards North Korea, as is claimed by both domestic and foreign critics? Why has there been a counterintuitive improvement in relations between North and South? What roles, if any, do foreign powers such as the US and Japan have in inter-Korean relations? This book is a thematic analysis of the intertwined fates of North and South Korea that attempts to answer these and other questions.

Objectives of the book and the series

As part of a series on the "global history of the present," the analysis in this book is focused on the "present," defined as the post-1989 years. It takes as its starting point the critical examination of the post-1989 narrative that has the United States proclaiming victory in the Cold War, some commentators hailing liberal democracy as the terminus of historical evolution, and others announcing the dawn of a new age of globalization in which states atrophy, information is borderless, and markets rule.[15] This requires analyzing pre-1989 causes of divergences and convergences with this narrative; examining the extent that post-1989 developments on the Korean peninsula adhere to the global narrative; and explaining the import of post-1989 trajectories.

Due to the series format and space restrictions, this book is not intended to be a detailed treatment of all the major issues and themes lacing the modern and contemporary histories of both

Koreas.[16] For example, issues such as religion, education, environment, gender, and literature, are either not discussed at all or not covered in great detail. Other books and articles in English on Korea provide monographic treatments of specific subjects: some of these are listed in the suggestions for further reading section at the end of the book.

Moreover, if we look at the sum of scholarly work on modern and contemporary histories of South and North Korea in Korean and Japanese, it should not come as a surprise that a thematic history like this one does not provide exhaustive details on all possible subjects. Not surprisingly, there are far more academic works on modern and contemporary Korean history written in Korean than in English. In addition, far more books and articles are published in Japanese than in English on modern and contemporary Korean history. The geographical proximity, the grammatical similarities between the two languages (although the sounds and intonations are quite different), and the complex imbrications in the histories of Japan and Korea, all combine to produce more popular culture flows, more cultural exchanges, and higher levels of interest in modern Korean history in Japan than in English-speaking countries. There are often differences in the types of questions and issues individual scholars are interested in, and in the base knowledge of most readers in South Korea and Japan. But even with this qualifier, it would be safe to say that analyses that overlook scholarship in Korean and Japanese cannot avoid empirical limitations – simply put, not all relevant or important information is available in English.

However, claims to "speak for Koreans" or represent a "Korean view" that occasionally garnish some English-language works are spurious at best. Unlike several works on South Korea and North Korea published in English, this book incorporates information and interpretations from a variety of works and sources in English, Korean, Japanese, and Chinese; it should not be seen as embodying a singular "Korean voice," or even "a third-party neutral" position. It is obvious yet necessary to point out that not all South Koreans have the same views on historical issues. In fact, many of the debates among scholars in South Korea on modern historical issues – especially anything related to the colonial period, assessment of the contributions of past presidents, the significance of democratic moments and movements, recent North Korean politics, and unification policies – eclipse anything comparable published in English for their intensity, depth, ferocity, and acrimony.

To condense a wealth of material and views into a relative short space may invite criticism, but despite the cumulative scholarship on the histories of South and North Korea, the regularity with which North Korea appears in international news headlines, and the extent to which South Korean products infuse everyday life in the West, public knowledge about the two Koreas beyond simple stereotypes can sometimes be surprisingly limited. The language barrier and limited access to sources of reliable information – especially on North Korea – have created a market that can at times be cluttered by works based on thin empirical research and buttressed by thick ideological conviction. Amidst the rush to repackage the remnants of the Cold War as a front line for the "war on terror," it is increasingly important to cast aside preconceptions generated by repetitive and simplistic coverage, and to look beneath the surface caricatures into the more complex depths of the histories of the two Koreas.

Organization

The organization of the book is as follows. The first four chapters outline the polarization processes. Chapters 1 and 2 focus on South Korea. The first chapter analyzes the democratization process, and the second, the wide spectrum of socio-economic changes. The next two chapters assess history in North Korea. Chapter 3 looks at the political history of North Korea, while Chapter 4 examines the socio-economic issues.

Chapter 5 turns to the decussation effects – the apparent improvement of relations between South and North. It examines the impact of popular representations in both countries, the decline of anti-communist education in the South, and the significance of the generational gap in the South on inter-Korean relations. The Conclusion briefly reflects on some aspects of the relations between the histories of the two Koreas and the present.

Background History

How did a previously unified peninsula become separated into two nation-states in the first place?[17] For most of its recorded history, despite repeated invasions by foreign powers, the Korean peninsula has generally been under unified rule, its inhabitants using the same language and sharing many, if not all, of their customs. The use of the term "reunification" in English (just "unification" – *t'ongil* – in Korean) thus refers to the long history of the peninsula as a single, unified state, and implies that the North–South division since 1945 is a relatively brief interregnum in its overall history.

Pre-modern history

The Korean peninsula is roughly the size of the UK in land area.[18] It protrudes southwards from the northeast edge of the Asian continent, with two large rivers – the Yalu and the Tumen – providing a natural boundary to the north with China and Russia. Archaeological evidence suggests Paleolithic humans lived on the peninsula from some 400,000 to 500,000 years ago, but the probable ethnic ancestors of contemporary Koreans, Neolithic people, did not arrive until sometime between 5,000 and 6,000 BC. Walled towns evolved into confederated kingdoms, the most powerful of which were Old Chosŏn, which emerged as a unified entity around 500 BC, and Koguryŏ, established in 37 BC.

The period of the Three Kingdoms began around 350 to 400 AD. Koguryŏ, which controlled the north, Paekche, the southwest, and Silla, the southeast, constantly jockeyed for power. Following a series of wars, Silla defeated the other two kingdoms with the assistance of the Chinese T'ang dynasty in 668 AD, so that for the first time the peninsula was unified under one authoritarian monarchy. By 676, Unified Silla drove out the T'ang armies, which had been ordered to remain in an attempt to occupy the entire peninsula. Unified Silla lasted until 900, when two groups of rebels easily toppled a political and economic system that had become desiccated. One of the rebel groups eventually emerged as the new unifier, and founded the Koryŏ dynasty, which lasted from 924 to 1392. Despite suffering defeat at the hands of the Mongols in the 1200s, the dynasty maintained control of much of the peninsula as a tributary state.

As a result of a successful coup led by a Koryŏ general, the Chosŏn dynasty was established in 1392, and governed the Korean peninsula until its colonization by Japan in 1910. During the same six hundred-year span, four dynasties rose and dispersed in Japan: the Muromachi (1338–1573), Momoyama (1568–1600), Tokugawa (1642–1848), and Meiji (1868–1912). In China, the Han Chinese Ming (1368–1644) and the Manchu Qing (1644–1911) dynasties acted as suzerains to Korea. Considering that the Chosŏn dynasty faced numerous rebellions from within, was devastated by invasions by the Japanese in the 1590s, was defeated by the Manchus in the 1620s and 1630s, was forced to open its ports from the 1870s on by Japan and Western powers under unequal treaties, and had two wars waged by outside powers in its territory (the Sino-Japanese War of 1894–95, and the Russo-Japanese War of 1904–05), it is remarkable that the dynasty outlasted its dynastic contemporaries in East Asia, and ruled over a unified country for six hundred years.

Colonial period

Through the late-nineteenth century, the Chosŏn state's reformers initiated several modernization projects, but before these could produce significant results, Japan forced Korea into Protectorate status in 1905 after its victory over Russia in the Russo-Japanese War. Korean armed guerrilla resistance broke out against Japanese control, reaching a peak in 1907 and 1908, while elites initiated various self-strengthening movements to stave off colonization. Despite the Korean resistance, Japan, armed with international support and wielding greater military power, officially colonized Korea in 1910; it ruled over Korea until its defeat in World War Two on August 15, 1945.

The thirty-five years of colonial rule created the foundations for the division of the peninsula in 1945. To simplify, the Japanese Government General developed the northern half for heavy industry and mining, while promoting light industries and agriculture in the south. The development of the economy created new socio-economic classes based on capitalism, enriching some, impoverishing others, and creating a new group of industrial laborers.[19] Colonial-era Seoul began to emerge in the late 1920s as the center of capitalist production and consumption.[20] Furthermore, the colonial state's strategy of divide-and-rule magnified the political and ideological divisions between Koreans that started to emerge in the 1920s.[21] By 1945, the chasm between leftist independence movements, many tied to the Korean Communist Party, and liberal capitalist Koreans, often more compromising and conservative, bifurcated Korean intellectual and political elites.[22]

Liberation and division

Liberation did not bring unification. Several factors converged to create a division at the 38th parallel that mirrored the political divisions that rived Korea. First, the aforementioned preconditions served as fertile grounds for ideological polarization to accelerate in the aftermath of even a temporary administrative division. The second factor was the dynamics of the latent Cold War, which fostered planning by both the US and the Soviet Union that to varying extents ignored sentiments on the ground. The third reason that Korea did not emerge as one independent nation was the collapse of domestic attempts to unify the political spectrum, which provided additional momentum to the long-term division.

In November 1943, the US, Britain, and China noted in the Cairo Declaration that Korea should become independent in "due course." Many Koreans interpreted this to mean independence upon liberation, while others noted the qualifying clause "due course" with great concern. US president Franklin Roosevelt proposed at the February 1945 Yalta conference between the US, Britain, and the Soviet Union that Korea be put under a trustee-ship composed of one representative each from the Soviet Union, the US, and China. The trusteeship, Roosevelt affirmed, would be in place for anywhere from twenty to fifty years before independence was granted. Such assessments were based on the US colonial experience in the Philippines, and also on a relative lack of preparation regarding Korea prior to 1945. Put simply, other than the role of Korean chemicals facilities in the Japanese war effort, successive US governments had been indifferent to the details of Japanese rule in Korea before 1945. Korea had never been a major market for US exports, other than Protestant missionaries, and had not been a source of materials or goods essential for the US. US president Harry Truman confirmed the terms of the Cairo Declaration agreed upon by his predecessor at the Potsdam Conference in July 1945.

As had been agreed by the Allies, the Soviet Union declared war on Japan on August 8, and rapidly advanced southward into the Korean peninsula. Meanwhile, the closest American troops were still in Okinawa, meaning they were several weeks behind the Soviets. On August 10th, two young American officers, Dean Rusk and Charles Bonesteel, under orders to produce a surrender line that was as far north of Seoul as possible, decided that the 38th parallel would be the most feasible line of temporary division. Using a National Geographic map, they were unaware that Russia and Japan had discussed using the same line in the mid-1890s as a possible line of division of imperialist spheres of influence in Korea. The stakes were high: if the Soviets did not accept the division, they could easily take over the entire peninsula before US forces could obtain a toehold. On August 11, to the surprise of the Americans, the Soviets accepted the terms.

Historians have surmised that this unexpectedly "generous" Soviet concession was in large part motivated by expectations of a reciprocal American generosity in relation to Soviet aspirations of occupying parts or all of Hokkaidō, the northernmost and second largest island in Japan. Whatever the reasons, by the time the Soviet armies rolled into Pyongyang on August 24, 1945, the lines of the temporary division of Korea had already been agreed on. On September 2, 1945, General Order No. 1, the first US public order to the Japanese Empire, included provisions regarding the division of Korea at the 38th parallel. The US occupying forces landed in the western port city of Inch'ŏn near Seoul on September 8, 1945, and proceeded to impose a curfew as one of the first orders of business. This curfew was to remain in place under various terms until 1982. While Soviet armies congratulated Koreans on their liberation, the American forces, and General Order No. 1, viewed Koreans as a defeated nation, a part of Japan that needed to be controlled, rather than liberated. In December 1945 in Moscow, the foreign ministers of the US, the Soviet Union, the UK, and China agreed to a five-year trusteeship for Korea, sending shockwaves among all Koreans.

The political process was inevitably influenced by the reactions of the two occupying armies on the ground to domestic political conditions. From August to September 1945, a Committee for the Preparation of Korean Independence laid the groundwork for a national government for an independent Korea. The organizational network of what were called "people's committees" served as the foundations for the Korean People's Republic (KPR), which was announced on September 6. When the Soviet and American troops entered Korea, they encountered a fledgling government already well entrenched in various parts of Korea, and operating as the *de facto* administrative body at the local level. Due to plans for land reform, conservative landlords were noticeably absent from the coalition government, but the Soviets had no objections to the KPR's platforms. In the northern half, the Soviets recognized the KPR, land reforms were implemented, and former colonial officials and collaborators had their properties confiscated.

The American occupying forces, in contrast, refused to recognize the KPR, and instead established the United States Army Military Government in Korea (USAMGIK). Working on the assumption that the KPR was a communist-run organization, USAMGIK proceeded to extinguish people's committees throughout the southern half, while at the same time, rampant inflation soured the opinions of many workers on the American trusteeship. Labor stoppages to demand wage increases to match inflation began in the summer of 1946, and were countered by force. These clashes culminated in massive strikes and demonstrations through the fall of 1946, during which many demonstrators, as well as policemen, were killed. USAMGIK even employed many Korean bureaucrats who had been colonial officials, and displayed little interest in removing collaborators from significant posts.

The domestic political conflicts were inflated by the arrival of two prominent exiles onto the scene. Kim Il-Sung (Kim Il-Sŏng) was introduced by the Soviets in Pyongyang as the hero of the guerrilla war against the Japanese on the northern borders, while Syngman Rhee (Yi Sŭng-Man), who had been in exile mainly in the United States during the colonial period, returned to Seoul at the age of seventy, riding a wave of reactionary anti-communist rhetoric. Each man proceeded, under the respective auspices of the Soviets and the Americans, to consolidate his power by eliminating political rivals. Navigating between these two charismatic and polarizing figures, moderate Korean politicians of the right and left launched an attempt to form a centrist coalition. The first joint meeting in July 1946 did little more than confirm that the five-point principles of the left and the eight-point platform of the right were worlds apart, especially over the main issues of trusteeship, how to deal with colonial collaborators, land reform, and requisitioning of assets owned by those deemed to have profiteered under colonial rule. By October 1946, the group had come up with seven agreed principles based on extensive compromise, but the proposals had become so diluted that they were unlikely to generate support from any side.

Meanwhile, the Soviet–US Joint Commission, established under the Moscow accord, met in 1946 and 1947, but made little progress. In a situation of diminishing flows of people and goods between the two zones and increasing Cold War tensions, crossing the 38th parallel without a permit was made illegal in May 1946. With both Korean politicians and the occupying armies intent on excluding either the political left or right from any future Korean government, and relations between the US and the Soviet Union deteriorating at a rapid pace around the world, the shift towards two separate countries gained momentum.

The US eventually succeeded in engineering a United Nations-approved election in just the southern half. Separate elections were held in May 1948 despite the protests of many Korean elites. A new constitution and a new republic, with Syngman Rhee as the new president, was announced on August 15, 1948. North Korea held its own elections on August 25, 1948, and declared the establishment of the Democratic People's Republic of Korea, with Kim Il-Sung as premier, in September of the same year.

Protests against these developments were understandably vehement. After decades of foreign meddling before 1910, and thirty-five years under colonial rule after, very few Koreans wanted trusteeship or a divided country. General strikes to protest the announcement of separate elections started in February 1948. Armed guerrilla resistance to separate elections and *de facto* division was particularly strong on the southern island of Cheju. Although Cheju is now a resort destination known for its unique cultural artefacts and beautiful natural scenery, over a span of a year from spring 1948 to spring 1949 leftists and rebel soldiers fought a sustained guerrilla campaign on the island against USAMGIK and the new South Korean government. An estimated 80,000 Cheju islanders were killed during the year. Another large-scale leftist insurgency in the southwestern province of South Chŏlla was brutally suppressed as well.

The Korean War

The long-term causes of the Korean War are still debated. There were incremental build-ups in rhetorical threats, and military tensions escalated between 1948 and 1950. South Korea initiated many of the small border skirmishes, and Syngman Rhee openly called for unification by military force. However, any suggestions that there is serious scholarly debate around who launched the immediate attack that started the war are groundless. There is little doubt North Korea launched the initial attack on June 25, 1950 that began the Korean War.[23]

Northern forces quickly drove south, and had nearly reached the southwestern port city of Pusan by August 1950. The US mobilized UN forces and turned the tide in September when General Douglas MacArthur carried out an ambitious behind-the-lines assault on Inch'ŏn. By October, the UN and South Korean combined forces had driven into the North, close to the Yalu River, before being pushed back by a Chinese counteroffensive. North Korean forces captured Seoul for a second time in January 1951, but the UN forces again pushed the North back to the 38th parallel by spring of the same year. For the following two years, the two sides remained locked in a bloody stalemate around the original border, while American planes regularly bombed the cities of the North.

A ceasefire agreement was eventually signed on July 27, 1953. Syngman Rhee, however, refused to sign the subsequent peace treaty, leaving the two Koreas to this day technically in a ceasefire agreement during an ongoing war. The border remained physically unaltered at the 38th parallel, but the Korean War marked an epochal moment in the history of war and the media, in that it was the first war to be covered through the infant medium of television. Of course, not all households had television sets in 1950–53, and television film had to be physically transported back to the broadcasting studios, but the Korean War remains the first major war to be broadcast through cathode-ray tubes directly into some living rooms.

What television did not and could not convey was the devastation, thorough and wide-ranging, wrought by the three years of fighting: the infrastructure of the entire peninsula was shredded, and the human toll, as mentioned above, reached the millions.

Even more than fifty years later, documentary evidence and testimonials were shedding light on many previously unknown massacres of civilians by both Northern and Southern forces. Families were torn asunder, homes were destroyed, princes were turned to paupers, and Koreans bludgeoned and bayoneted each other on the battlefields and in political cleansing campaigns. The scarring memories of the war reverberated throughout both countries through family stories and the formal educational system, and imbued both sides with a seething hatred of each other. Amidst the ruins of Seoul and Pyongyang in 1953, unification was a more distant and impossible dream than it had been three years before, with capitalist pigs and communist devils all seemingly trapped in a static diptych with no realistic scenarios for escape or unification in sight.

Over fifty years later, altered in content but not in basic frame, the Korean binary still remains.

1 | Pandora's Box?
South Korea's Democratization and Consolidation

Seoul was the capital of the Chosŏn dynasty for around six hundred years. It has been the locus of political, economic, and cultural activities since the establishment of South Korea in 1948. A succession of kings, aristocrats, colonial bureaucrats, charismatic politicians, and military dictators ruled from the seat of power in Seoul, and the physical legacies of their rule still dot the urban landscape amidst the densely packed apartments, automobiles, subways, skyscrapers, shops, and people. North of the Han River, it does not require a practiced eye to detect the sprawling restored royal grounds dating from the Chosŏn period, or the neoclassical architecture left behind by the Japanese colonial rulers. South of the Han, the dense forests of skyscrapers and apartment blocks are physical testaments to the massive development projects undertaken in the late 1960s and early 1970s.

However, it would take more effort to find among the innumerable streets monuments or memorials marking the most significant political transformation in South Korea's contemporary history. Most people in Seoul know where the main gate of Yonsei University is located, since it is known throughout the country as one of the top three universities in South Korea. There are likely far fewer people, though, who know the way to the unassuming concrete, four-storey building buried in the back streets about a fifteen-minute walk away from Yonsei University. The small entrance leads to a museum built in 2004 to honor Lee Han-Yŏl (Yi Han-Yŏl), a student activist who was killed in 1987 during pro-democracy demonstrations.

The relatively obscure location of a museum dedicated to a pro-democracy martyr is a contrast to everyday life at the time. Throughout the 1980s and into the early 1990s, the areas around the main gates of university campuses would often fill with thick clouds of tear gas as demonstrators and police clashed. The term "tear gas" is exceedingly misleading in its innocuousness. Once the tear gas grenades exploded, voluminous, white clouds enveloped demonstrators, and within a matter of seconds their eyes, noses, and throats burnt as if someone had poured liberal doses of undiluted acid onto their faces. Hours after a demonstration, even after the white smoke had dissipated and the air looked clear again, the sting from the remaining vapors caused passersby to become instantly and violently lachrymose.

These demonstrations and clashes were not restricted only to university campuses or only to Seoul. From 1960 on, students and laborers in various cities throughout South Korea, armed with rocks and Molotov cocktails, battled military police or private union-busters. In the 1970s, smoke-filled cafés that are no longer extant were the sites for innumerable and "illegal" discussions of democracy, and the streets around the major university campuses were the scenes of demonstrations and clashes between military police and student activists. And, the few times South Korea made the international news headlines throughout much of the 1980s were when particularly large-scale confrontations broke out between the masked students demonstrators and the helmeted riot police. In June 1987, anti-government and pro-democracy demonstrations reached record numbers and intensity.

During one such clash between demonstrators and riot police on June 9, 1987, in front of the main gate of Yonsei University, a tear gas grenade hit Lee Han-Yŏl directly on the head, critically injuring him. Demonstrations and street fighting escalated in the streets of Seoul – highways were closed off, demonstrators launched gas bombs at government buildings, and in some clashes students overpowered the riot police. A nationwide demonstration march on June 27 mobilized an estimated 1.8 million people throughout the country in 37 cities.

After days of intense demonstrations, on June 29, 1987 the South Korean government issued a "Democratization Declaration," an eight-point reform program that in essence established a blueprint for democratization. The unexpected announcement left the demonstrators scrambling to declare victory, while officials gathered to reform the constitution and implement the promises of direct presidential elections, protection of human rights, and reduction of restrictions on the press. Presidential terms became limited to one five-year stint under the new constitution. Lee Han-Yŏl died from his injuries in hospital on July 7, unable to witness the epochal changes about to come. On July 9, when his funeral procession ended in front of Seoul City Hall, an estimated 1 million people gathered to honor one of many martyrs for democracy in South Korea's history.

In the 1960s and 1970s, South Korea and North Korea were both ruled by authoritarian regimes: democratization after 1987 has launched South Korea on a clearly divergent path from the North. Previously noted for its combination of authoritarian governments and economic development (the so-called "developmental state"), South Korea is now widely seen as a case of successful democratization and democratic consolidation. If Polish advocates of combining authoritarianism with market reform were known in the late 1980s as the "South Korean" faction, some Cambodian NGOs (non-governmental organizations) dedicated to democratization in the twenty-first century consider South Korea to be a model for democratization.[1]

Despite an array of calls for caution and scepticism about democratic consolidation issued by domestic and foreign observers, democracy has taken root in South Korea. Four presidents have been elected under the 1987 Constitution – Roh Tae-Woo (No T'ae-U) in 1988, Kim Young-Sam (Kim Yŏng-Sam) in 1993, Kim Dae-Jung (Kim Tae-Jung) in 1998, and Roh Moo-Hyun (No Mu-Hyŏn) in 2003. Even with some obvious problems inherent in reducing complex nation-states into simplistic statistical rankings, a 2006 survey placed South Korea at 34 out of 150 countries on its democracy scale, just behind Japan at 32 and Israel at 33.[2]

In the South Korea of the twenty-first century, a whole generation has never tasted tear gas. Even if the occasional call for a military coup reverberates through a meeting hall in 2006, the danger of such an event happening in actuality seems distant. Academics and policy makers in South Korea study and debate the long-term significance of the events of 1987. Some scholars decry the "1987 system" as ultimately a top-down set of reforms that did not go far enough. Nonetheless, without a doubt, the most significant political change in South Korea after the mid-1980s was the transition from a series of authoritarian dictatorships to a functioning, sustainable democracy. The most significant not because democracy is the apogee of human achievement, the universal terminus for history, or because modernization theory has become retro-chic in some circles, but simply because 1987 marked an epochal transformation in the political structure and society of South Korea.

What factors explain how democratic transformation in South Korea, which widened the political gap with North Korea, occurred? How did democratic consolidation occur? What new developments emerged in South Korean politics during the process of democratic consolidation? This chapter focuses on the political dimensions in answering these questions. Chapter 2 will deal with the socio-economic aspects in more detail.

Democratization: 1960—1987

Why was it that democratic transformation occurred in South Korea in 1987 rather than 1989, and was it the inevitable outcome of the technological and moral efficacy of liberal democracy, as Francis Fukuyama argued in his *The End of History*?[3] The answer is that the democratization process had its roots firmly in domestic South Korean history, rather than being primarily caused by external pressures following the end of the Cold War in 1989. In addition, there was considerable individual agency and historical contingency: there was little that was inevitable about the process.

There are several views among academics on the causal factors behind democratization in South Korea. These generally revolve around discussions of socio-economic levels, the power and scale of the demonstrations, external intervention via US public declarations, and moral arguments. Rather than emphasize the primacy of one factor over another, it is best to see democratization in South Korea as a historically contingent convergence of multiple factors. In other words, several *necessary* but not *sufficient* variables had existed before. It was not until June 1987 that these collided into an epochal moment.

The "threshold model" suggests that collective action of any kind requires a certain critical mass before growing, as people make a series of choices based on seeing how many others are joining before deciding to participate in a movement. This helps explain both gradual and sudden change – somewhat akin to explaining how water warms up gradually before boiling, then seemingly suddenly turns to steam.[4] I would suggest that this model is the most appropriate one for explaining how the effects of cumulative resistance against forty years of authoritarian rule in South Korea boiled over in 1987 due to several key precedents and factors, ultimately resulting in the transformation into a democracy. Thus, a combination of four major factors was required to make democratization possible in 1987: the cumulative effect of decades of protest met by repression; the emergence of the middle class; the impact of foreign pressures and precedents; and internal divisions and miscalculations by the government.

Cumulative history and thresholds

First, it is important to acknowledge the impact of long-term trends and domestic precedents. South Korea had previous, albeit abbreviated, experiments in democracy before 1987. In many senses, the democratization process embodied Reinhold Niebuhr's statement that, "Nothing that is worth doing can be achieved in our lifetime; therefore we must be saved by hope."[5] Repeated cycles of repression and resistance infuse South Korean political history. Three strongmen had governed the country until 1987 – Syngman Rhee (Yi Sŭng-Man) from 1948 to 1960; Park Chung-Hee (Pak Chŏng-Hŭi) from 1961 to 1979; and Chun Doo-Hwan (Chŏn Tu-Hwan) from 1980 to 1987. Massive civic demonstrations challenged and eventually undermined all three regimes – in 1960, 1979–1980, and 1987. The first two regime changes failed to engender sustained democratic governments, but the memory of each – if not the direct outcome – contributed to the gradual attainment of the threshold point.

In April 1960, massive student demonstrations helped over-throw Syngman Rhee. Trading on the prestige that his independence activities during the colonial period gave him with the South Korean public, and armed with extraordinary powers under the anti-communist National Security Law, Rhee dominated the political landscape from 1948 to 1960, ruthlessly suppressing all significant rivals. The April Revolution was in large part a reflection of the public's disgust with widespread and constant corruption, but also a set of socio-economic changes. Improvements in the level of literacy, and increases in the number of educational institutions produced more students in higher education. Unemployment rates, however, remained high for university graduates, and economic development still appeared elusive.

Eight months before the March 15, 1960 presidential and vice presidential elections, Rhee executed one rival on charges of communist activities. The main opposition candidate for president died a month before the elections. Not surprisingly, Rhee won the presidential elections with 88% of the vote. However, the vice presidential election race between the opposition's Chang Myŏn and Rhee's right-hand man, the unpopular Lee Ki-Bung (Yi Ki-Bung), was widely expected to go Chang's way even with tainted ballots. When the result was announced as a landslide victory for Lee, there was little doubt that the election had been rigged.[6] On the same day, March 15, a massive demonstration to protest electoral corruption took place in the southeastern city of Masan. On April 11, a fishing boat in Masan harbor discovered the bloated body of sixteen-year-old Kim Chu-Yŏl. Protruding from one eye was a fragment of the tear gas canister that had hit him directly during the March 15 demonstrations. The discovery of the body and Rhee's denial of involvement sparked nationwide student protests. "Anti-communist" groups that had been fostered by Rhee clashed violently with students on April 18. On April 19, some 30,000 students marched toward the presidential office to protest the election rigging when military police fired on them, resulting in at least 124 deaths and over 558 injured. Outraged by the election rigging and the attack on unarmed students, the public called on Rhee to hold new elections or resign.[7] US officials urged Rhee to reform the government. Amidst the escalating pressure, on April 28 Lee Ki-Bung committed suicide with his entire family. Rhee finally stepped down on April 29, 1960.

The interim government announced a new constitution in June, and in late July, the popularly elected Chang Myŏn government took over the reins of power. It proved to be short-lived. There were several reasons for this, including the fact that the so-called April Revolution may have been more about protesting *against* corruption than about calling *for* systemic change. Chang Myŏn and his party were the beneficiaries, not the vanguard, of the April Revolution. In addition to issues of moral legitimacy, the new government was ulcerated with internal conflicts and hampered by economic woes. Its half-hearted purges of former Rhee loyalists, the proliferation of political demonstrations by left-leaning organizations under its watch, and seemingly vacillating leadership led to rising discontent among the citizens and the military. On May 16, 1961, Major General Park Chung-Hee, aided by his nephew-by-marriage Lieutenant General Kim Jong-Pil (Kim Chong-P'il), led 250 officers and 3,500 soldiers in a swift and effective coup that met with only token resistance. A paltry force of fifty military police was mobilized to defend the Chang government.[8]

In the twenty-first century, Kim Chu-Yŏl is largely forgotten even in the city of Masan.[9] Even more surprisingly, by 1963, just two years after the end of the experiment with democracy, some 86% of the students who had participated in the April Revolution agreed with the assertion that "Western" democracy was unsuitable for South Korea.[10] This can be explained by remembering that, as noted above, the protests had been *against* Rhee as much as they had been *for* democracy. Moreover, the socio-economic turmoil of 1960–61 highlighted with clarity the fact that democracy was not to be equated with economic growth or better material conditions for all. However, the legend of the April Revolution – that students were the guardians of political virtue and held the power to topple governments, that street demonstrations could make a difference – became a lodestar for subsequent generations of activists and demonstrators.

The second major attempt at democratization via demonstrations occurred during 1979–80. Although he was technically a civilian president from 1963 on, Park Chung-Hee together with his advisors ruled over South Korea with an iron fist for nearly twenty years, from the May 1961 coup until his assassination in October 1979. Park instituted a "Korean-style" democracy, which meant limited but relatively open party politics and elections from 1963 to 1971, followed by an openly repressive regime after winter 1971. While technically a victor of presidential elections in 1963, 1967, and 1971 in which he narrowly defeated his main rivals, Park was constantly under fire from opposition leaders and student activists, who questioned the legitimacy of the elections, especially those of 1967 and 1971.

Park needed additional sources of political legitimacy. He invoked two pillars from the very start: economic nationalism (or "GDP nationalism") and anti-communism. Enthusiastic in his subscription to modernization, Park also was wary of the assumption that the notion of development should incorporate "Western" notions of democracy and human rights. Economic development in the 1960s provided Park with ample fuel for his "GDP nationalism," the use of economic objectives to mobilize human resources and nationalist sentiments. However, a combination of external factors – most notably the 1969 Nixon Doctrine (which, in light of the Vietnam War, reaffirmed US treaty commitments but at the same time urged allies to assume primary responsibility for fighting their own battles rather than relying on US forces), and the proposed withdrawal of around 40% of the American troops stationed in South Korea – plus domestic factors, such as the growing strength of the opposition party, convinced Park of the need to armor himself with further powers.[11] In December 1971, Park declared a state of emergency. In October 1972, he pushed through a new constitution which granted the president the power to appoint one-third of the National Assembly, removed term limits for presidents, and changed direct presidential elections to indirect ones through an electoral college. The new constitution, called the "Yusin" ("restoration" or "revitalization" in Korean), in essence made Park the ruler of South Korea for life.

Torture of suspected opponents of the regime became everyday practice. People would go missing for days – the lucky ones would show up back at their homes, badly bruised but alive. In one particularly sensational case, opposition leader Kim Dae-Jung, who had been a very vocal critic of Park after being defeated narrowly in the 1971 presidential election, was kidnapped from his Tokyo hotel room on August 8, 1973 by members of the Korean Central Intelligence Agency (KCIA). Kim narrowly escaped execution because of the last-minute intervention of US officials.[12] Despite such ruthless repression, opposition to Park continued throughout 1972–79 from labor unions, student activists, Christian organizations, and politicians. However, the repressive system survived such international transgressions, international criticism, and increasing domestic opposition. Park even survived assassination attempts – the first in 1968 when North Korean commandos attempted to penetrate the presidential residence and office, known as the Blue House (Ch'ŏngwadae), and the second in 1974 when a Korean resident of Japan who was affiliated with the North shot at Park. Park escaped physically unscathed but his wife, Yuk Yŏng-Su, was killed in the attack.[13]

Left alone with more time for his diary and increasingly paranoid musings, Park managed to retain his control over the reins of power. Park removed potential rivals from among his own supporters, most notably ousting Kim Jong-Pil from the premiership. The successful transformation of the economy during the 1960s had given way to a prolonged slowdown from the mid-1970s. The economic downturn was exacerbated by the second oil shock of 1979 which occurred in the wake of the Iranian Revolution. The middle class, whose numbers had increased from around 19% to 26% of the population between 1970 and 1979, became increasingly dissatisfied.[14] Labor protests proliferated, often leading to violent confrontations with police. In August 1979, the brutal police crackdown on striking female textile workers of the YH Trading Company resulted in the death of one worker. In the same month, police raided the headquarters of the opposition party, focusing their efforts in particular on party leader Kim Young-Sam's offices.

Demonstrations calling for Park to resign erupted in the southeastern cities of Pusan and Masan, leading to an emergency meeting between Park and a handful of advisors on October 26, 1979. Kim Jae-Kyu (Kim Chae-Kyu), the director of the KCIA, pleaded for a compromise response to the situation that did not involve armed action. Park's bodyguard Ch'a Chi-Ch'ŏl, who was widely believed to have the most influence on Park after 1974, insisted that tanks and paratroopers should be dispatched to extinguish the demonstrations. Park agreed. At this point, Kim pulled out his revolver and shot Park and Ch'a at point-blank range, killing them both. Kim Jae-Kyu was arrested, tried, and found guilty by the Supreme Court after Major General Chun Doo-Hwan seized power (see below). Kim and four accomplices were executed for treason in 1980.

The death of one dictator did not give birth to a sustained democracy, but to a brief and ultimately ineffective interim government which lasted for all of two months, and was followed by another military dictatorship. On December 12, 1979, with some 7,500 troops at their disposal, Major General Chun Doo-Hwan, along with Major General Roh Tae-Woo, the commander of the Ninth Division that defended the key area between the DMZ and Seoul, led a coup within the army against their superiors in what came to be known as the "12-12 Incident." Once in control over the army, Chun proceeded to consolidate his powers by appointing himself director of the powerful KCIA in April 1980. A series of labor and student demonstrations ensued, prompting Chun to extend martial law throughout the country on May 17, 1980, arresting twenty-six politicians, shutting down the National Assembly, and imposing stringent censorship on the press.

Starting May 18, large-scale demonstrations against Chun broke out in Kwangju, the capital of South Chǒlla province in the southwest. Clashes between armed soldiers and unarmed demonstrators escalated over the next few days. Army units completely surrounded the city, and on May 27, paratroopers and tanks moved in *en masse* against the "democracy fighters," shooting and bayoneting civilians. Horrific accounts of indiscriminate slaughter of civilians by soldiers would only become public later.[15] The demonstrations involved an estimated 100,000 people and some 20,000 soldiers in what came to be known as the Kwangju Massacre or the May 18 Uprising. The government count acknowledged nearly 200 dead, but many estimates put the final death toll at somewhere between 1,000 and 2,000. It seems clear that many of the demonstrators in Kwangju were as outraged by the escalating violence used by soldiers against unarmed protestors as they were interested in systemic political reform. Some accounts even emphasize the lingering bitterness between residents of Kwangju and the student activists who had gathered there to help fuel the demonstrations.

As was the case with the Tiananmen Square demonstrations of 1989 in China, Kwangju itself did not directly result in regime change. Chun became *de facto* president in August 1980. Then, modeling himself on Park Chung-Hee, Chun resigned his military office, and was elected under a new constitution as the president in February 1981. Among many steps to strengthen his hold on power, Chun arrested and tried opposition leader Kim Dae-Jung on trumped-up charges of sedition, and sentenced him to death. Kim's sentence was commuted under strong pressure from the US government and overseas grassroots organizations. Kim was forced into exile abroad from 1982 to 1985. In another measure designed to consolidate his power, Chun forced the mergers of several newspapers and periodicals, and simply shut down around 25% of all publications.[16]

However, the Kwangju Massacre severely damaged the Chun government from its very inception. While Park had taken power in a bloodless coup, Chun had done so through the massacre of citizens. The memories of the massacre also provided powerful symbolic capital for opposition leaders to draw on, and its legacies informed Chun's own reluctance to use armed force to suppress the 1987 demonstrations.[17] Perhaps most important, accounts of the Kwangju Massacre, along with other counternarratives, were transmitted to the next generation through discussions within families and the erection of public memorials such as gravestones and plaques. These accounts in turn inspired many students to join pro-democracy organizations in the mid-1980s.[18]

Another of the legacies of Kwangju was a spurt in anti-American sentiment and a subsequent radicalization of the student movement.[19] The extent of US involvement or acquiescence in Chun's maneuvers is still under heated dispute. There are several contradictory accounts regarding how much US officials knew about troop movements beforehand and when exactly they learned of the massacres in Kwangju. However, the key point is that all contemporary reports and memoirs by US officials, whether they deny or acknowledge significant prior knowledge of Chun's moves, indicate that the overwhelming concern among US officials was not the violation of human rights or the massacre of unarmed civilians, but the possibility of North Korea using the crisis to launch an attack against South Korea.[20]

Seeking sources of legitimacy to distract from the blood-drenched beginnings of his regime, Chun turned to the precedents set by Park Chung-Hee. He stressed the importance of economic recovery from the recession of 1979–80, and the need to maintain national security to defend the country from intrusions from the North. Starting in late 1983 and early 1984, mirroring to some extent Park's limited liberalization in the 1960s and infused with confidence after seeing rapid economic growth rates, Chun implemented a series of political liberalization policies.[21] One of the earliest reforms was the 1982 termination of the 10 PM curfew that had been in place since 1945. Chun also established professional baseball and soccer leagues in 1982 and 1983 respectively in an effort to divert attention away from issues such as democratization and towards sports results. Armed with record economic growth rates for 1983, Chun embarked on a set of more substantive liberalization policies. In 1983 and 1984, he permitted anti-government professors to return to their universities, pardoned some political prisoners, and lifted the ban on political activities imposed on some 84 opposition politicians that he had banned in 1980. Many of these politicians joined the New Korea Democratic Party (hereafter NKDP), the first meaningful opposition party allowed under the Chun regime, when it was established in January 1985 under the leadership of Kim Young-Sam and Kim Dae-Jung. Chun's calculation was that providing the opposition with operating room would help exacerbate its internal divisions.

Rather than increase the popularity of the ruling party or fragment the opposition, however, these reforms provided a window for anti-Chun groups.[22] Chun's party suffered a near defeat to the opposition NKDP in the National Assembly elections of February 1985. Over the course of 1985 and 1986, the NKDP and opposition grassroots organizations (a variety of political interests often referred to by the general term of "*minjung*" movements or groups) campaigned for a constitutional amendment that would allow direct presidential elections. Chun initially agreed these demands in 1986, but in April 1987, he attempted to renege on his promise. This triggered angry reactions from opposition forces and prompted massive street demonstrations. When Chun announced on June 2, 1987 that Roh Tae-Woo, his close friend and co-conspirator of the coup, would be his successor, public fears that the elections would be rigged to ensure Roh's succession grew.

Moreover, individual cases of torture came to light. Female activists had been tortured and raped before, but in July 1986 Kwŏn In-Suk became the first women to bring charges against the government. Despite government censorship of the press, details of her story were printed in the newspapers, sparking a public outcry. Then, in January 1987, the death of Pak Chong-ch'ŏl, a student at Seoul National University, angered the public. He had been suffocated by policemen who repeated dunked his head into a large tub of water, and crushed his throat against the rim of the tub. The attending medical examiner contradicted the police denials, and the mass media picked up the story, eventually forcing the police to acknowledge that they had tortured and killed Pak Chong-ch'ŏl.

Thus, the cumulative history of state oppression and the sacrifices of individual activists, transmitted through the medium of families and mass media, culminated in June 1987 with the largest street demonstrations witnessed in South Korea. These in turn led to a new constitution (October 1987), direct presidential elections (December 1987), and new National Assembly elections (April 1988). Past precedents and collective memory alone are insufficient, however, to explain the massive numbers who participated in the 1987 demonstrations.

Emergence of the middle class

The 1987 democratization was also made possible by a second factor – fundamental changes in socio-economic demographics. Growth in education, per capita income from the decades of economic growth, and high rates of urbanization resulting in the growth in the numbers of white-collar workers and urban small businesses, combined with relatively low investment into social capital to create a wellspring of discontent with authoritarian rule. While intellectuals and students had participated in previous attempts at popular democratization in 1960 and 1980, the number of middle-class protestors – professors, non-activist students, and white-collar workers – was much larger in the 1987 demon-strations. Furthermore, greater urbanization meant greater ease in mobilizing support for grassroots and oppositional organizations, and better access to and circulation of nongovernmental sources of information. Some 28% of the population lived in cities in 1960, and 57% in 1980. By 1990, the urban population accounted for 75% of the total population. There are a variety of views on the impact of urbanization on voter turnout; however, some indica-tions of the utility of urban bases for oppositional groups is reflected in one study that concluded urban residents in South Korea were less likely to vote but more likely to vote for the opposition party if they did vote.[23] Moreover, the urban middle class was now a much larger proportion of the population than in 1960 or 1980. For example, 66% of the population worked in agriculture or other primary industries in 1960 and 38% in 1980. By 1990, this percentage had dropped to 20%. The results vary according to each survey, but as of 1987 some 66–70% of the South Korea population saw itself as middle class.[24]

Domestic and foreign media hailed 1987 as a "middle-class revolution," and Roh Tae-Woo himself acknowledged that citizens wanted to see a settlement of accounts for past sacrifices.[25] It would be unwise, however, to tidy away the complex dynamics of the democratization process under one such convenient rubric. After all, a diverse range of people and organizations, including religious groups, student associations, labor unions, and others, all participated in the process. Moreover, the category "middle class" encompassed a diverse range of political and economic interests.[26] Nonetheless, the long-term changes in the socio-economic structure of the country certainly contributed to the massive support for the pro-democracy demonstrators in 1987.

External Pressure

The third factor behind the 1987 democratization process was foreign attention and pressure magnified by the upcoming 1988 Summer Olympics. Despite the negative foreign press coverage the Chun regime received in 1980 as a result of Kwangju, in 1981 Seoul defeated Nagoya, Japan, for the right to host the 1988 Summer Olympic Games.[27] Chun began intensive efforts to ensure the success of this international media event.

In foreign policy, Chun wanted to ensure the presence of the communist bloc at the Olympics. While suggestions that South and North Korea field joint teams in some sports were quickly rebuffed, South Korea secured normalization treaties with Eastern European countries just before the Olympics. For example, the South Korea–Hungary normalization agreement was signed on September 13, 1988, just four days before the opening ceremony of the Seoul Olympics.

In terms of domestic policy, Chun knew that hosting the events amidst street demonstrations and tear gas was not going to generate the international prestige that he craved.[28] The "practice-run" Asian Games held in September and October 1986 had been a widely acclaimed success, but street demonstrations had been strictly held in abeyance by abundant security forces during the events. In August 1988, looking for a less visually disruptive means of ensuring the success of the Olympic games, Roh asked opposition politicians for a truce until the end of the games. An announcement of an agreement among all four major political parties to this effect was made public on September 2, 1988.

The so-called "snowball effect," positive foreign precedents reinforcing the events in South Korea, is often cited as a possible factor in the democratization process. The street demonstrations of the 1986 "people power" revolution in the Philippines were certainly inspirational. Korean civic organizations that organized the demonstrations for direct presidential elections did use the Philippines' National Citizens' Movement for Free Elections, the umbrella organization of 500,000 people that had been instrumental in piloting the "people's power" movement that ended the twenty-one-year reign of Ferdinand Marcos, as a benchmark for their own strategies.[29] However, it should also be noted that by the same token, the Philippines precedent also amplified Chun Doo-Hwan's concerns, and amplified the harshness of his crackdowns against student demonstrators in 1986.

The most important source of foreign pressure was undoubtedly the US. Unlike in 1980, the US position was clear and consistent in warning Chun against the use of military force to quell demonstrations. US President Ronald Reagan wrote a letter to Chun on June 19 that gently but firmly urged a peaceful resolution to the current crisis. The US Assistant Secretary of State for East Asian and Pacific Affairs, Gaston Sigur, met with Chun in person on June 25, sternly warning against the use of the armed forces to quell demonstrations.[30]

Internal divisions in the government

Fourth and finally, there were some indications of a significant if not major split between moderates and hardliners within the government. On June 19, 1987, Chun ordered some of his military units to stand by to prepare to attack demonstrators in Seoul. However, according to some accounts, he met with internal dissent. Roh Tae-Woo and others opposed the mobilization of army units against citizens. Chun determined that compromise was the best course of action. Chun, according to the recollections of his secretary in 1992, calculated that if he had Roh take credit for the democratization declaration of June 29, Roh could strengthen his candidacy for president. Moreover, Chun was convinced that given the likelihood that Kim Young-Sam and Kim Dae-Jung would not be able to agree to combine forces and would therefore split the oppositional vote, direct presidential elections would mathematically favor Roh.[31]

Whether Chun actually had such political acumen or whether his secretary's account was an attempt retroactively to improve Chun's image is difficult to verify. However, the results of the hard-fought December 1987 presidential elections hewed closely to what Chun's secretary claimed was the government's prognostication. Roh obtained victory with around 37% of the votes, while the two main opposition candidates, Kim Young-Sam and Kim Dae-Jung, unable to come to an agreement, captured 28% and 27% respectively. In February 1988 Roh replaced Chun as president; it was the first peaceful transition of power in South Korea's history.

Democratic Consolidation: 1987–2002

Given that four presidents have been elected under the 1987 constitution, the process of democratic consolidation can be called an overall success. As already mentioned, Roh Tae-Woo was the first to be elected under the 1987 system. In the 1992 election Kim Young-Sam, who had surprised many observers by merging his party with Roh Tae-Woo's government party and Kim Jong-Pil's conservative opposition party in 1990, was voted in as president with 41% of the votes to his old rival Kim Dae-Jung's 33%. In December 1997, in his fourth presidential election campaign, Kim Dae-Jung edged out the conservative candidate, Lee Hoi-Chang (Yi Hoe-Ch'ang) by a margin of 40% to 39% with the help of Kim Jong-Pil, who brought anywhere from an 11% to a 20% increase in the southeastern regions where Kim Dae-Jung had never fared well. In December 2002, in an even more surprising outcome, Roh Moo-Hyun triumphed over Lee Hoi-Chang by a narrow margin of 49% to 47% of the votes, becoming the fourth president under the 1987 constitution.

Most important, sustainable democracy emerged despite problems with corruption, lingering historical issues, and political parties that formed and disbanded at a high rate. Not only did a new systemic stability emerge, but military intervention in domestic politics was defused as a threat.

Nonetheless, the process of democratic consolidation was hardly smooth. Although democratization was driven by popular pressure, once the focus shifted to direct presidential elections and the new constitution in late 1987, familiar politicians hammered out the compromises and implemented the reforms. Civil society, in relative terms at least, was shunted aside as politicians constructed what is known in South Korea as the "1987 system." In addition, political parties formed and merged with a frequency that hindered democratic consolidation. The fact that parties often formed based on political expediency or personal networks rather than on clearly defined platforms also muddled the workings of a democratic political system.

The transition from Roh Tae-Woo to Kim Young-Sam

While Roh initially implemented a series of political liberalization reforms, because of his deep connections with Chun he never gained the legitimacy he yearned. Roh's image was eroded by his so-called "Protect the System" declaration in December 1988, which signalled a crackdown on civil society once the truce during the Olympics ceased. In 1988 and 1989 labor strikes and student demonstrations reached a peak in frequency, as demonstrators threw Molotov cocktails at riot police, who in turn launched tear gas at their opponents. The statistics for official arrests of dissidents for violations of the National Security Law averaged 5.4 persons per day for 1989. In contrast, the 1988 average number of arrests of dissidents per day was 2.6 persons, and, for 1987, 1.6.[32] Ultimately, Roh's government was seen as a continuation, albeit garbed in a softer, more diplomatic aura, of previous authoritarian regimes.

Thus, in January 1990, when Kim Young-Sam, the opposition leader who had castigated Roh as a "criminal" and a military dictator, merged his political party with Roh's ruling party and that of another opposition leader, Kim Jong-Pil (Park Chung-Hee's former prime minister), the public was initially surprised. Roh, as the head of a minority government, had wanted to solidify his power through an alliance with at least one of the "three Kims," and found a willing partner in Kim Young-Sam. The new ruling party, named the Democratic Liberal Party (DLP) after Japan's long-ruling Liberal Democratic Party, won the 1992 elections with Kim Young-Sam as its presidential candidate. Several explanations exist for why Kim Young-Sam emerged victorious, such as an electorate looking for political continuity during a period of economic uncertainty, anti-communist bias that worked against Kim Dae-Jung (who had been labeled a communist by a succession of authoritarian regimes), and significant regional biases in voting patterns (Kim Dae-Jung had traditionally received more support from the southwest provinces, while Kim Young-Sam drew his support from the southeast). Kim Young-Sam was, regardless, widely seen as a step in the right direction, the first civilian president since 1961 to hold office.[33]

Difficulties in democratic consolidation under Kim Young-Sam

Upon his inauguration, Kim launched a series of reforms that stabilized military–civilian relations by firing military officials known to have political ambitions.[34] He also implemented a series of reforms in 1993 and 1994 that promised to curb bribery and corruption. A 1993 measure mandating the use of real names for bank accounts and financial transactions made the flow of funds traceable. In addition, several laws that dealt with political funding, such as the Political Fund Law, were amended to strengthen their provisions. Kim also revived the Local Autonomy Act, which had been in abeyance since Park Chung-Hee took power in 1961. This provided local governments with the power to collect taxes and fees, and for voters to vote directly for provincial governors, mayors, and city councillors.

However, the honeymoon period ended quickly. In some respects, a series of manmade disasters signaled the end of the popularity of the Kim Young-Sam administration. Among the most significant, in October 1994 the Sŏngsu Bridge in Seoul, which was opened in 1979 to carry traffic across the Han River, collapsed during the morning rush hour, killing thirty-two people. In April 1995, there was a major explosion when a gas line was accidentally sheared open during construction work on the subway in the southeastern city of Taegu. In June 1995, all five above-ground floors of the Samp'ung department store in Seoul collapsed in an instant into its four basement floors, killing over 500 people. In several cases, the problem was not just the original fraudulent construction or dangerous renovation, but also the fact that inspectors during both the Roh and the Kim Young-Sam governments approved bridges as safe or additional floors to department stores as legal in exchange for bribes.

Recent history also came back to haunt Kim Young-Sam. He had repeatedly stated that the track records of Chun and Roh would have to be "left to the judgement of history." As it turned out, such declarations were based less on magnanimity and more on political expediency. In October 1995, after revelations by a National Assembly member that Roh had had at his personal disposal a slush fund of roughly $500 million, Roh acknowledged that he had accumulated around $650 million, and apologized to the nation. Subsequent investigations revealed that the top conglomerates had made regular "contributions" to Roh during his presidency. Although Kim Young-Sam denied having received any money directly, he essentially acknowledged that his 1992 campaign had received large sums of money from Roh. Even more surprising, Kim Dae-Jung admitted that he had received $2.5 million from Roh during the 1992 elections.

Demonstrations erupted around the country calling for the punishment of Chun and Roh for corruption, for the Kwangju Massacre, and for the military coup in 1980. Fearing political instability, in 1996 Kim Young-Sam used the National Security Law to suppress major student organizations.

More effectively, Kim managed a volte-face, now claiming that he would "rectify history" by promulgating a special law that would allow the courts to prosecute the two former presidents. Detractors decried this as an obvious move to bolster an administration dropping precipitously in popularity, but the National Assembly quickly passed special legislation for dealing with political bribery, the Kwangju Massacre, and the December 1979 coup. Roh and Chun, along with fourteen co-defendants, were arrested and charged with corruption, insurrection, and treason. Both denied guilt on all counts and refused to provide key information. In August 1996, the two main defendants were found guilty of all charges in what was called the "trial of the century." A series of appeals extended the case to April 1997, when the Supreme Court upheld previous rulings. On December 20, 1997, after the presidential elections, both Roh and Chun were granted a presidential pardon by president Kim Young-Sam and president-elect Kim Dae-Jung for a "grand national reconciliation."

While the trial symbolized the transfer of power from the military to the civilian government, it did not produce much meaningful closure for recent history, and left Kim Young-Sam in a precarious position due to his past connections with Roh. When another bribery scandal, this one involving several of his top officials and his second eldest son, hit the front pages, Kim was left a lame-duck president waiting out his time. Hanbo Steel, the second largest steelmaker in South Korea, went bankrupt in January 1997 under the weight of a $6 billion debt. The president of Hanbo was accused of bribing government officials to receive large loans at preferential interest rates. Several top officials in the Kim Young-Sam administration were implicated, and Kim Young-Sam's second-eldest son was convicted of bribery and influence peddling. Although the scandal exposed the extent of corruption still latent in South Korean politics, the fact that the son of a sitting president could be put on trial reflected the extent to which the independence of the judiciary had evolved since 1989.

In economic policy, Kim Young-Sam launched an ambitious *segyehwa* or "globalization" policy in 1995 that aimed to raise all aspects of South Korea to the "global" standard, and make it more competitive in the world market. Politicians and pundits raised concerns about whether the country was prepared to dive into full-scale global competition, whether membership in the Organization of Economic Cooperation and Development (OECD) would bring greater rewards or more pain. Membership required South Korea to adhere to international standards and procedures in finance, foreign investment, securities, the environment, and labor; in addition, domestic markets had to be opened according to an agreed timetable. These obstacles were navigated, and South

Korea joined the OECD in fall 1996 as its 29th member, the only East Asian country other than Japan to join the club.

However, entrance into the OECD spurred nearly indiscriminate diversification and borrowing by the large conglomerates, called the *chaebŏl*, resulting in dangerously high debt-to-equity ratios (for more details see Chapter 2). The economy took a steep nosedive in early 1996. The attempt to pass a new revised labor law that allowed for more layoffs prompted a series of strikes in December 1996; these peaked in January 1997, but a series of strikes through the year did not help matters. Conditions worsened during 1997 with eleven bankruptcies of mid-tier *chaebŏl*. The reasons for the 1997 financial crisis are multiple, as I will discuss in Chapter 2, but the announcement in November 1997 that South Korea would seek an International Monetary Fund (IMF) bailout was received as a traumatic event, a stomach blow to the GDP nationalism that had driven South Korea for the past several decades. The revelation that some government officials had ignored earlier warnings about the possibility of an imminent financial crisis (contained in internal reports issued in the summer of 1997) further enraged the public.

The return of Kim Dae-Jung

The failure in outcomes, if not in processes, of the Kim Young-Sam years created conditions favorable for a change in government. Kim Dae-Jung, who had announced his retirement from politics after his 1992 defeat, announced his intention to run in the December 1997 presidential election. Kim Dae-Jung was no longer the young liberal firebrand he had been in 1971, when he had lost his first presidential election. Years of tribulation had not tempered his ambition, but had rendered him more pragmatic and compromising. Kim Dae-Jung this time allied with Kim Jong-Pil for the election, and this move proved to be one of several key factors in his narrow victory over the government party candidate, Lee Hoi-Chang. A third major candidate who ended up with 20% of the vote took away a significant portion of the conservative vote from Lee. Furthermore, Lee's reputation was damaged when the media widely reported that his sons had managed to evade mandatory military service. Kim Dae-Jung's campaign took advantage of this to air a 30-minute video, "A Mother's Tears," the night before the vote, about a mother who had lost her son during his tour of duty in the army and did not mince her words in expressing her anger at Lee.

Upon his election victory, Kim Dae-Jung was hailed in the international media as the "Nelson Mandela of Asia." Although the most tenacious and celebrated opposition politician who became president, Kim was a complex mix of conservative and progressive values, hardly the radical some mass media portrayed him to be. For example, in exchange for supporting him, Kim Dae-Jung had promised to appoint Kim Jong-Pil as prime minister if elected. The alliance was the height of irony – a man who had founded the KCIA, and a man who had been kidnapped by the same organization joined in the same political campaign.

Moreover, when faced with opposition to the appointing of Kim Jong-Pil as premier, Kim Dae-Jung and his party used highly questionable tactics to block an opposing vote, and Kim unilaterally appointed Kim Jong-Pil as "acting" prime minister in March 1998. Kim Jong-Pil was later approved as "full" prime minister, in September of the same year, but the initial ploy, combined with Kim Dae-Jung's unwillingness to abolish the National Security Law, indicated that democratic consolidation was still influenced by ends-oriented rather than procedural politics.

New Trends in Democracy

What new trajectories characterized South Korean politics during the process of democratic consolidation? First, NGOs proliferated and became a significant force within Korean politics. NGOs expanded in scope and diversity, including ones that extensively utilized the Internet and digital communications technology. The rights of workers, women, children, and migrant workers increased overall, even if in fitful spurts, in large part because of NGO activities. Some NGOs focused on fostering improvements in gender equality and others on raising awareness of environmental issues, while their numbers, diversity, and politicization increased.

Second, the Internet and other digital communications technologies became increasingly important in politics. Politicians and NGOs recognized the importance of nimble management of the Internet, often termed "cyberpolitics" – maintaining good websites, using the Internet for lobbying, or for mobilizing supporters. This does not imply that the actual substance of policy discussions or the politicians themselves were somehow more innately "progressive," but merely that the medium and the space of debate increased in diversity.

Third, South Korea moved very quickly along the trajectory of other post-democratization countries: initial electoral enthusiasm followed by decreasing overall voter turnout, especially among younger eligible voters. Generational differences amplified by frequent and major changes also polarized South Korean society. In particular, the range of attitudes towards North Korea often varied by age cohort, exacerbating intergenerational schisms.

NGOs and civil society

The first prominent characteristic of South Korea's post-1987 democracy has been the proliferation of NGOs. Even if Kim Dae-Jung launched his government in 1997 with questionable tactics, democratic consolidation was greatly aided by a civil society that had flourished since 1987. While numbers do not tell the whole story, there has been an undeniable explosion in the number of NGOs since 1987. Only around 9% of the roughly 7,600-plus NGOs in operation today in South Korea existed before 1987, and only 25% were formed before 1990. Over 60% of all NGOs in South Korea have websites, and many of the major ones have multilingual sites. As of 1999, some 67% of all NGOs were concentrated in Seoul, but by 2003 this proportion had declined to 50%, indicating that the organizational form had taken root throughout the country.

The growth of NGOs since the late 1980s is a phenomenon that has not been unique to South Korea. The numbers of NGOs worldwide has been increasing in the post-Cold War years, most notably in post-authoritarian states. For example, estimates of the number of NGOs established in Eastern European countries between 1988 and 1995 hover around 100,000. As was the case in South Korea, in many of these countries increasing government liberalization of censorship, regulations that promoted the formation of civil associations, and financial subsidies combined with the increasing participation of the middle class in politics to fuel the proliferation of domestic NGOs.

In South Korea the deradicalization of NGOs in the post-1987 years was the most significant factor that contributed to making them more accessible to the majority of the population. There had been plenty of NGOs even under dictatorial rule during the 1970s and 1980s, with universities, churches, and labor union offices all sites of civic organization.[35] Radical, loosely class-based social movements called the "people's movement" (*minjung undong*) were the primary form of non-governmental organized activities.[36] As more of the middle class became involved in politics and social issues (as discussed above), many NGOs moved away from radical and leftist programs to more centrist agendas that were both a result of widening political involvement and a strategy to attract wider support.[37]

For example, one of the largest and most influential of the NGOs, the Citizens' Coalition for Economic Justice (CCEJ), was established in July 1989 with an explicitly non-radical platform. Its main aims are the promotion of a more equitable distribution of economic benefits, the promotion of anti-corruption policies and campaigns, and the prioritization concerns related to daily livelihood rather than class struggle. Supported by 60,000 members as of 2006, the CCEJ issues annual assessments of government policies, including Kim Dae-Jung's Sunshine Policy of sustained engagement with North Korea, and lobbies for specific cases. Two other NGOs formerly known for their more radical orientation, the Korean Teachers and Education Workers Union (KTU) and the Korean Peasant Movement Coalition, announced more mainstream positions. Moreover, several NGOs, both radical and mainstream, have personnel crossovers and combine their resources depending on the policy area.[38]

However, unlike the situation in Ukraine during the Orange Revolution of winter 2004, where Serbian radical student groups allied with Ukrainian student organizations, and controversy remains regarding the size and significance of US funding for Ukranian NGOs, there were no significant international linkages between South Korean domestic NGOs and international NGOs (INGOs).[39] Most South Korean NGOs developed from domestic concerns, agendas, and funds. Although they have on occasion mobilized international norms and standards, Korea NGOs have generally not had extensive ties or conflicts with INGOs, as has been the case in some countries such as Malaysia.[40]

Although they have hardly displaced the functions of the state, as was suggested in some of the literature in the 1990s,[41] some larger NGOs have had significant impact on politics and policy. Several NGOs in the fields of women's issues, the environment, and fair elections have played major roles in successfully lobbying for legislation. The Korean Women's Association United (KWAU) was established in 1987 and has pushed for gender equity bills, including the 1999 Anti-Gender Discrimination Law. The 1987 Equal Wage Law improved gender equity in pay, but the promulgation of the 1999 Anti-Gender Discrimination Law was needed to continue progress in attaining overall gender equity in hiring and other areas. Environmental NGOs also grew in size and influence. The Korean Federation for Environmental Movement (KFEM), established in 1993, has conducted several successful anti-pollution campaigns, including a successful campaign in 1997 to urge Taiwan to cancel its agreement to ship nuclear waste to North Korea.[42] Other NGOs, such as advocacy groups for physically disabled people or for rights of homosexuals, were established in 2000 under the auspices of the 2000 NPO (Non-Profit Organization) Law that standardized government approval procedures for establishing NPOs.[43]

In politics, the Citizens' Coalition for Fair Election (CCFE) served as a watchdog for corruption or coercion during the election campaigning in 1992. This led to the formation of NGOs such as the People's Solidarity for Participatory Democracy (PSPD), in 1994, which effectively pushed for anti-corruption measures. The PSPD combined with the Citizens' Alliance for the 2000 General Elections (CAGE) to issue via the Internet during the 2000 elections a blacklist of politicians with records of having received bribes or of influence peddling. As a result of active campaigning and the intensive media coverage of CAGE, 59 out of 89 blacklisted candidates were defeated.[44]

Admittedly, proliferation of and effective lobbying by NGOs do not necessarily promote democratic politics. Critics claim that NGOs in general may actually fracture society by fostering greater group polarization, as like-minded people gather to confirm that their views on a given policy issue are indeed correct and those of their opponents are incorrect.[45] As smaller NGOs (under ten full-time employees) constitute the majority, the opportunities to interact with others with differing opinions may decrease as well, further augmenting the effects of social atomization.[46] In addition, many of the larger NGOs with more than 10,000 members (which form around 10% of the total of NGOs) are very professionalized and nearly citizenless given the tenuous connections to their grassroots supporters.[47]

Furthermore, increasing politicization and partisanship have resulted in the NGO organizational form becoming co-opted as a tool for political mobilization. Government liberalization and subsidies helped the growth of NGOs, but they were for the most part opposed to government policies. More recently, civil society has increasingly become cluttered with a variety of cleavages, as both left and right have used NGOs as a medium for mobilizing support. Both sides decry what they see as a dilution of their ideas in the practice of current NGOs, and establish rival or splinter groups. This has resulted in the emergence of NGOs linked to specific politicians and political parties, such as booster clubs for candidates during an election, as was the case for Roh Moo-Hyun during the 2002 presidential election, or NGOs such as Citizens United for Better Society (CUBS), established in 2000 to promote anti-communist and free market agendas, which were allied explicitly with conservative opposition parties.

In this increasingly politicized environment, some of the smaller NGOs, such as the Refuge PNAN, which works to help all foreign asylum seekers (rather than just North Koreans) to South Korea, simply do not attract much support from the general public. Indeed, some of the larger NGOs in South Korea now find themselves in the awkward position of representing a new orthodoxy, as first-mover advantages and economies of scale help sustain their operations, while newer and smaller NGOs face greater hurdles for mere survival.

Given the increasing diversity of voices among NGOs, critics of the current political system inevitably hear a confusion of voices rather than coherent or cohesive debate. However, the apparently chaotic profusion of views actually reflects the increasing diversity in intellectual, material, and political views in South Korea. It is this broadened spectrum that has allowed NGOs and civil society to play significant, if not exclusive or definitive, roles in South Korea.

The media, the Internet, and politics

The second notable trend in post-1987 South Korea has been the resonances between specific forms of media and politics. In the 1987 elections, Roh Tae-Woo made effective use of political posters and advertising. In 1992, the three main print newspapers, *Chosŏn Ilbo*, *Tonga Ilbo*, and *Chungang Ilbo*, supported Kim Young-Sam, which provided momentum for his campaign. In 1997, Kim Dae-Jung used television to garner votes: his campaign made strategic use of the first presidential debates broadcast on television, short political advertisements, and longer paid announcements. The December 2002 presidential election victory for Roh Moo-Hyun came as a surprise to many, since the print newspapers had Lee Hoi-Chang ahead on all polls going into the voting. Several factors explain Roh's victory, but one of the most prominent ones was the use of the Internet by Roh's supporter club, Nosamo.

Nosamo, which is an abbreviation for "those who love Roh Moo-Hyun," was established in April 2000 as the first political fan club in South Korea. The core members were primarily in their twenties through forties, comfortable with using the Internet to transmit information and to expand membership. Roh, a high school graduate who never attended university, had been a lawyer since passing the difficult bar exam in 1975. Coming from an impoverished background, Roh had captured a seat in the National Assembly in 1988, but lost his seat in the April 2000 National Assembly elections, prompting his supporters to form Nosamo.[48]

With the presidential election looming in 2002, Roh won the candidacy of the ruling Millennial Democratic Party (MDP) because of widespread support among regular party members. The power brokers of the MDP, who had joined mainly because of personal connections to Kim Dae-Jung, were not so enthusiastic about the upstart candidate. Leading up to December 2002, traditional media outlets projected Lee Hoi-Chang as the victor, while Internet news and websites predicted Roh Moo-Hyun would win. Supported by Nosamo and OhmyNews, the first major Internet "citizens' press" – a media outlet whose reporters were not accredited journalists – Roh's popularity in the virtual world was essentially unchallenged.[49] However, many pundits doubted whether the virtual support would translate into real votes for Roh. Support was also generated by a last-minute betrayal by another presidential candidate who had pledged to support Roh then backed out, and by an intensive campaign via the Internet and cell phones. Roh managed a narrow victory over Lee. This rare political upset could be seen as a race not just between the old guard and new reformist politicians, but also between old and new media.

The emergence of Internet politics, or the "Netizen" and the "Cyberian society," has been one of the more distinctive elements of South Korea democracy. In a country that has the highest Internet broadband penetration rate and per capita cell phone usage rate in the world, and a 68% Internet penetration rate (good for 16th in the world), information technology proved to be an extremely convenient medium for social and political mobilization.[50]

Previously, voting patterns had been primarily based largely on the region of origin of the candidates. The extent of regional bias in previous elections has been questioned. On the one hand, many scholars and journalists speak of the political and economic biases that have concentrated power and money in Seoul and in the southeast, while keeping the southwestern provinces in the margins. On the other, some argue that actual distributions of income and voting patterns show that the impact of regional interests on voter behavior has been greatly exaggerated.[51] Whichever is the case, what is clear is that Netizen networks helped catapult Roh Moo-Hyun to national prominence by generating grassroots support across the nation, as evidenced by the strong support Roh received in the southwestern provinces, despite the fact that he was from Pusan, the largest city of the southeast.

Roh broke off from the MDP and formed his own party, the Uri Party or Our Open Party (OOP), in November 2003. The conservative Grand National Party (GNP), formally called the Democratic Liberal Party (the ruling party during Kim Young-San's presidency), and the MDP allied to impeach Roh, via a vote in the National Assembly in March 2004, for illegal electioneering and incompetence. Netizens again used the Internet and mobile communications to organize rallies to support Roh, including one gathering in late March that assembled some 250,000 people.

Meanwhile, the pro-impeachment demonstration on the same day attracted 2,000 people. The April 2004 general elections produced a majority for the OOP in the National Assembly, giving Roh a stronger hand; meanwhile, the Constitutional Court eventually overturned the impeachment in May 2004. Some conservatives called for a military coup to rid the country of Roh, but despite the seemingly irreparable political fissures, the weapons of choice remained the Internet, demonstrations, and elections, rather than armed insurrection.

Some qualifications about the successful use of the Internet and cell phones to organize demonstrations may be necessary, since the overall impact of such web-based politics remains open to further analysis. The numbers of members in a fan club, for example, may not necessarily correlate with the current number of active members, and having sophisticated websites does not ensure frequency of hits or positive reception. Nonetheless, almost all leading politicians are now armed with professionally developed websites, and many are also supported by their own Internet-based fan clubs.

Post-democratic trajectories

The third salient development in South Korean democracy has been the development of standard post-democratic consolidation patterns, including a drop in voter turnout and a widening of the political spectrum. In the South Korean case, this trajectory has been extremely rapid because of the emergence of a generational gap, both actual and perceived. The usual generational differences in political orientation, often explainable by different stages of the life cycle, have been magnified by the compressed change experienced over the past fifty years. Consequently, there has been rapid political alienation resulting in lower voter turnouts among younger eligible voters, and increasing domestic political polarization.

Political participation, at least in terms of voter turnout, has been declining rapidly. The presidential election of 1987 recorded a 89% voter turnout rate among eligible voters, while the 1992 election registered an 82% turnout, and the 1997 presidential election in which Kim Dae-Jung emerged victorious generated an 81% turnout rate. The 2002 presidential elections saw a steep decline to 71%, despite the widespread use of new communications technologies. In National Assembly elections, this pattern of electoral alienation has been even more pronounced. The 1988 elections generated a 76% turnout, while the 1992 elections saw 72% vote. In 1996, this dropped to 65% and in 2000 to 57%. The 2004 general elections rebounded slightly to 61%. For local elections, the voter participation rate dropped from 68% in 1995 to 49% in 2002.

Differences in presidential election systems, as well as timing and specific conditions, affect turnout and outcome, but as rough points of comparison, it is worth noting that other new democracies in Asia such as Taiwan and the Philippines had turnout rates of 80% and 84% respectively for their 2004 presidential elections. Among the older democracies the US had a 80% rate for the 1972 presidential election; by the 2004 election, this had dropped to 55%. The South Korean trend in voter turnouts might be closest to many of the new democracies in Eastern Europe, such as Slovenia, where turnout dropped from 86% in 1992 to 65% in 2002, or Bulgaria, which went from 75% in 1992 to 55% in 2001.

Voter disinterest trajectories in South Korea vary over three major age cohorts. First, the most active in voting are those over 50 with either memories of the Korean War or intensive saturation in anti-communist education. This cohort generally tends to be most supportive of US foreign policy in Asia and more wary of North Korea. Second, there are the voters under 30 who essentially grew up with democracy and relative economic comfort. The alienation from politics in South Korea has been most significant among the voters in this age category. For example, in the 1996 National Assembly elections (65% overall turnout rate), 78% of those in the 50 and over category voted, while only 50% of eligible voters in the 20–29 category voted.[52] In the 2004 general elections, the 50–59 group voted at a rate of 83%, while the 20–29 group was at 37%. As is the case in most other democratic countries, those under 30 are often seen as being more consumerist, individualistic, and indifferent towards politics. When the younger generations do cast votes, the general trend is that they tend to favor the more progressive and less conservative candidates. This group generally favors a conciliatory approach to North Korea.

The third cohort, the so-called "386" generation, is currently the most influential. Named after the Intel Pentium Central Processing Units (the 80-386) that were popular in the 1990s, "386" refers to people in their 30s when the term originated, now mostly in their 40s (the 3), who graduated from university in the 1980s (the 8), and were born in the 1960s (the 6). The 386ers witnessed both dictatorial rule and democratization, and grew up during a period of rapid economic growth. They were educated in the aftermath of the Kwangju Massacre, and many participated in the pro-democratization, anti-government demonstrations in the 1980s. If older generations are defined by the epochal moments such as liberation from Japanese colonial rule, the Korean War, or the oppressive Yusin system instituted by Park Chung-Hee in 1972, the 386ers are the cohort most closely linked with democratization. Unlike the older generations, the 386ers are comfortable in using the Internet and other digital communications technologies, which allows them to use various media for political mobilization.

Even more important, the 386ers form the most significant proportion of the electorate. According to the National Statistical Office, those in their 30s and 40s account for roughly 33% of the total population; they are the largest single segment of the population. Moreover a long-term demographic shift means that those aged 20 to 39 constitute over 50% of eligible voters in South Korea; given the lower voter turnout rates of those under 30, the 386ers are likely to have the most impact.

Further, there has been a relatively rapid generational transition in political office. While most of Roh's cabinet ministers have largely been in their 50s, many presidential advisory councils and committees to the government are composed largely of 386ers. In addition, the number of National Assembly members under 50 increased from 29% in 2000 to 43% in 2004, also reflecting the generational transition under way in politics.

South Korea's North Korea policy is the most galvanizing issue, one that regularly highlights the intergenerational differences. In early 2004, public opinion surveys indicated that those over 50 are more likely to support the conservative GNP, and disapprove of Roh Moo-Hyun and the OOP. Just as important, 386ers are more inclined to favor a conciliatory approach to North Korea, the so-called Sunshine Policy, while the older generation tends to be more hostile towards Kim Jong-Il and Roh Moo-Hyun's North Korea policy. Anti-Roh or anti-North Korea demonstrations showed a preponderance of older men, while the anti-American or pro-Sunshine Policy demonstrations, in contrast, were composed largely of people in their 20s through the 40s.

Yet generational differences can serve as a convenient explanation for political conflicts that ultimately shuts down further enquiry. In one instance, a November 2004 poll indicated that only 22% of the respondents felt that Roh Moo-Hyun was doing a good job. Among those aged 20 to 29, Roh scored 29%; from those in the 30–39 category, he earned 24% support; and for those 50 and above, 24%. Interestingly, among those between 40 and 49, only 12% supported Roh. This result runs counter to general assumptions of a linear correlation between age and relative support of President Roh.[53] In fact, in the 2002 elections, Roh had received the same percentage of votes from those in their 40s as had his counterpart, Lee Hoi-Chang, indicating that while younger voters did support Roh, generational differences are only one of many major variables that explain the political dynamics in South Korea's post-1987 democracy.

Conclusion

Democratization in South Korea was not the result of the kind of export of "freedom" and "democracy" that occurred in Iraq in 2003, nor was it the result of liberalization policies pushed through by the IMF or any other international agency. Rather, individuals and organizations whose roots were firmly planted in domestic history propelled the transformation process in 1987. Kim Chu-Yŏl, Lee Han-Yŏl, and countless others who participated in anti-government and pro-democracy activities cannot be categorized as just victims or beneficiaries of globalization.

An important logical implication of this interpretation is that it is extremely important that we do not view the process of democratization in South Korea as simply a product of reactions against US interventionism, or as a reflection of a desire to be more like the US. This is not to overlook the impact that actions of individual American officials, Korean access to US technologies and markets, and consumption of notions of democracy via the 1948 constitution has had on the history of South Korea. However, not all changes in recent world history, despite the impressions generated by both supporters and critics, revolve strictly around the US and its foreign policies.

Some critics protest that conservatives have hijacked democracy in South Korea and that the country remains mired in the legacies of authoritarian rule.[54] Given the shifts in demographic structure, the gradual generational transition in political power, and the voter turnout patterns, the differences between those in their 30s and 40s (the 386ers), and those in their 50s and 60s, it seems likely, will continue to fuel the process of political polarization rather than convergence. Others claim that the 1987 system sorely lacks institutionalized forms of consensus formation. The regularity of violent confrontations and disputes among politicians and the public regarding policy towards North Korea, as we shall see later in this book, indicates that it may be necessary for any president to suture some of the ideological and political ruptures. Undeniably, problems do remain, as reflected by the fact that despite its efforts the Roh Moo-Hyun government has, like its predecessors, been unable to abolish the National Security Law.

Ultimately, however, the accusations which conservatives and radicals regularly launch at each other that the other side is undermining democracy and corrupting civil society reflect less the problems with democracy and more the dramatic broadening of the political spectrum since 1987.[55] Despite the vitriol flying back and forth between conservatives and progressives, despite the fissures between left and right, and despite the drift apart of old and young, the fact that such tensions can be expressed in public is an important testimony to the rapidity and intensity of changes in South Korea's political system over the past twenty years. The space for discussion has expanded widely, a clear contrast to the tightly controlled political and social system of North Korea. Although some of the rhetoric in South Korea might give the impression that democracy has been a Pandora's box, a source of numerous unforeseen troubles, it should be remembered that in most versions of the myth, the last item that fluttered out was hope.

2 | Altered States
Economic and Social Change in South Korea

Seoul seems to be a city of light and speed. Corporate headquarters gleam above glittering neon billboards, while a cacophonic stream of modern motorized traffic permeates the streets. The capitalist and the consumer can find sanctuary and occasion for joy everywhere. Department stores and boutiques in the fashionable Apkujondong neighborhood are laden with a cornucopia of goods. The traditional markets, such as the Namdaemun and Tongdaemun markets, buzz with activity. A 2005 population estimate of metropolitan areas placed Seoul as the fourth largest in the world with 23 million people – 48% of the entire country – while a world 2005 cost-of-living survey ranked it as the fifth most expensive city in the world. In its current configuration, the city is divided into a northern and southern side along the meandering Han river. Some twenty bridges cross the Han river, and the entire city is latticed by an intricate and massive rail and subway network, estimated to carry some 1.6 billion passengers a year.

Standing in the streets surging with life, it would be hard to imagine that several economists of the 1950s plaintively labeled South Korea a perpetually backward "mendicant economy," living off aid money from the US.[1] During the 1950s and the 1960s, academics spilled much ink attempting to explain why development was not occurring despite the millions of aid money flowing into the country, while American politicians questioned the burdens US taxpayers had to bear for what looked to be a veritable economic black hole. Twenty-first-century Seoul, so liberally dotted with monuments of capitalism and consumerism, might be difficult to imagine for anyone from the 1950s, even as lingering fragments from a fevered dream. The seemingly overnight transformation has generated the misleading, if catchy, moniker "the Miracle on the Han" – inspired by "the Miracle on the Rhine," the rapid post-World War Two recovery of West Germany (rather than the ecological recovery of the same river in the 1990s).

The 1997 financial crisis seemingly blanched off much of the lustre. On the brink of insolvency when foreign creditors began withdrawing their loans, the South Korean government asked the IMF for assistance in November 1997. The $59 billion bailout package was at that time the largest in the history of the IMF. On the heels of the crisis, journalistic headlines and academic works asked whether South Korean economic growth had been "a miracle or a mirage." The question itself, for all its meretricious and alliterative power, is far too simple to serve as a useful starting point other than in a heuristic sense, since the obvious answer was that South Korea's economic transformation over the past several decades had never been either.

It would be difficult to ignore the fact that development in South Korea had been sustained over several decades, fueled by the unstinting efforts and sacrifices of millions of ordinary people rather than by a miraculous incantation. The notions of a "miracle" must also be tempered by the awareness of the high costs to the environment, labor rights, and human rights. It would also take near-superhuman effort to dismiss as a "mirage" the fact that the structure of the South Korean economy had irreversibly changed over the past few decades.

South Korea's relatively quick recovery from the IMF period of 1997 to 1999, culminating in the last payment for the IMF loans three years ahead of schedule, in summer 2001, restored the country to its status as a paragon of development and exemplar to countries aspiring for better material conditions. The "watershed" crisis seems to be of limited consequence ten years after, an eternity in today's attention-deficient world. South Korea's economy was ranked anywhere from 10th to 14th in the world for 2005, depending on the survey and method of measurement. It has maintained healthy growth rates for most of the period from 1989 to 2006, with only 1998 recording minus growth. All this stands in stark contrast to the smaller, less open economy of North Korea.

This chapter analyzes South Korea's post-1989 socio-economic history by focusing on four key words of transformation – development, crisis, cool, and multiethnicity. The first section examines South Korean economic development up to 1997, and the second dissects the causes of the 1997 financial crisis and the subsequent recovery. In the third section, I explain the rise of the entertainment industry on the heels of the financial crisis, the so-called "Korean Wave." The entertainment industry helped drive the economic recovery, and has done as much to project South Korea's image abroad as has its other exports. The fourth section looks at the demographic trends that are causing an accelerated transformation of South Korea into a more multiethnic society in reality, if not in official policy and everyday practice.

Economic Development, 1960–97

How did the South Korean economy grow? During the 1980s and 1990s, academics and journalists flocked to South Korea to search for the causal alchemy behind the metamorphosis of post-Korean War slag into late-industrial gold. Among the range of explanations offered, the roles of effective economic planning and timely intervention by a government dedicated to development – the "developmental state" model – became one of the most commonly cited. Others included the impact of "export-led development" and, more controversially, the role of culture, or "Confucian capitalism," on attitudes towards work, authority, and education. References to Asian "tigers" and "dragons" abounded, as did more specialized invocations of a 1930s Japanese economic theory of development called the "flying geese model" – which emphasized the role of trade of declining industries from one country to another as the lead country moved up the value-added chain.[2] Aside from these marriages of economics and zoology, the importance of market mechanisms versus industrial policy, the impact of supply-side factors versus demand-side factors, and total factor productivity increases versus increases in factor inputs, formed other lines of debate.

Historical legacies

As was the case with democratization, the origins of development and growth can be traced back to long before 1989. The question of when exactly Korean development began and the extent of the continuities between pre-colonial, colonial, post-liberation, and post-Korean War economies remain open for further exploration by historians.

At least four periods have been identified by various scholars as possible starting points for the story of Korea's economic development. This topic has been riven by intense debates in South Korean academia because of the view of economic development as a desirable outcome, and the association of colonialism or authoritarianism with normatively negative processes.

The first view situates the start of economic development in the late Chosŏn period. Commercial activity flourished in the late Chosŏn period, and the Chosŏn government had initiated some model manufacturing factories, but Korea was colonized by Japan before these prototypes could affect the entire economy. While the commercial roots of economic growth were certainly grounded in this period, sustained growth of the manufacturing sector did not occur on a large scale before the 1930s.

The second view locates the start of sustained development in the 1920s and 1930s under Japanese colonial rule. Under Japanese rule, while some attempts were made to promote manufacturing in the 1920s, it was not until the 1930s that there was sustained investment in manufacturing and heavy industry. Why and how the colonial state invested in manufacturing, and who ultimately profited from such development remain points of heated debate among academics and the public, but few disagree that there were significant increases in output in manufacturing and heavy industry. In this sense, the initial start to economic development, narrowly defined as structural transition from an agrarian to an industrial society, can be said to have begun in earnest during the 1930s.

There is a problem in linking the development during the colonial period to the post-1953 years due to the extensive damage to the infrastructure incurred during the Korean War – the war destroyed around 25% of capital stock or 85% of South Korea's 1953 gross national product (GNP). Also, heavy industries and power sources were generally concentrated in the northern half of the peninsula, leaving South Korea with little access to power once the peninsula was divided. Moreover, decolonization disrupted existing trade and supply routes with Japan. It is possible to argue that the more important legacy took the form of human capital and organizational form: the entrepreneurial know-how lodged in the minds of businessmen and government officials and the developmental state model. For example, the similarities in organizational structure between Park Chung-Hee's developmental state of the 1960s and the 1930s colonial administrative structure could be explained by Park Chung-Hee's early education in a Japanese military academy in Manchuria.[3] However, further empirical research is required to demonstrate that colonial experiences had a major impact on post-1960s development policy.

A third view emphasizes the role of capital accumulation and embryonic economic planning in the 1950s. The orthodox view had been that Syngman Rhee's policies and US aid had not generated consistent growth in Korea in the post-war years.[4] Revisionist views posit that the capital accumulation and fiscal reform that was necessary for post-1961 growth occurred from 1953 to 1960 rather than in the 1930s.[5] These scholars point to the existence of drafts for economic plans under Chang Myŏn that Park adapted for his own use after the coup, and to the continuities between bureaucracies of the 1950s and the 1960s, to argue that there was no spike in the level of prescience or effectiveness of industrial policy after 1961, but only a reduction in transaction costs due to policies based on personal networks.[6]

The fourth and majority view is that the development of the 1960s was not directly related to the preceding periods. Scholars who adhere to this view emphasize the damage suffered during the Korean War, the poor economic record under Rhee, and the convergence of state and market in the 1960s. Park's dictatorship rested on shaky stilts of legitimacy, but he was armed with the power to repress protest and maintain autonomy for its economic bureaucrats. Development also coincided with favorable international conditions, leading the central role of exports in development.

The developmental state and export-led development in the 1960s

Despite the various views on the starting point of development, what is undeniable is that starting in the 1960s, growth rates increased with alacrity. Park Chung-Hee deliberately promoted economic nationalism, making development the first priority, and unwittingly echoing the developmental economic historian Alexander Gerschenkron's proposition that the later the country starts on development, the stronger the need for a powerful ideology of development to act as a cohesive force that insures the input of all domestic actors involved.[7] Economic planning offices were newly established or expanded. The planners in them identified strategic industries and targeted firms that would receive preferential loans at low interest rates.

Park's developmental state targeted export industries for growth. The post-1953 recovery from war had been based on US aid and restrictions on manufacturing imports that were intended to provide shelter to infant domestic industries, a policy often referred to as import substitution industrialization (ISI). The shift in emphasis from ISI to export-led development (ELD) in the light industries meant that export firms were given preferential loans.[8] The injection of capital from funds and loans obtained from Japan after normalization of relations in 1965, combined with imports of technology from Japan and the US in the 1960s, also spurred growth, as did the government policy to devalue the currency and unify the official and the black market exchange rates.[9] Relatively easy access to the US market was also essential during this time, and a spike in demand from spillover effects of the Vietnam War were also crucial to the success of this strategy.[10]

High interest rates were also used to promote domestic savings, while consumer goods were given relatively little priority. As a result, the export sector grew rapidly and per capita output doubled during the 1960s, but the consumer goods and social welfare sectors remained relatively underdeveloped. Labor and human rights were systematically repressed through the 1960s and the 1970s, keeping wages down and providing a competitive advantage for exports.

Heavy industries and trade in the 1970s and 1980s

Starting in the early 1970s, Park emphasized heavy and chemical industries (HCI), essentially a form of ISI. The HCI drive resulted in a fundamental change in economic structure. The share of primary industries such as farming, fishing, and mining declined from 45% in 1960 to 25% in 1975, while the share of manufacturing output for heavy industries rose from 30% in 1963 to 76% in 1996. The government directed banks to provide low-interest loans to targeted *chaebŏl* that had been assigned specific tasks in developing the HCI. High levels of investment were required but the HCI drive increased capacity and output in industries such as steel, shipbuilding, and electronics. It also created economic distortions, such as inflation, high debt loads, and reduced savings, and it hampered the growth of consumer goods manufacturing. The demand for skilled workers grew with the HCI drive, driving up domestic wages. As a result, wage gaps between skilled and unskilled workers widened through the 1970s, creating greater inequality but also expanding the middle class.

Growth rates in the 1980s were equally impressive, but this time driven mainly by exports. Chun and Roh attempted to stabilize the economy from the legacies of the HCI drive by deregulating trade and finance, and at the same time rationalizing through government-mandated mergers of large firms in specific industries. Piecemeal liberalization proved effective in terms of generating high growth rates, but market concentration ensued as large *chaebŏl* such as Hyundai, Daewoo, Samsung, and LG increasingly bought up smaller rivals, leaving the small and medium-sized enterprises sector underdeveloped.[11] Wages increased, the size of the middle class expanded, labor rights continued to be suppressed, occasional corruption scandals surfaced, and credit issues accumulated. Exports continued to expand in volume and value, but the trade deficits began to mount after 1986.

The confluence of these trends resulted in a marked slowdown in South Korea's economy in 1989. After three consecutive years of 12% growth in GNP, in 1989 the rate fell to 7%. Increasing wages, frequent work stoppages, and skyrocketing inflation also contributed to a drop in export growth rates from 36% and 28% respectively in 1987 and 1988, to 2.6% in 1989. The current account balance, which had shifted from chronic deficit to surpluses after 1986, reverted back to a deficit in 1990. As noted in Chapter 1, Roh met the downturn and the associated labor strife with a clampdown that did not dissipate the sense of economic uncertainty.

Labor

Labor rights had been controlled and suppressed by the government over the decades. The low wages that characterized labor repression had worked in conjunction with export promotion policies to facilitate development. Not surprisingly, there were no powerful independent labor unions under Park's rule. The Federation of Korean Trade Unions (FKTU), organized by the government in 1961, had essentially been a corporatist extension of the state into labor. Not surprisingly, the FKTU had difficulty gaining recognition as an independent workers' body, despite the fervent efforts of Park to promote it as such. Although workers in general had accepted or endured poor working conditions and low wages over the years, protests and demonstrations occurred regularly. In 1970, during one of the numerous labor demonstrations in the face of violent police retaliation, a twenty-year-old man, Chŏn T'ae-Il, immolated himself, becoming a martyr for labor rights.

The combination of government oppression and the restricted forms of labor organization prompted a number of independent unions to form. These eventually joined to form the Korean Confederation of Trade Unions (KCTU) in 1995. Although the Kim Young-Sam government only recognized the FKTU (the KCTU did not gain legal recognition until 1999), both the FKTU and the KCTU occasionally cooperated in lobbying for changes to labor laws. Naturally, FKTU membership declined as the KCTU took a more radical stance against the government, culminating in the nationwide general strike that began in December 1996. This became the largest strike in South Korean history as some 1,900 unions and 750,000 members joined at its peak in January 1997. Both the OECD and the International Labor Organization (ILO) urged the South Korean government to improve labor conditions and rights to meet international standards.

South Korea was able to achieve these and other socioeconomic transformations through a combination of several factors: effective industrial policy; government control of finances; an emphasis on education that produced a large skilled labor pool; government repression of labor rights; an emphasis on output increases at the expense of environmental degradation; timely inputs of Japanese parts, technology, and capital; US support and markets; high savings and investment rates; high productive inputs; favorable market opportunities; an ideology of economic nationalism; and predominant values that allowed for the mobilization of society for development.[12]

The economy grew at an average annual rate of around 10% from 1965 to 1970 in terms of real GDP growth; 8% from 1971 to 1980; 10% from 1981 to 1990; and 7% from 1991 to 1997. This sustained economic growth performance was matched only by Taiwan and two city-states, Hong Kong and Singapore. Per capita income increased over a hundred fold: from US$105 in 1965 to US$11,380 in 1996. South Korea became an industrialized country, a significant section of the population considered themselves middle class, and rapid urbanization occurred as workers conglomerated in industrial centers. Life expectancy increased from 54 in 1960 to 72 in 1997. Much of the growth could be attributed to increases in the use of productive inputs – physical capital in particular – rather than to productivity advances, but there had been no collapse of a specific industry before 1997, and all projections pointed toward continued growth in 1997 and 1998.

1997 Financial Crisis and Recovery

What then caused the 1997 financial crisis? And how did the country recover so quickly? Predictably, there remains considerable debate about the causes of the 1997 financial crisis, and about whether there has been a full recovery since then.[13]

Causes of the 1997 financial crisis

Much of the discussion revolves around assessments of whether Kim Young-Sam's liberalization program of the mid-1990s failed because it was incomplete or because it was ill-conceived. One perspective argues that the developmental state was designed for catching-up, not for maintaining growth as an industrialized society, and that the 1997 crisis was a warning that government intervention based on national interests rather than on market logic was no longer a viable approach for maintaining growth. The logical follow-on from this assertion is that the Kim Young-Sam liberalizing reforms were undermined by *insufficient* adherence to neoliberal principals.

The opposing view is that there was essentially *excessive* liberalization at the wrong time, making South Korea vulnerable to volatile international capital flows at a time when the state's capacity to intervene in foreign exchange markets had already been eroded. Liberalization of capital accounts caused rapid accumulation of short-term external debts at high interest rates, so-called "hot money." This, together with a highly leveraged corporate sector and the banking sector destabilized by the financial repression, provided the backdrop for the financial crisis of 1997.

The answer seems to be a combination of both. The immediate cause of the crisis was an outflow of capital as a result of the chain reactions from the financial crisis that started in Thailand in July 1997, spread to Hong Kong in October of the same year, and eventually reached South Korea in November. In particular, loans from Japanese banks to South Korea dropped from $22 billion in December 1996 to $9 billion one year later.

Regional disparity within South Korea was not an issue in generating the crisis. Regional income distribution has long been assumed to be unequal, tilted in favor of the capital city and the southeastern provinces, the original hometowns of successive rulers such as Park Chung-Hee, Chun Doo-Hwan, Roh Tae-Woo, and Kim Young-Sam. The imagined geography of regional distinctiveness did help form political cliques and generate concrete political tensions. Moreover, pork barrel projects and favorable loans distributed on the basis of personal connections were not uncommon. However, a recent study found that overall, the income distribution between regions was generally equitable between 1986 and 1995.[14] The marked increase in independent labor activism was also not a primary cause of the 1997 financial crisis.

The basic conditions for crisis had been firmly established before 1997 by the unsuccessful financial liberalization undertaken by the Kim Young-Sam administration. When Kim Young-Sam announced his *segyehwa* or "globalization" policy in 1995, his idea was to raise South Korea to global standards and make the country more competitive in the world market. Under this new banner, the government embarked on a series of liberalizing policies, and became an active actor in international economic organizations.[15] South Korea had previously participated in the Uruguay Round trade talks, and the formation of the Asia Pacific Economic Cooperation (APEC) in 1989, but became even more active under the *segyehwa* campaign, reflected in its participation in the launching of the World Trade Organization (WTO) in 1995. It also lobbied hard for admission into the OECD, on the grounds that South Korea had reached the $10,000 per capita GDP required for membership in 1995. The OECD requested adherence to several preconditions for membership, one of which was the opening of financial markets. Given access to more foreign loans, the *chaebŏl* expanded capacity and increased assets without regard for profitability. The *chaebŏl* eventually saddled themselves with high debt-to-equity ratios: the 1997 average ratio of the top 30 conglomerates was over 500%.[16] The situation was compounded by the fact that many of the conglomerates were run by aging founders whose powers of discernment seemed to be fading, or second- or third-generation owners whose inexperience led to questionable decisions.

As firms failed to meet their debt payments, a series of bankruptcies rocked the economy. Starting with the bankruptcy of Hanbo Steel in January 1997, and culminating in the collapse of Daewoo, the third largest *chaebŏl* in November 2000, nearly 50% of the top 30 *chaebŏl* became insolvent over a three-year span. Buried by the increasing volume of non-performing assets, domestic banks found themselves in increasingly vulnerable positions by the time the Korean currency, the *wŏn*, took a precipitous drop of some 45% in value in October 1997. Overall, South Korea's ratio of short-term foreign borrowing to foreign exchange reserves was 285%, much higher than Thailand's at 135% and the Philippines at 105%.

In addition to the highly exposed financial position of domestic banks and the *chaebŏl*, declining exports compounded matters. Relying on export growth rather than research-and-development (R&D) investment as it had in the past meant that the South Korean economy was vulnerable to currency fluctuations. In particular, South Korean products competed with Japanese products in export markets; consequently, South Korean export firms were vulnerable to fluctuations in the value of the yen. It was no surprise then that the devaluation of the yen in 1996 adversely affected South Korean export firms. Wages also increased dramatically, at an average rate of 18% annually throughout the 1990s. The subsequent sudden increase in disposable income among Koreans induced excessive private spending and a corollary inflation.

On November 21, 1997, Kim Young-Sam asked the IMF for loans. The public reaction was shock, with some people even likening the "IMF Period" to the Korean War. Kim Young-Sam asserted that his officials had hidden the seriousness of the liquidity crisis from him, but the arrest of his former deputy prime minister and minister of finance, Kang Kyŏng-Sik, and senior presidential economic advisor Kim In-Ho for hiding information obtained earlier in the year about the potential seriousness of the crisis, did not resolve matters. On December 3, 1997, the IMF agreed to provide a $59 billion package to South Korea. The IMF-mandated reforms included the stabilization and liberalization of the financial market, reform of the *chaebŏl* through consolidation and downsizing, and increasing the flexibility of the labor market by institutionalizing layoffs, early retirements, and irregularization of the workforce.

Two years later, in December 1999, Kim Dae-Jung announced the end of the financial crisis. Macro-economic statistics indicate an impressive return to form for the South Korean economy, with record growth rates, low inflation, improved unemployment data, and record inflows of foreign investment. The 1998 real GDP registered minus 7% growth, but growth had recovered to a positive 10% rate by 1999, and the average from 1999 to 2006 was 6%. Admittedly, growth rates were no longer in double digits, but if we take South Korea's real GDP growth for 2004 (4.6%), for example, and compare it against that of the world (5.6%), the OECD (3.2%), and the EU (2.4%) for the same year, it appears that South Korea's performance still compares favorably to the OECD average. Unemployment, which had hovered around 3% for the decade, skyrocketed to 7% in 1998, with a concomitant 9% drop in real wages. However, by 2000, unemployment had dropped back to 4%. As for the *chaebŏl*, assets of larger groups such as Kia and Daewoo were purchased by domestic or foreign firms. In 2005 and 2006, in surveys on trust and influence among powerful institutions, top *chaebŏl* such as Hyundai, Samsung, SK, and LG ranked in the top five in both categories, ahead of many government institutions and NGOs.[17]

Post-1997 recovery

So how did the post-1997 recovery come about, and what socio-economic changes emerged after 1997? Here again, we encounter several views. One approach asserts that although there have been changes in the contents of economic policy, the fundamental objectives and methods have not fundamentally departed from those of the developmental state.[18] The 1997 crisis, from this perspective, was not paradigm shifting, but simply another in a series of economic shocks encountered by the South Korean developmental state, such as the Oil Shocks of 1973–74 and 1979.

In contrast, a second view sees the post-1997 government policies not as continuations but as new policies that were firmly committed to structural reform and market liberalization.[19] Moreover, this view depicts the economic results as positive in the long run, as such reforms promote more stability in banking practices and greater corporate accountability. A third perspective agrees that neoliberal reforms have been implemented. However, scholars of this position emphasize the exacerbation of a range of socio-economic problems, such as rising inequality, decreasing investment spending, increasing foreign ownership of Korean assets, and suppression of labor rights masquerading under the misleadingly bland rubric of "labor flexibility."[20]

The record of mixed methods and results should be acknowledged. In general, the policies in the post-IMF period were clearly designed to reform banking and corporate behavior. The Kim Dae-Jung government forced the *chaebŏl* to sell nonessential firms in order to improve their debt-to-equity rations to below 200%. When negotiations between firms bogged down, the government intervened directly to facilitate mergers. Various forms of legislation were passed to reform finance, banking, labor, corporate law, social welfare, and other areas.

While not all of these measures produced the intended results, there have been areas of notable success. For example, there was a steep increase in foreign direct investment (FDI), from $3 billion in 1996 to $16 billion in 1999.[21] Before 1997, foreign investors had been concerned by political instability, constant labor strife, rapidly rising wages, and bureaucratic red tape. The switch from using foreign loans to inducing FDI greatly reduced the risk of the South Korean economy being affected by changing interest rates or sudden demands for loans repayment, and allowed some of the risk to be shouldered by foreign firms.

At the same time, there have been severe social costs. Beyond the rhetorical criticism of the IMF as an imperial occupying force,[22] the Kim Young-Sam administration's failure to develop social safety nets during the mid-1990s left South Korean workers most vulnerable during the years of high unemployment, 1997 and 1998. The quick recovery of the unemployment rate was somewhat deceiving since many companies laid off workers, reduced hours for more senior workers, and transformed many full-time positions to part-time ones.[23] The Kim Dae-Jung government appeared at first to be inclusive in its policies toward labor in forming a Tripartite Commission between government, business, and labor to examine industrial relations. However, Kim Dae-Jung's neoliberal mandate placed the government in direct conflict with labor. Although the Tripartite Commission announced a compromise framework for recovery in February 1998, this was rejected by the KCTU. The number of labor disputes doubled from 520 during the Kim Young-Sam years (1993–1997) to 1,130 in the Kim Dae-Jung years (1998–2002).[24] The projected number of labor disputes under the five years of the Roh Moo-Hyun government is around 1,800.

Moreover, economic inequality rose significantly after the 1997 crisis. Development in South Korea had been achieved with relatively low levels of inequality in income distribution.[25] Despite minimal social welfare policies throughout the authoritarian period, the percentage of people living in poverty decreased from roughly 40% in 1965 to 10% in 1980.[26] Before the 1997 crisis, this number remained at around 8%, but the percentage doubled to 16% in 1998.

The often-used Gini coefficient, which measures inequality via a number between 0 (perfect equality where everyone has the same income) and 1 (perfect inequality where one person has all the income, everyone else has nothing), also reflected the growing inequality.[27] After a decrease in income inequality starting in the late 1970s, the Gini coefficient rose significantly after the crisis. In 1996, the overall Gini index based on disposable income was 0.298, and in 1997, 0.283, but it rose to 0.320 in 1999, and 0.358 in 2000. Changes in the distribution of income have been notable in recent years throughout the world, driven largely by the emergence of skill-based technologies, the relative strength of labor, aging populations, and a range of other factors.[28] Income inequity has been particularly prominent in developing economies, including larger countries such as China, Russia, and India. Even then, South Korea at 0.358 in 2000 had the third-highest Gini coefficient among OECD countries, with only the US at 0.368 (2000) and Mexico at 0.494 (in 1998) higher.[29]

South Korea also scored poorly on other measures, such as the poverty rate (those earning less than 40% of the average income for all households): this was 7.7% in 1996, but lurched up to 12% in 2000. In this category, South Korea was the second-highest among OECD countries, as the US had actually dropped from 12% (1994) to 10.8% (2000). Only Mexico was higher among the OECD member states, at 15% (1994) and 16.3% (1998). Other forms of Gini coefficient for categories such as "market income" increased for South Korea from 0.302 in 1996 to 0.374 in 2000. "Wealth distribution" Gini indexes were even worse, reaching the high 0.500s and 0.600s by 2000.[30] All this has been exacerbated by the fact that South Korea only spends roughly 10% of its annual budget on social welfare, a stark contrast to the 40–50% rates found in social welfare states such as Sweden, Canada, and Germany, and lower than Mexico, which spends an estimated 20%.

The Korean Wave

Out of the seemingly splintered fragments of the developmentalist dream there arose in the late-1990s a new cultural and economic champion for South Korea – the entertainment industry. The "Korea Wave," or *Hallyu* has seen the diffusion of South Korean popular music, television dramas, films, and other forms of popular culture into the rest of Asia, and to a lesser extent, other parts of the world.

In a country still feeling the aftereffects of the IMF crisis, the seemingly unexpected overseas success of the entertainment sector in the 1990s was met with largely celebratory media coverage. In fact, the socio-economic difficulties brought on by high unemployment and uncertain social welfare services during the post-IMF period provided the backdrop for some works, such as the independent film *Sympathy for Mr. Vengeance* (2002) by director Park Chan-Wook (Pak Ch'an-Uk), the TV drama/comedy series *Super Rookie* (2005), and, to some extent, the blockbuster hit that signaled the renaissance of the South Korean film industry, *Shiri* (1999).[31]

Major US studios have bought remake rights to South Korean films, such as Universal which acquired the rights to *The Host* (2006) and Steven Spielberg's DreamWorks which bought *A Tale of Two Sisters* (2003). South Korean film directors have also won prestigious awards at major international film festivals such as Berlin, Venice, and Cannes, most notably the prodigious Im Kwon-Taek (Im Kwŏn-T'aek) who won the Best Director award for *Chihwaseon* at the 2002 Cannes festival, and director Park Chan-Wook who received the Grand Jury Prize for *Old Boy* at Cannes in 2004 .

Statistics indicate that in 1998 some 43 domestic films were shown, with only 25% of the market share, in contrast to the 290 imported movies which captured 75% of the market. The tide shifted in 1999 with the massive commercial success of *Shiri*: 49 domestic films accounted for 40% of total admissions. By 2004, domestic films captured 60% of the market share, and in 2006, Korean films took 65%. This commercial success is a pointed contrast to other markets within the OECD, such as Mexico, in which domestic films accounted for 14% of the market in 2000, and the EU, in which "domestic" films usually account for around 20% of the market. The fact that South Korean films have done well in international film festivals, and the growth of the domestic market from around 48 million admissions in 1993 to nearly 167 million in 2006, attracted attention from Hollywood.[32]

South Korea's successful hosting of and fourth-place finish in the Korea–Japan soccer World Cup in 2002, was another factor in its rapid resurrection of its image as a dynamic country through the medium of popular culture. The burgeoning popularity of South Korean films, TV dramas, and pop songs gained fans in China, Taiwan, Singapore, Hong Kong, Vietnam, and Japan, and has continued to attract coverage from Korean and other Asian mass media (English-language coverage tends to be several years behind the latest trends), while academic conferences on the subject are held with increasing frequency (although, the initial surge in the popularity of Korean cultural commodities having declined in Japan, there have recently been conferences on the "Post-Korean Wave").

In this section, I first trace the emergence of the Korean Wave, and, second, explain its growth. Third, I analyze some of the discourses within South Korea that attempt to link popular culture flows with notions of "soft power" or the growth of "pan-Asian" consumer communities.

Defining the Korean Wave

What is the Korean Wave? Simply put, Korean popular culture products of various media and genres have become increasingly popular in several Asian markets, generating some spillover effects such as increased enrolments overseas in Korean language classes and more tourists bound for South Korea, especially from other Asian countries. According to South Korean government estimates, the Korean Wave pushed up export earnings of cultural commodities from around $13 million in 1999 to $38 million in 2003.

TV dramas have constituted the majority of the cultural exports. While there have been some fluctuations, Taiwan has generally been the largest export market. As of 2003, 25% of the dramas exported were sold to Taiwan, 19% to China, 19% to Japan, and 3% to Hong Kong. Roughly 75% of exports were to Asian countries, although Egypt, Mexico, Canada, and the US also imported Korean dramas. In film, South Korean commercial blockbusters have invigorated domestic movie theaters, DVD sales, and the film production industry, making South Korea, according to some estimates, the seventh largest film market in the world.

The term "Korean Wave" first emerged in China, with the sudden popularity of the first Korean dramas aired in China, in 1997, on the national Chinese Central Television Station. A subsequent rebroadcast of the same shows in 1998 generated even more interest. Hit dramas in China and Taiwan, and the rising popularity of Korean musical performers resulted in the proliferation of the term "Korean Wave" in Chinese mass media by 1999. The popularity of South Korean dramas, films, and pop music spread to other places in the region, including Hong Kong, Singapore, Vietnam, Indonesia, and Japan.

Several points must be kept in mind when defining the Korean Wave. First, it is important to remember that the Korean Wave does not spring from one undifferentiated fountain of cool, but is composed of a myriad of formats, genres, agendas, and artistic visions. The term "Korean Wave" itself may not be particularly meaningful considering that within South Korea's film output alone there are art house films, commercial blockbusters, comedies, and melodramas. Simply to stuff them all under the rubric of "Korean" is as meaningful as assuming that such disparate films as *Legally Blonde* and *Mulholland Drive* (both released in 2001) can somehow be meaningfully captured under the rubric "American films" simply because they were produced in the US and directed by Americans. The films *Christmas in August* and *Shiri* happen to have the same male lead actor, Han Suk-Kyu (Han Sŏk-Kyu), but could not be more different in mood and pacing. The former is an arthouse film, while the latter is a full-blown action thriller. Within music, some popular South Korean music stars are known as hip-hop artists, and others are better known for their pop ballads. All this diversity means that the fan bases within the so-called Korean Wave can often be discrete and unrelated. For example, there is little overlap between the demographics of Japanese fans of BoA, the Korean pop singer who has had a record tally of number-one albums in Japan, and Japanese fans of South Korean melodramas.

Second, in many of the markets, it took many years for Korean TV shows or films to develop a following. For example, although Taiwan liberalized its TV market in 1993, a flood of well-produced Japanese shows initially dominated the market. The first South Korean dramas shown in Taiwan in 1997 generated little in the way of sustained interest: it was not until 1999 that the viewing ratings improved enough to generate a steady stream of imports. The first Korean drama to be broadcast on Japanese TV was the drama *Jealousy*, shown in 1993 by a station in Fukuoka (the largest city on the island of Kyushu). Some Korean films, such as the art house minimalist drama *Christmas in August* (1998), drew praise from critics and fans alike in Japan, but it was not until the action/romance blockbuster *Shiri* (1999) that some Korean films became large-scale commercial successes in Japan. Further, the buildup to the 2002 World Cup involved several joint productions between Japanese and South Korean television stations. These developments culminated in the monumental success of the TV melodrama *Winter Sonata* (2002) when it was broadcast first on Japanese satellite TV in 2003 and on regular TV in 2004. Japanese media coverage gravitated around the fan culture that developed around the series among its ardent viewers, further fueling the diffusion of South Korean popular culture.

A third qualifier in defining the Korean Wave is that not all Korean cultural commodities do well in terms of box office receipts in overseas markets, even those with significant numbers of fans of South Korean popular culture. The suspense/drama film *JSA* (2000) was a hit in South Korea, breaking the box office records that had been set by *Shiri*. In Japan, however, it generated around half the box office receipts of *Shiri*. The gangster film set in Pusan, *Friend* (2001), was a huge domestic hit, breaking the records that had been set by *JSA*, but it failed to draw audiences in Taiwan, and closed after three days.[33] Some blockbusters that were hits in South Korea, such as *Silmido* (2003) and *The Host* (2006), were severe disappointments in Japan, generating around one-third or less of the revenues of *Shiri*.

Fourth, the Korean Wave is restricted to specific forms of media. So far, it has been made up largely of TV dramas, films, and popular music. Other fields of entertainment such as feature-length animation, animation programs, and console video game software are still dominated by Japanese companies. Subcontracting or in-between animation work has long been the staple of the South Korean animation industry, but animation feature films written, directed, and produced by Korean production companies have failed to make an impact on domestic or overseas markets. While consoles and console video games are still dominated by Japanese firms and Microsoft's X-Box, South Korean firms have been the leading providers for online or broadband computer games. The videogaming culture in South Korea is abuzz with activity, with several specialized TV channels that show online games played by professionals, an estimated 26,000 Internet cafés called "PC Rooms" dotting the country, and professional game leagues with the top players earning annual incomes estimated to be around US$200,000. However, online games are often overlooked in discussions of the Korean Wave, although this field may prove to have the biggest economic impact among the popular culture products that comprise the Korean Wave, especially given the rapid expansion of the video/computer gaming market in China.

Fifth, the Korean Wave has not obliterated the competition from Hollywood or imported films. Generally, it is estimated that Hollywood accounts for some 85% of the global film market, and the South Korean market has continued to import the standard Hollywood blockbusters and less commercial films. For example, in 2004 *Troy* and *Shrek 2* placed second and third respectively for annual box office receipts in South Korea. Some Japanese films have done well in South Korea also, especially the films of the famed animator Miyazaki Hayao. In terms of numbers, imported films continue to outnumber domestic releases: in 2005, for example, 83 domestic films and 213 imported films were screened.

Sources of the Korean Wave

What helped generate this Korean Wave? Given the diversity in range of products and audiences outlined above, it would be a mistake to attribute the same explanations to all the commercial or critical successes. However, at the risk of simplification, three common factors can be identified: the diffusion of new communications technology, the development of the domestic industry, and state policies.

The advent of digital communications has facilitated the flow of images and dreams of resplendent capitalist luxury and eternal love across geographical distances. There has been a proliferation of satellite and cable TV stations; illegal and legal Internet uploads of TV dramas; distribution of DVDs of foreign TV shows and films with subtitles by fans; and multilingual virtual advertising on the Internet through official and unofficial websites. The Internet has also paved the way for the formation of transnational fan clubs using e-mail and chatting technologies. This technology has also allowed diasporic communities, especially in Hawai'i and the North American mainland, to consume Korean dramas and films. In particular, the increase in the number of satellite stations in countries such as Japan and Taiwan during the latter half of the 1990s, created a niche in which Korean dramas, priced lower than their Japanese counterparts but with similar production values, could thrive.

In addition to changes in technology and regional market structure, the survival of the South Korean film, television, and music industries in overcoming various challenges over the decades meant that the Korean Wave did not emerge without any foundations. Despite government censorship of films, music, and TV which severely limited the range of expression, there still were limited exports of low-budget movies in the 1960s and 1970s, and some South Korean singers, most notably Lee Mi-Ja in the 1960s and early 1970s, and Cho Yong-P'il in the 1980s, had hit singles in Japan. In the early 1990s, some Japanese fans even began to go to South Korea to attend concerts of musicians such as Sŏ T'aeji and the Boys or Kim Kŏn-Mo.[34]

For the film industry, the easing of government control on artistic expression and on imports provided opportunities and challenges for domestic producers in the post-1987 period. Initially, the South Korean film industry faced what looked to be certain extinction when, after years of pressure from the US, the government allowed direct imports from Hollywood to start in 1988. South Korean film companies initially responded by producing high volumes of movies: 110 films were produced in South Korea in 1990 and 121 in 1991, up from an average of 90 per year in the 1980s. However, the market share for these hundred plus films was only around 20%, down by nearly half from the peak of 40% in 1983.[35] By 1995, the number of films had dropped to 64, with around 20% of the market share. There were occasional domestic hits, such as Im Kwon-Taek's *Sŏpy'ŏnjae* (1993), which topped 1 million admissions, and won Im international acclaim; however, the downward trajectory of the domestic film industry continued. In 1993, the 63 domestic films that were released captured only 16% of the total national admissions.

Moreover, Kim Young-Sam's *segyehwa* drive of the mid-1990s meant that enforcement of plagiarism and intellectual property rights laws became stricter, resulting in several TV shows becoming enshrouded in controversy. To make matters worse, the Kim Dae-Jung administration implemented a three-stage plan for allowing imports of Japanese cultural products beginning in October 1998. Pirate tapes and CDs of Japanese music and movies had always abounded on the streets, but the new official policy forced producers to acknowledge Japanese templates for some shows and pay rebroadcasting fees.[36] Several programs were investigated for plagiarism in 1999. One drama was canceled after ten of its twelve episodes had been aired when it was discovered that it was a replica of a Japanese hit drama.

In the long run, this competition from imported shows and new standards of "originality" ultimately strengthened the South Korean entertainment industry. For example, *Shiri* clearly takes some of the elements of the French blockbuster films of Luc Besson such as *La Femme Nikita* (1990) and *Leon* (1994), with more familiar elements of romantic melodrama, and sets them in somewhat plausible contemporary South Korean settings. The director of the cult film festival hit *Save the Green Planet* (2003), Jang Jun-Hwan (Chang Chun-Hwan), was originally inspired by some of the problems he saw with characterization in Rob Reiner's *Misery* (1990), and by a website that claimed that Leonardo DiCaprio was an alien sent from outer space to enrapture all Earth females. *Winter Sonata*, the biggest single *Hallyu* success story, incorporates some elements of a popular Japanese TV melodrama, the 1991 *Always in My Heart* (more widely known by its Japanese title, *Kimi no Nawa*). The programmer who first decided to import *Winter Sonata* for the Japanese market stated that some of the common tropes between the two dramas convinced her to import the show.

Many scholars and journalists point to government policy, especially the screen quota, as the main reason for not only the survival but also the growth of the domestic film industry. It is true that there has been a screen quota system in place since 1966, when the Park Chung-Hee government mandated that domestic films had to be shown for at least 90 days during the year (later expanded to 146 days). The monitoring of the screen quota system was ramped up in 1993 during the nadir of the film industry to ensure that domestic films were actually screened for the legislated number of days per year.[37] After extensive negotiations and years of pressure from the US government, the screen quota was reduced to 73 days (around 20% of annual screening days) in July 2006 in exchange for progress on the Free Trade Agreement between the two countries.

A 1994 advisory board report to Kim Young-Sam noted that a blockbuster such as *Jurassic Park* generated total revenues equivalent to the sale of 1.5 million Hyundai cars. The government promulgated the Motion Picture Promotion Law in 1995 to provide subsidies for film production, and established the School of Film and Multimedia in the same year at the Korean National University of Arts to foster the next generation of producers, directors, and technicians. The government also helped start two major international film festivals – the Pusan International Film Festival in 1996 and the Puch'ŏn Fantastic Film Festival, featuring mainly science fiction and fantasy films, in 1997. Both festivals have proved to be successful and stable, promoting the study and popularity of Korean films within the country and abroad. The Kim Young-Sam administration also encouraged the *chaebŏl* to invest into film and media industries. This investment lasted for only a few years, as the IMF period saw the conglomerates withdraw from film under Kim Dae-Jung's directives for the *chaebŏl* to rationalize their operations. However, even after their exit, less-personalized, larger-scale business management practices in the film industry remained, helping the commercial viability of production and distribution companies.[38] The Kim Dae-Jung government also provided some $150 million to support film and television broadcasting under the Basic Law for the Culture Industry Promotion in 1999.

It seems clear that these government measures aided the film industry, especially during 1993 and 1994 when the very survival of the domestic film industry seemed to be in danger. However, the screen quota system and government policies alone cannot account for the emergence of the Korean Wave. The initial screen quota system in the 1960s actually decreased the capital available to domestic production companies as prior to 1966 many film companies had used revenues from imported films to finance their own productions.[39] Moreover, many prominent South Korean directors, including Im Kwon-Taek, debuted in the 1980s, before the wave of government initiatives began. Other currently prominent directors entered the film industry in the early 1990s. Director Kang Je-Gyu (Kang Che-Gyu), responsible for blockbusters such as *Shiri* and *Taeguki – Brotherhood of War* (2004), made his first professional foray into film as a screenwriter for a 1990 film, and his directorial debut came in 1996, only a year after government institutions to train filmmakers were founded. Furthermore, as noted above, many South Korean directors recount as their influences a rich mélange of foreign films, shows, and books, as well as their experiences working on earlier domestic productions.

The South Korean Ministry of Culture and Tourism worked with KBS (the Korean Broadcasting System, the equivalent to the BBC in the UK) to export *Winter Sonata* to markets such as Egypt. However, the success of South Korean TV dramas in Egypt started with a drama, *Autumn Story* (2000), which was a hit before the ministry's promotion campaign. Japanese fan reaction to the same shows also started well before the South Korean government jumped on the bandwagon. The sensible conclusion is that government support facilitated the growth of domestic industries, but hardly constitutes the sole, or even most important factor. In addition to government support, other ingredients, such as improvements in communications technology, development of export markets, resonances with audiences, and improvements in the quality of domestic productions, were all required.

Reactions to the Korean Wave

Aside from fan or viewer enthusiasm, what have been some of the reactions to the Korean Wave? The discourse has been diverse, but it is possible to divide it into nationalist, regionalist, dismissive, and protectionist views. As noted above, enamored to a large extent with the possibilities of "soft power" (the ability of a country to influence the perceptions or behaviors of another through cultural or ideological means), many South Korean officials and journalists have actively promoted the Korean Wave. Nationalist perspectives focus on either the Wave's power to generate positive effects in image politics, or the effects on the balance of payments, or its potential for drawing foreigners in towards more "traditional" arts. Tourism has increased, as has enrolment in Korean language classes in Taiwan, Japan, and other countries; *Hallyu* stars serve as spokesmodels for various products such as automobiles and cell phones.

The problem, however, with the concept of "soft power" is that it seems to assume that audiences have little autonomy or diversity. While audiences can be influenced in their views of other countries via cultural commodities, at the same time audience segmentation and variation cannot be entirely discounted either. South Korea may be the first to attempt to become a "dream society of icons and aesthetic experience,"[40] but such rhetoric conveniently elides the language barriers, and the often-conflicting meanings generated by governments, producers, and consumers out of the same movie or TV series.

South Korean artists have for the most part displayed their Korean origins proudly on their sleeves.[41] However, several scholars argue that it is the "Asian" context that is more important than anything innately Korean about the cultural commodities. The Korean Wave, according to this view, allows Asian middle classes to discover and reinforce their values as they expand in numbers and income. The "Asian" settings and context help viewers make sense of modernity in its multiple manifestations, or guide dreams and aspirations through the spectacles of dazzling material luxury of the "modernized Korea" that is portrayed in the shows. Some observers also suggest that the Korean Wave should be used to help create and reinforce an "Asian bloc" or a common "Asian identity" that would compete with other regional blocs forming around the world.[42]

It may also be true that South Korean dramas and films have succeeded in Asian markets precisely because they are similar to Hollywood films, not because of anything uniquely "Korean" about them other than their site of production. Many of the TV shows present an image of a "Westernized" Asia rather than of the current realities of South Korea itself. Nonetheless, considering that some Korean dramas and films have had moderate levels of success in Mexico, Egypt, and Russia, looking for reasons beyond cultural proximity to explain the emergence of the Korean Wave and coeval Asian modernities seems necessary. Such an effort would require considerably more detailed audience studies and wariness against exaggerating the effects of Korean cultural commodities on perceptions of South Korea in those countries.

In an era where the tocsin against the Hollywood domination of the collective imagination has become a familiar sound, South Korea's emergence as a vibrant film producer has been embraced by some elements of the international media as a refreshing alternative. However, another reaction has been one of disappointment, especially from several North American film critics. These critics lament that the Korean blockbusters are too similar to the standard Hollywood film. Certainly, there are familiar lighting and camera techniques: for example, the overall visual atmosphere of director

Chang Yun-Hyŏn's *Tell Me Something* (1999) is reminiscent of David Fincher's *Seven* (1995). The problem is that many film critics never define what constitutes originality; nor do they seem able to grapple with their sometimes Orientalist expectations of what constitutes an "authentic" Korean film.

Meanwhile, many foreign governments have expressed concerns about the impact of the proliferation of South Korean dramas on domestic production in their own countries. Whether it is the repeated calls by Japanese bureaucrats for a new industrial policy to promote cultural industries, Vietnamese officials complaining about the hedonistic capitalist lifestyles depicted in South Korean TV dramas, or China limiting the broadcast of "foreign" animation and shows during prime time, attempts by governments and other public organizations to regulate and control the production, dissemination, and reception of cultural commodities abound. In Japan, a comic book (a widely used medium of expression for all ages in Japan) called *Hate the Korean Wave* (*Ken-Kanryū*) was published in 2005. This became the best-selling book in Japan for that year and spawned considerable controversy, eliciting criticism from both the political left and the political right in Japan for various inaccuracies contained within it.[43]

Popular culture and "real life," or text and context, are certainly not divorced from each other. The impact of popular culture cannot be calibrated merely on the basis of revenues or film festival awards, or the number of members in a fan club; but since 1999 popular culture has become one of South Korea's highest-profile exports. The domestic market has become one of the most vibrant in the world, and new box office records are set virtually every year. The Korean Wave has affected South Korea's image overseas, especially in Asia, and has drawn tourists to various sites associated with TV dramas. Marriage brokers promising to introduce Japanese women to South Korean men have sprung up as a result of the popularity of *Winter Sonata*.

If popular culture is in some senses the private life of the nation-state, then South Korea has been using the medium of popular culture to attempt to digest issues of mimicry/hybridity, history, and socio-economic change. South Korean blockbusters have often adapted the tropes and techniques familiarized by Hollywood to compete successfully against American films in domestic markets.

Some films, such as *Memories of Murder* (2003), have grappled with unresolved issues related to everyday forms of violence during the period of authoritarian rule. Other more recent films and TV dramas such as *You Are My Sunshine* (2005) and *The Bride from Hanoi* (2005) have depicted the growing trend of older bachelors in the rural areas seeking brides from abroad.

Demographic Change

As hinted at in shows such as *The Bride from Hanoi*, South Korea is fast becoming increasingly multiethnic, whether it wants to or not. By this I do not mean that there are simply more non-Korean restaurants in the cities, or that more global designer labels are available in the boutiques: if anything, although generally well stocked with the usual fashion brand names, for a city of its size Seoul has surprisingly few "ethnic" restaurants other than Japanese and Chinese. This multicultural and multiethnic trajectory is not a consequence of the successes or failures of the Kim Young-Sam government's globalization policies or the results of the 2002 World Cup. Nor is it something washed up from the high tide of the Korean Wave. Fundamental shifts in demographics, namely a sustained labor shortage, aging population, and a sex ratio imbalance, have made multiculturalism and multiethnicity central issues in South Korean society.

However, it was probably not until the spring 2006 visit to South Korea by Hines Ward of the Pittsburgh Steelers, the winner of the Most Valuable Player award for the 2006 American Super Bowl, that a rush of media coverage and debate about the boundaries of "Korean" identity began. Ward, who is the child of an African American GI father and a Korean mother, has been credited with being a catalyst for encouraging South Koreans to shift from a homogenous, blood-based view of ethnicity to a more multicultural and open one. Ward partnered with Pearl S. Buck International – an INGO founded in 1964 by the Nobel and Pulitzer prize-winning writer with a long history of supporting the rights of international and "mixed race" children and promoting their adoption – to raise awareness of the importance of substantive multiculturalism in South Korea. Upon hearing Ward's story, several South Koreans responded that it was time for South Koreans to cast aside their "pride" in being a "homogenous society" and to change towards a more multicultural view of Korean identity. Also, some mixed-race (mainly Caucasian American and Korean) stars have become more visible in South Korea since the mid-2000s. For example, one of the most popular male actors in television since the mid-2000s is Daniel Henney, whose father is English American and whose mother is Korean American.

History of multiethnicity in Korea

However, injunctions to openness must also be combined with acknowledgement that multiethnic elements of South Korea's history have been marginalized for decades. Admittedly, the population of ethnic minorities in modern South Korean history has never been large. At the same time, it would be misleading simply to accept the notion that South Korea has always been a "homogenous" culture, only now challenged by waves of immigrants borne on the waves of globalization.

Leaving aside issues from pre-modern history such as the intermarriages between Mongols and Koryŏ dynasty nobility, South Korea was a multiethnic country at its inception in 1948. During the colonial period, marriages between Koreans and Japanese were encouraged by the colonial state. The number of officially registered interethnic couples was around 400 in 1925, and 1,750 in 1937.[44]

Some of the marriages may not have produced children, but given the number of interethnic couples married between 1910 and 1945, there must still have been at least a thousand children who might be described as multiethnic or multiracial during the immediate post-liberation period in South Korea. Such families and children were never publicly acknowledged as multiethnic, although their descendants might know, for example, that one of their grandmothers was Japanese.

Japanese wives of Korean men who stayed in South Korea after liberation also form a small minority community. Estimates of their current numbers are 1,000, although the estimates are affected by their age and the fact that many hide their ancestry. As of 1991, around two-thirds had either South Korean citizenship or dual citizenship, but many lived in relatively impoverished conditions, especially if their spouses had died.[45] There is a home that houses a handful of Japanese wives in Kyŏngju that has been run by a Christian Korean foundation since its establishment in 1972,[46] but this particular legacy from the colonial period has not been addressed as a part of Korean multiethnicity.

In addition, there has been a population of resident Chinese in Korea since the 1890s. In 1970, an estimated 33,000 to 40,000 ethnic Chinese lived in South Korea, mainly in Inch'ŏn, Seoul, and Pusan.[47] The Park Chung-Hee government issued laws in the 1960s limiting land ownership by foreigners, and it dispersed Chinese stores and restaurants in downtown Seoul during urban reforms of the early 1970s. This forced many Chinese to migrate to the US, Australia, and Taiwan. In 1999, Kim Dae-Jung removed restrictions on foreign ownership of land, but the population of Chinese in South Korea had already declined to 21,000 by 1990. Although some 90% of the Chinese were originally from Shandong province on the northeast coast of mainland China, the majority were given Taiwanese passports in 1949 when the Chinese Communist Party took control of China. Most retain their Taiwanese passports to this day, although a small number have Chinese or South Korean passports. Historically, they have had difficulty finding employment, with the result that the majority now operate or work in Chinese restaurants. Their conditions, however, have generally improved from 2000 or so because of the boom in interest in China; the recently restored Chinatown in Inch'ŏn has become a somewhat popular tourist destination.[48]

Multiethnic heritage also stems from the Korean War and the Vietnam War. Among its many legacies, the Korean War initially left some 40,000 "mixed-race" children or "GI babies." These children actually constituted the majority of the Korean babies who were sent abroad for adoption between 1955 and 1965, especially as orphans were not granted South Korean citizenship under the family registry laws.[49]

Between 1964 and 1975, some of the 400,000 Korean soldiers and civilians who were in Vietnam sired children with local Vietnamese women. At the end of the war, the soldiers and the South Korean government did little to support these children's lives. Estimates of their numbers range greatly, from as low as 2,000 to as high as 30,000. The term *Lai Daihan* is used in South Korea and Vietnam to describe these children who are now in their thirties and forties, but it is problematic due to the pejorative nuances (*Lai* means "mixed-breed" and *Daihan* refers to Korea).

They live for the most part in Vietnam, and the extent of the discrimination against them has been debated. In many accounts, they are portrayed as facing constant discrimination in Vietnam as "children of the enemy", for their visually different appearance, and for being fatherless. According to this view they have less access to education and receive fewer work opportunities. On the other hand, one South Korean NGO that works with the *Lai Daihan* in Vietnam has asserted that some media outlets and NGOs exaggerate their plight in an attempt to dramatize their stories.[50] The ones that do find their way to South Korea to live with their fathers face even more difficulties with language, culture, and employment.

Out of South Korea's 2006 total population of around 49 million, only an estimated 5,000 are Amerasians. However, many of them, especially those whose parents are not Caucasian, still face pervasive discrimination in everyday life, have high dropout rates from schools, have difficulties in obtaining employment, and suffer from high suicide rates.

Labor shortage

The labor shortage that emerged by the late 1980s, especially in the labor-intensive, unskilled sector, also triggered changes in the human landscape. Previously, as mentioned above, migrants from the rural areas had filled labor opportunities in the urban areas. In fact, South Korea had been an exporter of labor, sending nurses to West Germany in the 1950s and construction workers to the Middle East in the 1970s and 1980s on term-limited contracts. The situation changed during the late 1980s, as foreign migrant workers increasingly filled labor shortages in the so-called "3D" (dirty, difficult, dangerous) jobs within smaller firms. Smaller firms in labor-intensive industries have been particularly reliant on migrant laborers from China, the Philippines, Nepal, and other countries within Asia.

In December 1997, soon after the inauguration of Kim Dae-Jung as president, the government issued an order for all illegal workers to leave South Korea by the end of March 1998, offering temporarily to freeze its policy of fining those who had overstayed their visas or entered the country illegally if they voluntarily left before the announced deadline. This measure reflected Kim Dae-Jung's response to the 1997 crisis: to limit the number of people the state was responsible for and to promote an atmosphere of economic nationalism. Small businesses, represented by the Korean Federation of Small Businesses (KFSB), protested the move, as it would deprive them of a cheap labor supply. An estimated 370,000 foreign workers, most of them illegal, remained in South Korea as of February 1998 despite the order.[51] As of 2005, around 550,000 foreigners resided in South Korea, roughly 1% of the total population.

Like many countries, South Korea needs foreign workers, but seems loath to accept them. By 2020, according to the Bank of Korea, there will be a labor shortage to the tune of 4.7 workers per firm. NGOs, such as the Joint Committee on Migrant Workers in Korea (JCMK) founded in July 1995, have been active in lobbying the government for legislative reform and in campaigning for greater public awareness of the need to improve the rights of foreign migrant workers.[52] There have been some improvements: foreigners who have had permanent resident status for more than three years, such as Chinese residents of South Korea with Taiwanese nationality, were granted the right to vote in local elections under an electoral law revision in June 2005. Yet foreign migrant workers continue to battle prejudice in everyday contexts.[53]

Aging population

The second factor affecting the demographic profile of South Korea is the rapid graying of the population, which has created a dire need for legally working, therefore tax-paying, adult laborers. South Korea's fertility rates are the lowest among industrialized countries at an average of 1.08 per woman as of August 2006. Since the accepted population maintenance threshold is 2.1 children per woman, South Korea's low fertility rate has serious implications for the future.

Although anti-natal effects of industrial society and global mobility are evident across most industrialized countries, statistical evidence indicates that South Korea already has the fastest-aging population in the world. If the proportion of the population who are aged 65 and older reaches 7% of the total population, a society is considered "aging." When this proportion reaches 14%, the category changes to "aged," and when it reaches 20%, the society is considered "super aged." South Korea reached the 7% mark in 2000, and is projected to reach 14% in 2019. South Korea's National Statistics Office projects that the country will reach the 20% benchmark for a "super aged" society by 2026. Thus South Korea will take only 19 years to go from 7% to 14%, when France took 115 years, Sweden 85 years, the US 75 years, and the UK 45 years to traverse the same transformation. The closest comparison is with Japan, which took 26 years to go from 7% to 14%. As a result of accelerating changes in the dependency ratio (the number of working to non-working people), the current average of three working people between the ages of 25 and 54 supporting one elderly person over the age of 55 will change to one person supporting one elderly person by 2026.

This drastic demographic transformation, both historical and projected, has been propelled by several long-term trends. Increases in life expectancy, decreasing mortality rates, low fertility rates, later median age of marriage, are just some of the demographic factors that have been converging since the early 1960s.[54] Increases in educational and employment opportunities for women have also resulted in fewer and later marriages. In combination with the increasing cost of living and of raising children, more lifestyle choices of younger people do not include having children. Increasing divorce rates overall may also be contributing to the decrease in fertility. There were some 12,000 divorces in 1970, 46,000 in 1980, 68,000 in 1990, and 145,000 in 2002, with increasing numbers of divorces initiated by women.[55]

The reasons for this trend are several: increasing opportunities for education, more employment for women, improved rights for women, and financial distress from the IMF crisis, among others. In fact, South Korea's divorce rate per 1,000 placed it second in the world after only the US in world statistics in 2002. Especially as younger couples may marry and divorce before having babies, the increasing rates of divorce can only lower the fertility rate.

Sex ratio imbalance

A third factor engendering the emergence of a multiethnic South Korea has been the imbalance in the sex ratio, which has been an issue of government concern since the mid-1990s. The "normal" average sex ratio at birth is 105 males to 100 females. The country has historically had similarly imbalanced sex ratios to those of China and Taiwan, but South Korea became one of the first countries to report very high imbalances of sex ratios at birth, since the introduction of sex-selective technology and fertility decline in South Korea occurred earlier than in other Asian countries.[56] "Traditional" preferences for male children, especially first-born sons, to carry on the family line motivated the initial sex preference. This cultural preference was reinforced and reflected in the family household registry system called the *hoju* (literally, "head of the family"), which banned women from legally representing their households until the law was reformed in the spring of 2006. This meant that, for example, aged widows were registered under the names of their eldest sons in official documents, and children of divorced mothers could not be registered to their own family or even their stepfather's.

The introduction of sex-selection technologies amplified the male preference. Ultrasound spread in the cities in the mid-1980s, and was reported to have reached rural areas by 1990.[57] Moreover, the data indicated that people sex-selected regardless of birth order. The preference applied in the first pregnancy because there was a traditional preference for the first-born to be male; the tendency to sex-select rose for third and fourth births as parents tried to ensure that they produced a son. In 1992, the sex ratio for fourth births in South Korea was an astounding 229, whereas the overall ratio was 114. Relatively high-quality medical facilities and accurate vital information registration also meant that differential gender mortality and underreporting did not contribute to these skewered sex ratios.

From the mid-1990s, the government launched a public awareness campaign warning of the dangers of such distortion, and began to enforce strictly laws forbidding the use of sex selection technologies. A widespread and influential media campaign also focused on the anticipated shortage of brides. These efforts led to a decline in the sex ratio imbalance from 116 in 1998 to 108 in 2004.

Nonetheless, due to the distorted sex ratio, the government predicts a "marriage crunch" for around 2010. There has already been an increase in the number of registered "international" marriages, from roughly 15,0000 in 2001 to 43,000 in 2005, according to the National Statistics Office. While these numbers are 11% of the total number of marriages in 2005, increasing numbers of men in the rural areas have been marrying foreign brides, as has been the case in Japan and Taiwan for some time. Korean farmers generally have small plots with large debts; many urban women are not willing to give up the comforts and the opportunities of the city in order to marry into relative poverty.

Some 40% of rural Korean men now marry non-Koreans, many of whom are from Vietnam or the Philippines, or are ethnic Koreans from China and Japan. The children of these marriages between a Korean national and another Asian national are widely called "Kosians" (an abbreviation of Korean Asian), a term coined by some "intercultural" families in 1997 to refer to themselves, but also criticized by some as racially discriminatory. Currently, there are an estimated 35,000 "mixed-race" children in South Korea, according to the INGO Pearl S. Buck International, but by 2020, the government predicts that some 33% or 1.7 million of all babies born in South Korea will be "Kosians." For some "mail-order" brides, these arranged marriages have turned out well: but according to reports from several NGOs, the majority of the foreign brides suffer from abuse and depression, resulting in alienation, divorce, and, sometimes, death.

Conclusion

The South Korean economy and society since 1989 has experienced long-term economic growth despite the 1997 crisis, a rapid expansion of the cultural industries, and massive demographic change. Admittedly, cities everywhere around the world are increasingly marked by their striking abilities to illustrate spatially the gap between luxury and misery, with homeless people panhandling in front of designer brand boutiques, or slums sprawling behind soaring skyscrapers – and Seoul is no exception. Social problems abound throughout the country: divorce rates have increased steadily since 1997, with the leading cause cited as "financial issues," while among married couples increasingly both partners work to support the cost of raising children. Further, the rapid changes experienced by South Koreans have produced relatively distinct cohorts and generations who have been stamped by different epochal events, and raised within very different material and ideological environments. This has amplified the growing economic inequities.

Nevertheless, while recognizing the seriousness of the problems in South Korean society, it would also make sense to move beyond the bounds of solipsistic national criticism. South Korea's record and trajectory have been comparable to Japan's although the pace of change has been far faster. Compared to the socio-economic situation of a country like South Africa, where some eight million are homeless and over five million are HIV positive, the South Korean situation would seem to be better in most respects. The warnings against the power of the prevalent miasma that reduces Africa to repetitive images of "poverty" and "backwardness" should be heeded. But in relative terms at least, if South Korea is a country that is weary from its pursuit of development and the changes it has experienced under "turbo-charged" capitalism, other countries in the world currently face far greater systemic challenges.

Clearly, amidst South Korea's accelerated changes in terms of population aging, low fertility rates, labor shortages, divorce rates, and "international" marriages, clinging to the myth of a single "pure" race of Koreans in a single nation-state is not a feasible vision for the future. In addition, acknowledging a multicultural and a multiethnic South Korea might help the integration of North Koreans into South Korea, since North Koreans bring with them a culture that marks them as potentially a different ethnic group than South Koreans.

The demographic transformations challenge officials and the public to go beyond seeing globalization as shorthand for national competitiveness in export markets, or for increasing the diversity of consumer products from around the world, to see globalization instead as an opportunity to restructure South Korea's national identity in a manner that acknowledges realities on the ground and the mistakes of the recent past. The reality is that the IMF period, even if it was not comparable to the Korean War or the colonial period in terms of material devastation, has undeniably left South Korea's economy and society in an irrevocably altered state.

3 | Holy Trinity
North Korean Politics after 1989

If I had my ideal world I would not allow weapons and atom bombs
anymore.
I would destroy all terrorists with the Hollywood star Jean-Claude van
Damme.
I would make people stop taking drugs.
I would even destroy the word "DRUG" to make people forget about it.
I would make everybody get good jobs.
Everybody would be happy: no more war, no more dying, no more
crying.
Then I would make a rule (Do not believe in God.) God doesn't help
and there is no God.
I would make people believe in themselves, and they would work hard
for their happiness and success waiting in their future.
I would make the whole world use only one language, which would be
Korean, and I would make all people have the same amount of
money: no rich people, no poor people.
Only in my ideal world can the people have freedom and live very
happily.

Chol Pak (Grade 7), "My Ideal World" (1996) [1]

All the children in the class were assigned the same theme, to
write a poem about "My Ideal World." At the time he wrote this
poem, Chol Pak, born in 1981, was fifteen, a bit older than the
average age of thirteen for the Grade 7 class at the International
School in Berne, Switzerland. From the poem, we can glean that he
was against war, liked movies of the Belgian action star, opposed
drugs, wanted full employment, was an ardent atheist and a committed humanist, professed a belief in equality, and was either a
nationalistic Korean or someone who detested having to write in
English. The last line is, perhaps deliberately, ambiguous – did it
mean that he wanted people to be happy only in his ideal world,
or was this a lament that only in his dreams could people live in
freedom and happiness?

I would suspect that most of us would be sheepish at the very least, possibly even mortified from embarrassment, if someone were to analyze poems we had written for some literature assignment in elementary school. So why subject this particular poem to close scrutiny? All things considered, this poem is very polished for a Grade 7 student, but its literary merits are not what make it significant for a chapter on the North Korean political system. It so happens that it was written by the person who is the most likely successor to the throne of power in North Korea. Chol Pak was the pseudonym of Kim Jong-Chol (Kim Chŏng-Ch'ŏl), the second-oldest son of Kim Jong-Il.

Now, some of the seemingly innocuous motifs in the poem take on a greater significance. There are the ironies: the belief in equity when North Korea is, according to most accounts, a highly hierarchical society; the anti-drugs sentiment when North Korea has been accused of manufacturing and dealing drugs; the invocation of a Hollywood action hero of the 1990s when many US officials have apparently been attempting to cast North Korea as the arch-villain in a Hollywood action film; and anti-atomic-bomb sentiment when North Korea has tested a nuclear weapon, albeit ten years after this poem was written. Then there are the resonances with Ludwig Feuerbach's critique of religion which stresses the human being as God.[2] There is no proof that Jong-Chol was familiar with Feuerbach's work in 1996, but North Korean intellectuals had begun stating at least as early as 1982 that they found Feuerbach more useful than Karl Marx because of the former's emphasis on the power of the human spirit rather than on historical materialism.[3]

Of course, even if the world may on occasion be seen in a grain of sand, the structure of North Korean politics and society cannot be understood entirely through the magic prism of one poem. People change, as do their ideas and their political standing (as does their willingness to engage in exercises such as the writing of poetry). Furthermore, contrary to official propaganda, the North Korean state has evolved over the years, and is not solely run by one man or one family. Reductionist approaches that focus solely on the eccentricities and the crimes of Kim Jong-Il or the members of the North Korean "royal family" may end up rendering the reader captive to caricatures rather than illuminating new spaces of understanding.

However, to overlook the impact of the only two leaders North Korea has known – and the potential future successor – would be a mistake. Even if political rule is not absolute, the power of the ruling family in the North is far greater than that of any political oligarchy in the South. This chapter will focus on the ruling family of North Korea, while attempting to avoid the two extreme positions that either stress the irrationality of Kim Jong-Il or emphasize the rationality of his reactions in the face of American imperialist aggression. Chapter 4 will delve into the other ruling organizations, the economy, and the society; the causes of the famine; and the nuclear issue.

Sources of information on North Korea

Accurate information on North Korea has been difficult to obtain – entry to the country is controlled, minders accompany visitors even when entry is gained, statistics can be problematic, intelligence is often sketchy, defectors' accounts are of questionable reliability, and ludicrous propaganda is abundant. Some of the challenges in analyzing North Korea are reflected in the now-discarded predictions, made by several observers, of imminent collapse in 1989 and 1994. Neither the disintegration of the Soviet Union nor Kim Il-Sung's death triggered a systemic collapse.

Ironically, the paucity of reliable information has not hampered the proliferation of North Korea "experts" within the last five years working in English. If anything, the relative lack of research rigor has facilitated the publication of books or the upload of blogs by nearly anyone who has ever visited North Korea. The cacophony of the information age has empowered the free expression of opinions, but it has also come with a corollary: if the noise has diminished the monopoly of one voice on any given subject, it has simultaneously amplified the need for any interested reader to discover ways to filter out posturing from research, hyperbole from reality.

More specifically, information on North Korea can be classified into several categories: North Korean official propaganda; defector accounts; visitor accounts; journalistic accounts in Korean and Japanese; journalistic accounts and policy papers in English; NGO reports in Korean, Japanese, and English; government reports in Korean; academic works in Korean and Japanese; and academic works in English. Although there are some thorough works in English by academics and journalists, a surprising number of published books and articles on North Korea are notable for their inability to engage with existing academic work, archival sources, or defector accounts published in Korean or Japanese.

The most reliable sources of information tend to be secondary works (whether written by academics or journalists) that go beyond simply describing their authors' experiences in North Korea and engage with sources in Korean or have access to information brought out of North Korea via NGO networks or relatives in Japan. Some specialists have also conducted extended fieldwork in the border areas of northeast China. South Korean and Japanese media also invariably have more detailed reports than the English-language media, but can also end up peddling sensational rumors and groundless defector accounts in great abundance. Defector accounts can be very useful: many recent academic works, especially in Korean and Japanese, have made judicious use of testimonies. However, some of the defectors embellish their accounts or fabricate information in order either to push up sales of books or to lobby for regime change. Individuals who have had fall-outs with Kim Jong-Il carry with them specific personal agendas as well, especially those who were close to power. Many of those who live in the Chinese borderlands are not free to speak on record, while others may provide a limited picture of life in North Korea, as many of the economic refugees tend to be from the northeast. Others, such as Kim Jong-Il's personal sushi chef, Fujimoto Kenji (a pseudonym), are more reliable: he spent nearly ten years in direct contact with the North Korean ruler and his family. However, Fujimoto's books provide great details but little in the way of analysis of what he witnessed. In writing this and the next chapter on North Korea, I relied on a combination of secondary, journalistic, and defector sources mainly published in Korean and Japanese, and to a lesser degree on sources in English (and Chinese); I cross-checked information whenever possible.

Analytical Approaches

Several labels have been used to explain the North Korean state. The eight most prominent of these might be called Stalinist, corporatist, personalist, ideological, guerrilla, Confucian, hermit, and theocratic. In this section I briefly summarize these, then propose an alternative label that captures the overarching dynamic of the North Korean political system, the "Holy Trinity."

Existing approaches

Although "Stalinism" is often left undefined in many journalistic accounts, and is often used as a loose synonym for totalitarianism, the term usually seems to refer to the cult of personality that surrounds Kim Il-Sung and Kim Jong-Il, and the emphasis on central economic planning.[4] While the Soviet Union launched a de-Stalinization program in the 1950s, North Korea, along with Albania and Romania, refused to abandon many elements of the system that was put in place in the aftermath of World War Two. Thought control remains in North Korea, but central control of the economy has deteriorated significantly. Further, while both Kim and Stalin shared a common penchant for grandiloquent monikers, the North Korean cult of personality was not merely an ossified version of Stalin's personality cult.

The "corporatist state" approach refers to the top-down variety of corporatism, based on a single-party, mass-mobilizing totalitarian set of policies.[5] There are in North Korea two token "non-communist" parties that serve as diplomatic arms of the ruling party, the Korean Workers' Party (KWP), but the larger problem with the corporatist approach is that while local branches of the KWP are still responsible for some political education programs, the locus of political activity has shifted to the Korean People's Army (KPA). Furthermore, the top-down controls have deteriorated (or relaxed), as indicated by the emergence of a merchant class whose members have accumulated some degree of personal wealth.

The "personalist state" approach emphasizes the North Korean theories on the role of the "absolute leader" or "great leader" (suryŏng), an individual who does not simply occupy an administrative post but possesses the qualities to take over as the "heart and brain" of the nation, with the people as the body.[6] Several scholars have pointed out the parallels between the North Korean ideology and the pre-1945 Japanese Emperor System and the ideology of the Kokutai, or "national body". However, this approach underplays the role of ideology.

In contrast, the "ideological state" approach emphasizes the role of the state ideology, Juche, which can loosely be defined as autonomy or autarky, in governing the state.[7] The significance of Juche is in some ways reflected in the fact that after being increasingly invoked from the mid-1960s on, it was granted a place in the 1972 North Korean constitution as the official state ideology. The problem here is that emphasizing primarily the ideology overlooks the role of the absolute leader as the material and spiritual embodiment of Juche.

The most systematically articulated version of the "guerrilla state" perspective argues that from the late 1960s to 1972, a "guerrilla band state" emerged with Kim Il-Sung as in essence a commander of a guerrilla band with absolute power over all resources. As in a guerrilla unit, the leader had the freedom to direct the militarization of the nation's economy in a guerrilla war against the American imperialists.[8] It is true that North Korea's leadership presents the country as being constantly at war against US imperialism. However, as is the case with the personalist state approach, the ideological underpinning of Juche can be obscured by the emphasis on the organizational structure.

In contrast, the "Confucian" perspective emphasizes the Confucian or "traditional" elements in North Korean politics, such as the emphasis on hierarchy, the parallels between the literati of the Chosŏn period and the intellectual class, and the use of a political geomancy that made places of birth of major figures, trees, and mountains such as Paekdusan (the Korean peninsula's highest) into sacred entities.[9] However, while an emphasis on historical continuities can generate insights, it can also obviate the need for actual analysis of more recent history. In lieu of historical contingency, culturally essentialist labels are used to explain complex convergences of various motivations and influences.

The sobriquet "Hermit Kingdom" has been brandished with gleeful abandon by nearly every other journalist or North Korea "watcher." North Korea is certainly isolated in relative terms. However, the label is highly misleading in that, first, as we shall see in Chapter 4, the North Korean economy was and remains highly dependent on foreign aid; and, second, North Korea actually was active in the Non-Aligned Movement in the 1960s, was host to various international visitors into the 1980s (admittedly on propagandistic tours), and even sent aid (mainly to African countries) in the 1970s and 1980s.[10] Also, over 150 countries have official relations with North Korea, including Canada and the UK.

Holy Trinity

All of the above approaches contain elements that are useful in any attempt to understand North Korea. However, I propose that the metaphor of the "Holy Trinity" most parsimoniously captures the dynamics of North Korea's politics. By this I do not mean to suggest anything divine, predestined, or inevitable about the process by which Kim Il-Sung and Kim Jong-Il have created and maintained power in North Korea. Nor is the point that the North Korean leadership views its own political system in these terms. Rather, the point is that this metaphor captures all of the factors listed in the alternative approaches by conceptually organizing them as a triumvirate at the core of the North Korea political system. It avoids culturally essentialist and empirically ungrounded assertions, and serves as a counter to approaches that emphasize only one factor.

In other words, to understand North Korea's post-1989 political history requires us to address the following three strands: how the founding Father, Kim Il-Sung, consolidated power; the role of the Holy Spirit, the ideology of Juche, in binding the "Holy Trinity" to the North Korean society; and how the Son, Kim Jong-Il, successfully managed the dynastic succession or "Ascension."

The most similar approach is the "Theocratic State" approach. However, this view identifies the Father as Kim Il-Sung, the Son as Kim Jong-Il, and the KWP as the Holy Spirit, in accordance with the official North Korean literature.[11] In the "Holy Trinity" formulation, Juche is the Holy Spirit that infuses all of society as one, not the KWP or the KPA. As the Son proceeds from the Father, the Holy Spirit proceeds from the Father and the Son – a fitting definition for the role of Juche. Potential candidates for the Second "Ascension" into the Trinity to succeed Kim Jong-Il are drawn from the extended Kim family, the so-called "royal family."

The Holy Trinity stands above a second triadic set, the two branches of the "Apostles," and the masses. The "Apostles" can be divided into upper echelons of the KWP, and the KPA: these elites rule over the rank and file members and the rest of the citizenry. Socialist countries, like other political systems, are not immune to interest-group politics.[12] North Korea is no exception: there are different coalitions within and across the KWP and the KPA over views on economic reform, security, and diplomacy. There are also vast differences between the top officials in both units and the mass party members or the regular soldiers in terms of status and material benefits. The living conditions of the masses display great range depending on status, loyalty, and location. Chapter 4 will deal with this second triad.

South Korea has experienced three coups and four democratic successions in the executive since 1948. In contrast, North Korea has experienced many purges, and possibly three failed coup attempts, but it has had one succession and is facing the prospect of a second succession in the near future. Moreover, the process of political succession itself remains far less codified in North Korea. Whether this pyramid, the Holy Trinity that sits atop the second trinity of the North Korean society, can handle a Second Ascension, constitutes one of the major challenges for regime survival.

The Father

How did Kim Il-Sung consolidate his power? Visitors to North Korea, who are almost all required either to place flowers or bow before the 23-meter-high, gold likeness of Kim Il-Sung, might assume that from the birth of North Korea in 1948 to his death on July 8, 1994, the Great Leader, Kim Il-Sung, reigned supreme over the country. However, Kim Il-Sung was not always worshipped as a deity.

It is possible to make the case that Kim Il-Sung's imprint on post-1945 history owes much of its existence to the division of the peninsula, since prominent political figures with more renowned pre-1945 careers congregated in Seoul, assuming that real power would be had there rather than in Pyongyang. Kim Il-Sung's apotheosis was a historically contingent product of the favorable circumstances, a loyal core support group, Soviet support, and political ruthlessness. In fact, the cult of personality did not emerge in full force until 1967, and the golden colossus itself was not unveiled until April 1972.

Soviet support and political patience

Born Kim Sŏng-Ju in 1912, Kim Il-Sung was not the sole or the preeminent leader, but he did gain considerable fame as a guerrilla leader fighting against the Japanese in the northern borderlands of colonial Korea.[13] As the Soviet ground forces drove into Korea in 1945, Grigory Mekler, a propaganda officer of the Soviet Army, interviewed various possible candidates for the post of leader, and concluded that Kim Il-Sung was the most appropriate leader on account of the combination of his expressed sympathies to communism and his political acumen. The backing of the Soviets meant access to their propaganda know-how and the knowledge among his rivals that to oppose Kim Il-Sung was to oppose the Soviet occupation forces.

Nonetheless, in the early post-Liberation period, Kim needed to use his political patience and dexterity to gain control of the KWP, the primary ruling organization. Initially, Kim forged an array of alliances, and manoeuvred the various rival groups into coalitions.[14] There were four major factions within North Korea before 1950. The smallest and least politically experienced was the Partisan Group, composed of two factions, Kim Il-Sung's Manchurian Partisans and the support network, called the Kapsan Group. The largest was the Domestic Group, the members of the Communist Party who had operated in colonial Korea and had moved to the North. The third was the Yanan Group, Koreans who had participated in the Chinese revolutionary war under Chinese Communist command. Lastly, there was the Soviet Korean Group, numbering around 400, Koreans who accompanied the Soviet military forces into Korea, then remained behind to help administer the fledgling country. Many of the Soviet Koreans were active in propaganda, helping establish Kim Il-Sung as the Stalin of North Korea.

Purging rivals

Kim Il-Sung attacked different groups from 1950 to 1967. Despite the fact that Kim mistakenly calculated that the US would not intervene in the Korean War to defend South Korea, he adroitly deflected the blame for this failure by launching expurgatory campaigns against rivals. The rival factions, especially the Domestic and Yanan Groups, were not united around one leader, making them vulnerable to attacks. Members of the Domestic Group had been under attack from 1948, but were particularly targeted after 1950, ostensibly for failing to start an insurgency in the South, and the group's leader was publicly executed in 1955. Key generals from the Yanan Group were purged for their military failures, while the leader of the Soviet Koreans committed suicide under suspicious circumstances in 1953. The excommunications continued from 1956 to 1960 following a failed political coup against Kim Il-Sung in 1956 by several of the leading members of the remnants of the Soviet and Yanan groups.[15]

The cult of personality and continued purges

1966–1972 marked the elevation of Kim Il-Sung to divine status: predictably, this process was accompanied by the purging of dissidents from within, this time some members of his Partisan Group. As early as the immediate post-Liberation period, parades celebrating liberation from Japanese colonial rule featured placards bearing portraits of both Kim and Stalin. However, after Stalin's death in 1953 and the decimation of rival groups, portraits of Stalin disappeared, while those of Kim Il-Sung proliferated. In the post-Stalin years, the Soviets often urged restraint in the use of the personality cult: Kim Il-Sung simply listened politely, then proceeded to ignore such suggestions.

The cult of personality was accompanied by the emergence of an ideological justification. The elevation in 1967 of Juche thought as the state doctrine began after the expulsion of leading members of the Kapsan faction within Kim's Partisan Group. The highest-ranking Kapsan Group member, Pak Kum-Chŏl, who occupied the number 4 slot in the KWP, had led the charge against the Yanan Group in the 1950s. While the reasons for his expulsion remain unclear, Pak found himself the subject of KWP criticism and apparently committed suicide in May 1967.[16]

In 1969 Kim also ousted several Partisan generals in the KPA who had advocated a more confrontational policy towards the South. In 1967, the North initiated several clashes within the DMZ, and also sent several spy incursions into the South. This culminated in the daring attempt to assassinate the South Korean president, Park Chung-Hee, in January 1968 when a group of Northern agents tried to infiltrate the presidential Blue House but were stopped around 500 meters from its gates. The failure of this mission paved the way for Kim to remove rival Partisan generals, such as Hŏ Pong-Hak, from their posts in February 1969. Several charges were leveled at the generals, the most prominent of which was the assertion that they had attempted to establish KPA independence from the KWP, and had been "counterrevolutionary" in their failure to follow orders.[17]

After consolidating his control over the KPA, in 1970, Kim further solidified Juche as the official ideology and his role as the absolute leader. Colossal statues of him were erected around the country, while his portraits looked down on every public hall.[18] The system had become so thoroughly saturated into the society that the Romanian ruler Nikolai Ceauşescu was apparently very impressed by the Great Leader's model of social control when he visited North Korea in 1971.[19]

In 1972, the golden colossus of Pyongyang was unveiled and the now-famous Kim Il-Sung badges were distributed to party members. North Korean propaganda states that the idea of the badge was Kim Jong-Il's but the similarities to the Mao Zedong badges of Cultural Revolution China were likely not coincidental. The difference was that Mao badges were not produced by the government, resulting in numerous shapes and types: in contrast, in North Korea the production and the distribution of the genuine Kim Il-Sung (and Kim Jong-Il) badges have been controlled by the state, resulting in only an estimated sixty to seventy different types.[20] There is apparently an intricate rank system attached to different shapes and types of Kim Il-Sung badges. In addition to the badges and the statues, in 1974 Kim Jong-Il started referring to "Kim Il-Sungism" in reference to all policies, movements, and ideas associated with his father, the principal component of which was Juche.

The cult of personality does seem undeniably odd, but it may be useful to view it in comparative context. A 2002 British documentary film, Game of Their Lives (2002), told the story of the 1966 North Korean team that did surprisingly well in the soccer World Cup of that year. The British film crew interviewed the surviving members of the team, or, more accurately, those who had survived both the ravages of time and various political purges (left unmentioned in the film). During the interview, team members suddenly burst into tears when they recalled the death of Kim Il-Sung, who had made possible their success. It was a jarring moment that reminded viewers that North Korea was indeed a very different country despite a shared love of soccer. At the same time, North Koreans might experience even more bewilderment when seeing sports players or entertainers in the "West" thanking God for the outcome of a big game or when receiving an award. After all, upon some reflection, it actually makes more sense that Kim Il-Sung would personally have been interested in the outcome of a specific soccer tournament, while it seems somewhat unlikely that God granted grace to one team or individual over another for specific games and awards shows.

Societal control

Kim Il-Sung turned the KWP, the police, and the KPA into engines of mass mobilization and informational control. The KWP membership accounted for some 17% of the total population by 1980, the highest percentage for a ruling party among socialist countries. Propaganda was piped into homes via publications, television programming, films, and radio broadcasts.

Print monthlies, dailies, and topical pamphlets for mass consumption propagated the Kim Il-Sung cult, while the television sets were fused to one channel. All newly purchased televisions and radios were registered with the local police and had their channels set. Radios could be re-altered to receive South Korean stations, but the fear of punishment (rather than the technical difficulty of removing the metal soldering) prevented people from making the necessary alterations.

Preparing for succession

Most important, throughout the 1970s Kim Il-Sung worked on paving a clear path for the Ascension of his Son, and with the help of the Son he diffused the Holy Spirit through the country. In fact, on his eightieth birthday, 15 April 1992, Kim Il-Sung noted in a public speech that laying the foundations for the dynastic succession had been one of the major achievements of his life. Considering the relative unpredictability and uncertainty of political succession in the Soviet Union and China, Kim Il-Sung could take some comfort in having laid out a long-term process for succession.

The process of establishing the Ascension was not simply a matter of the human God Kim Il-Sung anointing a successor, but an orchestrated, contingent, and incremental affair. Kim Jong-Il had been designated the successor in February 1974 by the KWP Politburo, but first Kim Jong-Il had had to prove his political mettle. Upon graduating from the Economics Department of Kim Il-Sung University in 1964, Kim Jong-Il held several positions in the KWP, eventually becoming the head of the Organization and Guidance Department in 1973, a position previously occupied by Kim Yŏng-Ju, the younger brother of Kim Il-Sung. Kim Jong-Il was also active in the various sixtieth birthday celebrations for the Father in 1972, and in propagating Juche in the name of his father. Jong-Il, aware that some of his Father's Partisan colleagues thought Jong-Il too young and inexperienced, also actively courted the support of some of the first-generation Partisans, in particular the KWP Number 3, O Chin-U.

The preparations for the public Ascension were handled with patience and care, but in actual terms, according to defector accounts and East German observations, the years 1974 to 1985 were characterized by joint rule between Kim Il-Sung and Kim Jong-Il. Kim Jong-Il had actually begun making personnel changes in the KWP and the KPA around 1970 with his father's approval, replacing older cadres with younger ones. This generational shift continued throughout the 1970s.[21] Around 1980, the arrangement changed so that Kim Jong-Il took up much of the administration. This transition accelerated after the death of one high-ranking Politbureau member, Kim Il, in 1984, the serious car accident of another, O Chin-U, in 1986, and Kim Il-Sung's heart attack in 1986.[22] Thus, while Kim Il-Sung held court for reporters until his death on July 8, 1994, it was Kim Jong-Il who made most of the executive decisions after 1986.

The reverberations from the fall of the Berlin Wall reached Pyongyang clearly, but the suddenness and the violence of Ceauşescu's fall in Romania had a greater impact on the Father and the Son. The "betrayal" by North Korea's main supporters, the Soviet Union and China, when they normalized relations with South Korea in 1990 and 1992 respectively, left the North Korean state on an apparently steady and inexorable course to disintegration. Observers across the political spectrum predicted the fall of the Kim dynasty. There were even rumours of a serious conflict in policy positions between the Father and the Son during the nuclear crisis of 1993–94, but allegations that Kim Jong-Il had his father assassinated seem to be based on evidence that is tenuous at the very best.

North Korea, in official terms at least, is ruled to this day by the willing ghost of the deceased Father, Kim Il-Sung. The 1998 constitution states that Kim Il-Sung is "the Eternal President of the Republic." From 1994 to 1997, Kim Jong-Il ruled in his capacity as the Chairman of the National Defense Commission, a title that he received in April 1993. It was not until the three-year mourning period for his father was over, on October 8, 1997, that Kim Jong-Il became Chairman of the KWP. Kim Il-Sung's mummy is housed in the sepulchral grandeur of a pyramidal mausoleum that is reminiscent of an Aztec temple or Lenin's tomb. A fitting epitaph for the leader who had made himself into a living god, this monument was built while millions of North Koreans starved.

In some senses, however, this was a necessary symbol for political survival for the Son. Rather than use the Father's death to differentiate himself from the Father, the Son incorporated the Father's ghost into his own Ascension. The Holy Spirit, the manifestation of the Father's will, had been directly transplanted into the Son, according to official accounts; therefore, while the body of the Father remains entombed, the Spirit of the Father still rules the country outside the walls of the mausoleum through the Son.

The Spirit

It is no coincidence that the right hand of the colossal statue of Kim Il-Sung in Pyongyang points towards the Juche Tower, a 170-meter obelisk soaring into the slate Pyongyang sky. Built in 1982 on the occasion of Kim Il-Sung's 70th birthday, the Tower, crowned with an artificial flame, is a required stop on tours like the golden colossus, with two or three bows usually elicited from visitors.

What are the main components of Juche? Juche is eschatological – that is, the Spirit infuses the present, but at the same time anticipates or promises a future, a pledge of the fulfilment of the already begun but not yet completed realization of all the precepts of Kimilsungism.[23] Further, according to the North Korean literature, Juche does not adhere to historical materialism, but accounts for the power of the human spirit. As mentioned above, the ideology came to be more inspired by Feuerbach than Marx. Second, autonomy, imagination, and awareness are the fundamental components of Juche. Third, a brain was required to integrate the people, and the Great Leader was connected to the Party (Army) and the people like a human body. As the embodiment of Juche, the Leader's destiny was to harmonize the organic state. Thus, the official position is that Juche is not a philosophy that attempts to address the meaning of existence or life, but a philosophy that explains the relationship between humans and the world, one that acknowledges the role of the human being in the world, unlike Marxism.

Origins of Juche

The concept of Juche made its first public appearance in a speech by Kim Il-Sung in December 1955, but Juche was not proposed as a systematic ideology until 1967. The December 1972 constitution marked the first time the concept of Juche was elevated to official status. The concept of Juche might be translated as "self-determination" or "autonomy as identity," which meant national, rather than individual or class, self-determination in politics, self-sufficiency in the economy, and self-defense in security, all initially fueled by Marxist revolution in the 1960s.

North Korean propaganda claims that Juche emerged immaculately conceived in Kim Il-Sung's mind amidst guerrilla activities in the 1930s. Some scholars trace the roots of Juche further back to "traditional" political thought developed in the nineteenth century to maintain autonomy during a period of Russian, Chinese, US, and Japanese imperialist expansion. Kim Il-Sung's statements contrasting Juche with "flunkeyism" – the attempt to maintain loyalty to Moscow or Beijing – display parallels with such nineteenth-century thought.

Hwang Jang-Yop (Hwang Chang-Yŏp), the leading ideologue of Juche under Kim Il-Sung, acknowledged to various foreign scholars after the fall of the Berlin Wall that Juche had not evolved from a moment of epiphany, or from a desire to obviate Marxism, but from more humble origins as a declaration of autonomy from both the Soviets and the Chinese. In addition to foreign policy agendas, the domestic political considerations required the mobilization of the Spirit to help support the emerging cult of the Father in the 1960s and 1970s.

The Father and the Spirit

With the rise of the personal cult, the fuel of revolution changed from Marxism to Kimilsungism. If Marxism was a doctrine for explaining historical processes driving revolution under material conditions, Juche, according to North Korean propaganda *circa* 1985, was a doctrine that would guide the activities of humans within a socialist country after revolution.[24] It is also possible to view the elevation of Kim Il-Sung as the font of Juche as a logical evolution of Leninist views on the role of the vanguard in the revolution: from a vanguard core elite to one absolute leader to embody the spirit of revolution.[25]

According to the official view, after the revolution, not all intellectuals or party elites could define Juche. The management of the socialist state obtained its legitimacy not from ideologues or a bureaucratic vanguard, but from the Father of the revolution – the Great Leader – and his Son. This highly concentrated form of revolutionary elitism proved to be a politically useful tautology: since those who were its material embodiments best interpreted the meaning of the Spirit, there was no need or room for debate whenever the Father or the Son issued an interpretation. As a consequence, there was no distinction between exegesis and eisegesis after the consolidation of the personal cult of Kim Il-Sung.

The Son and the Spirit

The Son, Kim Jong-Il, was particularly active in detailing the ever-changing "correct" interpretations of Juche, publishing countless articles on the subject starting in the late 1960s. In 1974, Kim Jong-Il announced "Ten Cardinal Principles" of a unified ideological system under Juche. Most of these ten principles stressed the role of the Great Leader and the need for unconditional loyalty. This evolved to a more explicitly distinct "human-centred" theory as outlined by Kim Jong-Il in 1982, partially as a result of the concerns raised about market reforms in China after 1978 under Deng Xiaoping.[26] A flurry of articles on "Surviving Our Way" followed in the 1980s, expressing the need for North Korea to adhere to its own version of socialism. This culminated in the 1986 treatise by Kim Jong-Il entitled "Theory of the Immortal Sociopolitical Body," which outlined the Great Leader as the brain, the KWP (or KPA) as the arms, and the masses as a body for an integrated triad.

Post-1989 changes in international context

The end of the Cold War in Europe, and the normalization of relations between South Korea and the former Soviet bloc, provided the impetus for further disavowal by North Korea of connections with Marxism or Leninism. The phrase "Our Own Socialism" began to appear in 1991, not coincidentally on the eve of Soviet Union–South Korea normalization.[27] The 1992 constitutional revision eliminated all references to Marxism or Leninism.

By the time of Kim Il-Sung's death in 1994, North Korean officials had had time to study the patterns of socialist collapse ranging from the disintegration of the Soviet Union to the defeat by election of Enver Hoxha's successor in Albania, Ramiz Alia, in April 1992. In 1994, Kim Jong-Il declared that the communist bloc in Eastern Europe failed due to the overemphasis on economic relations and the underestimation of moral and ideological dimensions and incentives.[28] Juche, needless to say, addressed this lacuna.

It helped that Juche was liberally spiced with heavy doses of anti-imperialism and nationalism. As Kim Jong-Il put it, "In order to establish Juche in thinking, it is necessary to possess a high sense of national dignity and revolutionary pride."[29] As was the case with Mao Zedong's brand of communism in the China of the 1930s, nationalism played a large role in generating mass support in North Korea. In the North Korean case, however, nationalism was continuously woven into the very fabric of the ideological framework, rather than allowed to lapse until the atrophy of communism and revived as ersatz ideology.[30]

Other embodiments of the Spirit

The material manifestations of the Spirit were varied. Efforts to export Juche took the form of propaganda distributed via meetings of the Non-Aligned Movement, and overseas Juche research groups formed often in conjunction with the contribution of aid money through the first half of the 1970s. All overseas Juche research groups were eventually placed under the supervision of the International Juche Research Centre established in Tokyo in 1978. The Academy of Juche Sciences was established in Pyong-yang in 1979 under Hwang's leadership, and the International Juche Foundation was incorporated in Geneva in 1993 to attract funding for Juche-related activities based on an initial $1 million contribution from a wealthy Lao businessman.

Some of the more striking infusions of the ideology into non-political arenas included the development of a Juche singing style and a Juche agricultural method (essentially expansion of arable land and collectivized, high-density farming). The Juche spirit apparently also animates Kim Jong-Il's theories of filmmaking.

The Spirit after the death of the Father

After the death of Kim Il-Sung, some ideological expansions of Juche, such as "Red Banner Thought" and the "Strong Nation" movement, emerged with the consent of Kim Jong-Il, while Kim Jong-Il personally reprimanded Hwang Jang-Yop (although without directly naming him) as an individual who had claimed too much personal credit for developing Juche and for mis-interpreting the origins of Juche.[31] Hwang, at the time Number 26 in the official KWP ranking and a member of the KWP Secretariat (one of the top three most powerful bodies in the KWP), defected on February 12, 1997. Hwang visited Japan in January 1997 for an international conference on Juche: on his way back to North Korea, he visited the South Korean embassy in Beijing to announce his intention to defect. After tense negotiations between China, North Korea, and South Korea, Hwang was sent to the Philippines then to Seoul on April 20, 1997. While there were several reasons for his defection, one of the primary ones was that Hwang was a member of the generation of Kim Il-Sung loyalists whose influence was clearly waning by 1997 as Kim Jong-Il replaced them with people more loyal to him.

Perhaps not coincidentally, after Hwang's defection Kim Jong-Il "returned" to Juche, toning down the attempt to propagate "Red Banner Thought" and other ideological subsidiaries. In 1997, Kim Jong-Il declared that Juche had in fact "clarified that the country and nation are the basic unit for shaping the destiny of the masses" in contrast to the original Marxist notion that the working class shared universal bonds.[32] In addition, a Juche calendar system was started in July 1997 at the official end of the period of mourning of Kim Il-Sung's death, with Kim Il-Sung's birth year, 1912, as year one (thus, 2002 was Juche Year 91), a system not unlike the Japanese practice of using the Emperor's reign name for its annual calendar (thus, Heisei 14 is 2002, as the Heisei Emperor's reign started in 1989).

Undoubtedly, all human beings are capable of erecting intricate sagas of self-deception, whether it is in the form of the hollow invocation of "freedom," "equality," or "justice" as rationales for wars, or the array of more quotidian excuses/explanations used in everyday life. The North Korean ruling elite seem to have carved out a particularly monumental illusion, but one with at least more ideological and political utility and coherence than the unholy mélange of ideas brandished on occasion by personalist rulers such as Jean Bedel Bokassa, the self-proclaimed emperor of the Central African Republic, or Idi Amin, the infamous tyrant of Uganda. The narcissism, imperial trappings, ruthless elimination of political rivals, misappropriation of religion, and succession maneuverings might be identified as common denominators, but the African personalist dictators did not have anything remotely resembling the ideological machinery of the North Korean state.[33]

After arriving in Seoul, Hwang accused Kim Jong-Il of twisting the idea of Juche for personal power and glorification.[34] This is a self-serving canard at best: the Spirit or Juche was intended to embody the will of the Father, inculcate loyalty to the Son, and facilitate regime survival and dynastic succession, not individual or class emancipation. The "abuses" of Juche appear to be the logical outcomes of an ideology or religion that stressed the role of the Human as God. More interestingly, there are indications that Kim Jong-Il knows the difference between reality and ritual. Even as a cascade of applause for him flowed around them at a concert in 1983, Kim Jong-Il turned to the film director Sin Sang-Ok and remarked, "This is all a lie."[35]

The Son

According to North Korean propaganda, Kim Jong-Il was born in 1942 in a secret base near the sacred Paekdusan, accompanied by a symphony of auroras and comets exploding in the heavens (presumably outshining the Star of Bethlehem). Known as the "Dear Leader" until his Ascension, Kim Jong-Il has been widely referred to since 1997 as the "General," despite his lack of military experience. The title "General" stems from the fact that during the three-year period of mourning for his Father, Kim Jong-Il ruled from his positions as Supreme Commander of the KPA (appointed April 1992), and the Chair of the National Defense Commission (appointed April 1993). He only became Chairman of the KWP in October 1997.

Extreme experiences that seem to be the product of a single villain's dreams or obsessions seem to hold an inherent fascination for most people; not surprisingly, Kim Jong-Il has been portrayed as the root of all evil, or as an endless source of surreal eccentricities. While there is certainly an element of the absurd in North Korean politics, the reporting on Kim Jong-Il can at times be nearly as absurd. Major journals and academic publications continue to repeat out-of-date or disproved information, such as news about his favorite cigarettes (although Kim stopped smoking in 1998 or 1999), or speculations about his having a fear of appearing in public (when the 2000 summit meeting with Kim Dae-Jung had already undermined such views).

The mesmerizing minutiae of Kim Jong-Il's life are less pertinent here than the answers to the question, how did the Son consolidate his power after the Ascension? Several factors facilitated the rare instance of a dynastic succession in a socialist state.

Twenty-five-year preparation

The first reason that the Son was able to inherit the reins of power is that, as has been mentioned before, the preparations for the Ascension took place over a twenty-year span during which Kim Jong-Il was active in the administration of the country, appointed loyalists into positions within the KWP and the KPA, and established his own public role as the "Dear Leader." Moreover, there was nothing automatic or culturally predetermined about his ascension. Kim Jong-Il's status as the eldest son did not assure him of his position as the successor.

Kim Jong-Il had to outperform his rivals to be anointed as the Son. His uncle, Kim Yŏng-Ju, ten years younger than Kim Il-Sung, had signed key documents during a period of reconciliation with the South in 1972, and had been widely considered to be the likely successor. However, possibly for health reasons and because of his political ineffectiveness in follow-up negotiations with the South, he disappeared from public office after 1975, and only reemerged in a ceremonial capacity in 1993. Kim Jong-Il also had to nudge out a stepbrother, Kim P'yŏng-Il. Kim Il-Sung had married a communist partisan, Kim Chŏng-Suk, in 1940, and the couple had Kim Jong-Il in 1942, a boy, P'yŏng-Il, in 1944, and a girl, Kyŏng-Hŭi, in 1946. P'yŏng-Il died in 1948 in a drowning accident in a backyard pool, and Kim Chŏng-Suk also died in 1949.[36] Kim Il-Sung officially remarried in 1963 to Kim Sŏng-Ae, but the couple had a daughter in 1952 and in 1953 a son, P'yŏng-Il (the name is written using a different Chinese character for the second syllable than appears in the name of the boy who died in 1948), followed by another son, Yŏng-Il, in 1955.[37] There are a range of accounts from defectors, but most agree that Kim Jong-Il had a troubled relationship with his stepmother, and was not particularly close to his step-siblings, especially the taller Kim P'yŏng-Il, who apparently was the Father's favorite while growing up.

Whether Kim P'yŏng-Il was ever seriously considered as a possible successor is difficult to determine. Again, there are conflicting defector accounts that claim that P'yŏng-Il, in charge of Kim Il-Sung's personal security for a time, was more popular than Jong-Il in the KPA, while others claim that P'yŏng-Il was never a serious candidate because the elites in both the KWP and the KPA all preferred Kim Jong-Il as he was the son of the beloved anti-Japanese partisan Kim Chŏng-Suk. While the Mother, Kim Chŏng-Suk, was not officially apotheosized as one of the Three Great Generals of Paekdusan (along with the Father and the Son) until December 1997, she had been an active communist guerrilla, unlike Kim Sŏng-Ae, who had been a KWP typist. What we do know is that starting in 1982, soon after Kim Jong-Il's public confirmation as successor, Pyŏng-Il spent most of his time abroad, primarily as ambassador to various European countries, and that after Kim Il-Sung's death, Kim Sŏng-Ae disappeared from the political scene.

It should be noted that the name "Kim Jong-Il" was not used in public statements until 1980: instead, pamphlets and publications referred to the mysterious "Party Center." It was not until the 6th

KWP Congress in October 1980 that Kim Jong-Il was introduced to the public as the official successor to Kim Il-Sung. During the Congress, the Son was also elected to the Standing Committee of the Politburo (the most powerful organ in the KWP), but into the number 4 spot, after number 1 Kim Il-Sung, number 2 Kim Il, and number 3 O Chin-U. In 1983, Jong-Il became the official number 2 in the Politburo, and after Kim Il's death in 1984, the use of honorifics in reference to the Son became increasingly widespread. By 1988, the same level and frequency of honorifics as used for Kim Il-Sung was used for Jong-Il.

Generational shifts in bureaucracy

The second reason why Kim Jong-Il was able to inherit and maintain the mantle of power was that between 1994 and 1998, Kim Jong-Il replaced many of his Father's stalwart supporters with individuals who were more personally loyal to him. This process was facilitated by the age of the first-generation Partisan loyalists who had fought alongside his father, and also by the Son's willingness to assert his authority in ruthless ways. On December 29, 1995, according to Kim Jong-Il's personal sushi chef, Fujimoto Kenji, Kim Jong-Il ordered the execution of twenty-five officials who opposed his succession to the North Korean throne.[38] Another indication of the persistence of purges is that in 1990, Kim Jong-Il gave each of twenty of his top aides a gold ring, with the promise that they should meet again in 2000 wearing the same rings: Fujimoto noticed that at least six of them were absent at the 2000 meeting. Also, Kim reportedly promoted over 1,100 of the current roster of 1,400 generals in the KPA, and many of them were elevated to their new posts in 1997 and 1998 as Kim Jong-Il was consolidating his hold on power.

Currently, Kim Jong-Il is supported by a larger set of officials or Apostles in both the KPA and the KWP who are sometimes called the "1980 group" as many of them began their rise up through the system in 1980 under Kim Il-Sung's directive to promote the second generation of leaders. The most prominent of these are number 2 Kim Yŏng-Nam, whose official title is President of the Presidium of the Supreme People's Assembly (the equivalent of the legislature), and number 3 Cho Myŏng-Rok, the First Vice Chair of the National Defense Commission and

Director of the Political Bureau of the KPA (internal watchdog of the KPA), who are both now close to eighty. Kim Yŏng-Nam, who had been one of Kim Il-Sung's trusted advisors, has in many ways become the *de facto* head of state, negotiating and signing various international agreements and making state visits. This may relate to Kim Il-Sung's advice to his son that in case of political or economic change, it was better to become something akin to a constitutional monarch than be possibly held accountable for the failures of specific policies. In fact, according to US Secretary of State Madeleine Albright, during her visit to North Korea in 2000 Kim Jong-Il indicated interest in Swedish or Thai models of constitutional monarchy. [39] The roster of the Apostles has changed over the years – for example, some KPA generals seen as close allies of Kim Il-Sung in the 1980s have moved down in the official rankings for state funeral processions, while the makeup of the members who accompany the Son on inspection trips and weekend trips to *dachas* (country retreats) has also changed.

The overall generational shift has also been reflected within the ranks of the Supreme People's Assembly. This has one representative for every 30,000 people, each representative on five-year terms. Of the 687 deputies elected in August 2003, 340 were first-time appointees, with around 50% of the total under the age of 50.

Military-First politics

The third factor that helped the Son to consolidate his power was that he retained Juche, as discussed above, but altered the dynamics of the second trinity by declaring a new political principle, Military-First Politics. The slogan "Military-First Politics" first appeared in August 1998 in the government daily *Rodong Sinmun*, and has since then been the cornerstone of North Korea under Kim Jong-Il. Whereas the KWP had been above the KPA under Kim Il-Sung, under the rule of the Son, the KPA has been given more power compared to the KWP.[40] Although the KWP maintains a presence in local administration, the KPA power in major policy-making decisions has been clearly ascendant since 1998. There are several probable reasons why Kim Jong-Il implemented these reforms. There was a temporary breakdown of law and order in 1995–96, as roaming vagabonds searched for food, and the food distribution system broke down. Kim Jong-Il publicly blamed the KWP in 1996 for problems with the food distribution system, although by some accounts the KWP's bureaucratic efficiency had started declining in the mid-1980s. Also, the Military-First ideology was required to obtain the loyalty of the KPA, as some KPA officers and intelligence directors were apparently disgruntled by Kim Jong-Il's policies. The potential seriousness of such discontent was reflected in the high ranks of some of those purged in 1998 for alleged profiteering: General Kim Yŏng-Ryong, the First Vice Director of the State Security Agency (domestic intelligence), and Kwŏn Hŭi-Kyŏng, the Director of Department 35 (foreign intelligence).[41] While some 130 KPA generals have reportedly defected over the past decade, most of these appear to be younger generals who had been affiliated with purged groups.

There have been some claims that Military-First Politics has been a source of dissent among the Apostles. Several defectors have claimed that the KPA and the KWP are locked in a power struggle. In addition, North Korean Foreign Ministry negotiators in two disputes – over the 1994 Agreed Framework and, in the same year, the return of the survivor of a US helicopter shot down by North Korea – claimed that the intransigence of the KPA was the primary hindrance in negotiations. On the other hand, there is some question as to whether this conflict can be divided along such clear organizational lines, or whether these statements were merely negotiating strategies. Kim Jong-Il himself claimed to Madeleine Albright that there was a split among hardliners and reformers within both the KPA and the Foreign Ministry as to whether or not relations with the US should be improved. It seems clear that there are at least two policy factions – one pushing for more economic reforms, and the other for the retention of the primacy of military priorities – but the most reliable defector accounts indicate that the actual fault lines may not fall neatly between the KPA and the KWP.

Societal control

Fourth, the Son has been relentless in his control of information and in the oppression of his own people, especially those with dubious lineage. Although Kim Jong-Il and his trusted aides have access to any number of cable and satellite channels, and Japanese and other foreign channels can be seen in the Pyongyang hotels for foreigners, information access to the outside world is highly restricted for ordinary North Korean citizens. The first state-sponsored Internet café opened in May 2002, and they now total six or seven.[42] But ordinary North Koreans are prevented from browsing on the Worldwide Web, as they are allowed to log on only to an intranet that carries only the websites of North Korea's major state institutions, including universities. Some South Korean dramas and films have reportedly circulated in North Korea, but the school grounds and the classrooms in Pyongyang still reverberate with songs of the General's greatness, and specific classes are devoted to the study of the three aspects of Kim Jong-Il's greatness (ideological, leadership, and aura).

Video footage of well-fed elite families with pet dogs in Pyongyang provides a stark contrast with footage of public executions in the regional cities. It was rumored that after 1995, Kim Jong-Il ordered shots to be fired into the heads of the executed, rather than the previous practice of aiming for the chest, to increase the impact on those watching.[43] Athletes who have not performed at respectable levels at international competitions have reportedly been sent for reeducation on potato farms for a year. The North Korean intelligence agencies monitor all potential dissident activity both domestically and abroad. For example, Lee Il-Nam (Yi Il-Nam, pseudonym Yi Han-Yŏng, the cousin of Kim Jong-Il's firstborn son, Kim Jong-Nam), who had defected in 1982, was shot dead outside his own apartment in a Seoul suburb in February 1997: the South Korean government concluded that this was the work of two North Korean agents. Lee had published a tell-all book in 1996, and his mother (the younger sister of Kim Jong-Nam's mother), had also defected in 1996.

Additional factors

Three additional factors helped Kim to maintain power. They are briefly outlined here, but will be discussed in more detail in Chapter 4. First, there is sufficient control of the economy by the Apostles and the Son himself to allow for the distribution of material comforts to the elites and to loyal KWP members.

Second, by developing missiles and nuclear weapons and

inviting US pressure, the Son has been able to maintain and even amplify the siege mentality within the country. In fact, several observers have suggested that the North Koreans deliberately initiated the missile crisis in 1994 by moving the equipment to a location that would be spotted by US satellites. Given the constant stream of anti-imperialist and anti-US rhetoric flowing through North Korea's educational and propaganda channels, having the US as an enemy helps bolster domestic control, not unlike the Eurasia–Oceania conflicts in George Orwell's novel *1984*. Even the famine of the mid-1990s was repackaged in the official propaganda as an "arduous march" that Kim Jong-Il led the people through, while the 2003 invasion of Iraq was fully used to highlight the very real threat of invasion from the US.

Third, Kim Jong-Il implemented a limited set of economic reforms in July 2002, which partially liberalized wages and prices, reorganized the various private markets into district markets, monetarized the economy, and allowed limited privatization. These reforms, combined with internal policing, have allowed the North Korean government to reassert some level of control over what had been a small but growing informal economy.

Although described as imperious, mercurial, and intelligent by the limited number of defectors who actually had direct interactions with him, Kim Jong-Il is only a crazy madman in some branches of the Western mass media. Even his detractors, including Hwang Jang-Yop, acknowledge the Son's craftiness and intelligence. Kim and his supporters, whether they are reformists or hardliners, know that regime survival is the more immediate and realistic goal, not the export of revolution to the South. In order to maintain the long-term viability of the regime, thorough preparations for a successful Second Ascension are crucial.

The Second Ascension

The succession issue – the question of who will replace Kim Jong-Il – has taken on momentum ever since the arrest and deportation of Kim Jong-Nam (Kim Chŏng-Nam) in Tokyo in May 2001 (see below). Kim Jong-Il was anointed successor in 1974 in front of the KWP, when the Father was sixty-two and he was thirty-two, although there are claims that he was first secretly approved by Kim Il-Sung in 1972. If we recall that Kim Il-Sung did not announce his successor to the public until 1980 (and discreetly at that), when Kim Il-Sung was close to seventy, it seems likely no public or final announcement will be made on the succession until at least 2014 or beyond. Kim Jong-Il recently stated that he would continue to rule for another ten to fifteen years, which would be consistent with this prediction and his own experiences with gradual preparation and incremental increases in responsibility. This does not mean, however, that there has not been jockeying among potential successors, or that Kim Jong-Il has not been thinking about future scenarios.

The extended royal family

Before we continue in the analysis of the candidates for the Second Ascension, it would be useful to untangle some of the branches of Kim Jong-Il's family. He has had at least five wives, although the legal status of each union is unclear. The accumulated defector accounts indicate that Kim Jong-Il had one daughter with his first wife/mistress, Hong Il-Chŏn, a leading intellectual. He had a son, Jong-Nam, in 1971 with his second wife, Sŏng Hye-Rim. Sŏng, who was a famed actress, was already married with a child when Jong-Il took a fancy to her. The third wife, the only one formally recognized by Kim Il-Sung, was Kim Yŏng-Suk. She gave birth to two daughters, Sŏl-Song in 1974, and Ch'un-Song in 1976.

Kim Jong-Il's fourth wife or mistress, Ko Yŏng-Hŭi, was born in Japan in 1953; she arrived with her family in North Korea in 1961. She was a star dancer in a prestigious national troupe before becoming Kim Jong-Il's fourth wife. Ko gave birth to two sons, Kim Jong-Chol in 1981, and Kim Jong-Un (Kim Chŏng-Un) in 1983, and a daughter, Il-Sun, in 1987. Currently, Kim Jong-Il is reported to have a fifth wife, Kim Ok, who has been his personal secretary for some time. One defector has claimed that there is also a sixth mistress/wife in her mid-thirties, Na Hye-Kyŏng.[44]

Kim Jong-Nam

The eldest son, Kim Jong-Nam, was initially considered the most likely successor as he had accompanied his father on inspection tours in the past, and had been described as being very similar in personality and temperament to the Son. Around the mid-1990s, the nickname "Little General" had been given to Jong-

Nam. Jong-Nam also guided Kim Jong-Il around Shanghai and Beijing during an unofficial visit in January 2001, and had apparently been active in the Korea Computer Center, the government computer hardware and software research institute. These details hinted at a potential reformer, until Jong-Nam was deported from Japan in May 2001 after being caught entering the country on a fake Dominican Republic passport. He explained that he and his family had wanted to visit the Disneyland near Tokyo. According to several accounts, Jong-Nam had previously entered Japan on numerous occasions using fake passports, and had been something of a regular customer at one particular Korean hostess bar in Tokyo, claiming to be a businessman. Many of the royal family allegedly travel regularly on fake passports, but Jong-Nam's *faux pas* of being caught reportedly angered Kim Jong-Il. Since then, Jong-Nam has lived in exile (albeit a luxurious one) in Beijing and Macao. Therefore, Jong-Nam has not been in a position to build domestic support for himself within either the KWP or the KPA over the past several years.

Some North Korea watchers still claim that due to Confucian hereditary practice, the eldest son must inherit the family title. However, Jong-Nam never had political support from a mother that had sway over Kim Jong-Il. Jong-Nam's mother, Sŏng Hye-Rim, had not been with Kim Jong-Il since 1974, and had spent most of the succeeding decades in Moscow receiving treatment for clinical depression until her death in 2002. More important, the emphasis on allegedly unchanging cultural norms overlooks the fact that Kim Jong-Il himself was not chosen just because he was the eldest but he had displayed the requisite loyalty and ambition, and the ability to beat out rivals. Further, even in the Confucian Chosŏn period, not all eldest sons were chosen as heirs. In several cases, the most capable son was selected – for example, King Sejong, known as the father of the Korean writing system, Han'gŭl, was the third son of the previous king.

There are conflicting reports about Jong-Nam's current political aspirations and his relationship with his father. One view, espoused by his clearly biased aunt (his mother's younger sister) and cousin, who both defected to the West in 1996, is that Jong-Nam is not interested in political power and only wants to live in comfort. The more dramatic accounts claim that Jong-Nam expressed a desire to push North Korea towards a market-oriented reform along the lines of China, a sentiment that allegedly triggered his father's anger. There are also reports that he currently feels bitter towards his father and makes frequent calls to his aunt on his father's side, Kim Kyŏng-Hŭi (Jong-Il's sister), for mutual commiserations – to Jong-Nam over his exile, and to Kyŏng-Hŭi over the nearly two-year exile of her husband, Chang Sŏng-T'aek, from the centre of power.[45]

Chang Sŏng-T'aek

Chang Sŏng-T'aek was for several years considered the *de facto* Number 2 in North Korean politics, and a possible successor to Kim Jong-Il. Chang had very close connections to the KPA because his oldest brother was the commanding officer of the Pyongyang-area Third Division, while another brother was also a high-ranking KPA officer. Chang was by all accounts very close to Kim Jong-Il, and headed various domestic economic reform projects and overseas trade missions. However, all of a sudden, on April 13, 2004 he was removed from his post as First Vice Director of the KWP Organization and Guidance Department. He was reappointed Vice Director of a less powerful public works department in January 2006.

Defectors have claimed wildly varying reasons for his temporary dismissal. One rumor was that he had become estranged from his wife, Kyŏng-Hŭi, and that the purge was somehow related to this. Another rumor that was reported as "fact" in many media outlets was that Chang and his wife had attempted a coup. Other observers have claimed that Chang's ouster was engineered by hard-liners opposed to the economic reforms that had been implemented by Chang and his coterie.

Yet another unsubstantiated claim was that there was an internal clash over Kim Jong-Il's attempted rapprochement with Japan in 2002. By 2004, it was clear that the policy had failed. But the malcontents could not criticize Kim Jong-Il, so turned their attention to a more vulnerable scapegoat, Chang, and alleged that he had misled the "General." Another account claimed that Chang was aligned with Kim Jong-Nam against Ko Yŏng-Hŭi and her children, thereby incurring Kim Jong-Il's wrath. However, there has been little corroboration of such conspiracy theories and claims that each faction is planning a coup. Either way, based on the order of name listings for ceremonial events, and his official position, it seems that while Chang has managed to return to the "royal court," his influence and power have diminished.

Sŏl-Song

At least one North Korea specialist in South Korea has noted that Kim Jong-Il's daughter, Sŏl-Song, might be a plausible candidate for the Ascension. She has accompanied her father on various domestic guidance trips to factories, and also on the trips to Russia and China. She majored in political economy at Kim Il-Sung University, and defectors have asserted that her intelligence and personality have made her Kim Jong-Il's favourite.[46] However, there have been no public efforts to elevate her status, and she does not hold a position within the KWP. She may serve as an advisor or consultant to the Second Son, whoever that might turn out to be, but there is little evidence concerning her relations with other successor candidates.

Kim Jong-Chol

Kim Jong-Chol, the author of the poem that starts this chapter, is the leading candidate for the Second Ascension. He attended the International School of Berne from 1993 to 1998, but did not become the focus of international media frenzy until June 2006, when a Japanese TV crew captured him attending four Eric Clapton concerts in Germany.

There are several indications that Jong-Chol is the most likely successor. First, there were reports in spring 2006 that a Kim Jong-Chol badge was issued to the top officials in the cabinet, the KWP, and the KPA in February 2006.[47] Second, a campaign started in summer 2002 to apotheosize Jong-Chol's mother, Ko Yŏng-Hŭi, as the KPA's "Revered Mother." Pamphlets of speeches for the KPA and the internal KPA monthly included extended discussions of the "Revered Mother" and her unstinting love for the Great Leader, Kim Il-Sung. Though the 'Revered Mother' went unnamed, mention of her dedicated support of Kim Jong-Il through the difficult eight years after 1994 (accompanying him to visit the KPA units right after the Father's death to uplift the troops) and other details indicate that the reference could not be to any other of Kim Jong-Il's wives, since Ko was the *de facto* First Lady from 1979 on.[48] While there is some question as to whether the campaign continued after her death from cancer in a Paris hospital in April 2004, the campaign is certainly consistent with the pattern of apotheosising the mother of the successor and the precedent of the deification of Kim Jong-Il's mother to lay the groundwork for the First Ascension.

A third indication that Jong-Chol is the most likely successor is that he has already occupied several positions within the KWP, possibly within the Organization and Guidance Department (but as yet not the Politburo or Party Central Committee).[49] Fourth, official North Korea media outlets have started a story that Kim Jong-Il originally thought of Military-First Politics in 1960, when he was still around eighteen. This may signal many things, but it may indicate some preparations for a young successor, such as Jong-Chol, who despite his youth could, with the requisite qualities, become the Second Son, or the next great leader. The fifth reason why Jong-Chol is the leading candidate is that the support network of Kim Jong-Il loyalists who would assist Jong-Chol's progress appears to be already in place. Lee Che-Kang (Yi Che-Kang), the Vice Director of the Organization and Guidance Department of the KWP, is the Number 2 within the entire party after having overseen the temporary purge of Chang Sŏng-T'aek. Lee and three generals who currently control the KPA in *de facto* terms all appear to support Jong-Chol. Moreover, there have been unverified reports that Kim Jong-Il has ordered the appointment of younger people of around Jong-Chol's age into the KWP and the KPA to create a loyal cohort.

Kim Jong-Un

There are some claims that Jong-Chol is not the favored candidate. For example, according to Kim Jong-Il's personal sushi chef, Fujimoto Kenji, the Son said of Jong-Chol's personality, "He's no good, too much like a girl." Kim Jong-Il at the time apparently preferred Ko Yŏng-Hŭi's second son, Jong-Un, for his ferocity and for similarities to his own personality.

The problem is that while Fujimoto defected or escaped from the North in 2001, many of these comments were made before 1996 when the heirs (or the "Princes" as they were called) were still children, and well before Kim Jong-Il was considering the issue of his successor. Also, Jong-Un was apparently quite considerate towards Fujimoto, even personally bringing him bottles of beer (Heineken at that) when Fujimoto said in passing once that they had run out of beer. Based on the same logic, it could be possible to argue that such "softness" towards an eventual "defector" should disqualify Jong-Un for political leadership.[50] Less facetiously, unlike his older brother, Jong-Un does not currently have a position within the KWP or the KPA: although he may eventually take up an official position, there are no indications that he is actively being groomed to be the successor.

Some North Korea watchers claim that bypassing Jong-Nam would be "destabilizing" for a "Confucian" society – this reflects a lack of understanding of North Korea's political history. As explained above, Kim Jong-Il was not simply appointed successor because he was the oldest, and even in the "Confucian" Chosŏn dynasty, the eldest royal son did not automatically inherit the throne. The more meaningful possible issue is that Jong-Chol and Jong-Un no longer have the direct support of their mother, Ko Yŏng-Hŭi. However, the "Revered Mother" campaign may dilute any negative effects from Ko's death on Jong-Chol's possible succession. Moreover, the current wife, Kim Ok, and Kim Jong-Il do not have any children, and are unlikely to have any in the future as Kim Ok was born in 1964 or 1965.[51]

As was the case with Kim Jong-Il's own Ascension, the process of appointing a successor for Kim Jong-Il will likely not be determined solely by fiat. The families of first-generation Partisan loyalists and other top officials wield some influence in the process. More important, the presence of poetry penned by North Korean authors espousing peace and equality notwithstanding, the emergence of a Gorbachev-like reformist figure from deep within the bowels of the North Korean system seems highly unlikely, at least for the foreseeable future.

Conclusion

While Seoul has now witnessed four peaceful presidential transitions via direct presidential elections, the North Korean executive succession remains a competitive yet labyrinthine process redolent of palace politics of old. Some defectors have claimed that there are insurgents and dissidents within North Korea ready to overthrow Kim Jong-Il. While some of the stories of assassination attempts on Kim Jong-Il and shoot-outs in Pyongyang between candidates for succession appear to be groundless, or based on a combination of deliberate misinformation, shoddy research, and wishful thinking, there are still persistent reports that there was an attempted coup in 1992 by a dozen Soviet-trained KPA officers, which led to KPA officers receiving their training in China after 1992. There was another reported coup attempt in 1995 by a KPA division in North Hamgyŏng province (in the northeast corner), although Kim Jong-Il asserted in 1998 during a closed meeting with a visiting delegation of North Korea-affiliated Korean residents in Japan that it was a just a small incident in which some officers had to be removed because of insufficient indoctrination.

The existence of discontent and embryonic coup plots notwithstanding, the political system has continued since 1948. George Orwell noted, "… hereditary aristocracies always have been short-lived, whereas adoptive organizations such as the Catholic Church have sometimes lasted for hundreds of thousands of years. The essence of oligarchical rule is not father-to-son inheritance but the persistence of a certain world-view and a certain way of life, imposed by the dead upon the living."[52] In North Korea, hereditary socialist aristocracies, adaptive oligarchical rule, and self-justifying world-views have been fused together into the Holy Trinity. North Korea's tenacity may lend itself to portrayals of a country captive to a petrified political system, but the system has evolved through reforms, purges, some resistance, and the continued flight of members of its elite. The Holy Trinity has evolved along with the system, but its continued talismanic power has clearly been the central element of post-1989 North Korean political history.

4 | Economic Tetralogies
Socioeconomic Conditions in North Korea

Video footage and eyewitness accounts of Pyongyang in 2007 indicate that direct evidence of the famines, missiles, and nuclear weapons that dominate the Western news headlines are absent from the streets. Granted, there are many easily discerned differences from Seoul: there are some street lamps, but the city is still near pitch dark at night; there are no neon signs, and maybe six billboards throughout the entire city – for the same car at that; although there are some food booths that sell sweet potatoes and other edibles across from the major hotel for foreigners, the numbers pale in comparison to Seoul's cornucopia of commerce; power outages in homes and on trains, although fewer than say two years ago, are still common; policewomen direct traffic at intersections devoid of traffic lights; and numerous banners displaying revolutionary realist paintings exhort citizens to be constantly vigilant against American imperialism.

While the major edifices of most cities in the industrialized world tend to celebrate the power of capital or serve as reminders of imperial legacies, in contrast Pyongyang's tallest building, the Ryukyŏng (Yukyŏng) Hotel, is an improbable ziggurat, an empty shell that is not even listed on the current official maps, a symbol of the failed attempt at limited economic opening in the late 1980s. This monolithic pyramid, which at 330 meters was the tallest hotel in the world at the time of its construction, sits dark and incomplete; because of problems with funding, contracts, and construction, not one of its 105 floors was ever opened for guests.

Nonetheless, expectations of endless vistas saturated with anxiety and desperation, of people seething with quiet but palpable anger at the casual savagery of the evil Kim Jong-Il, would be betrayed. The young university students walking to the campus of the Kim Il-Sung University in their uniforms do not seem to be emaciated or stunted. People in Pyongyang eat, laugh, walk, and breathe, like other human beings, although their wariness with visitors from the West contrasts with the relative openness they display to Chinese or Russian tourists.

The catch is that the residents of Pyongyang are the loyal, the privileged, the select, the few. The society is officially divided into three classes – workers, farmers, and intellectuals. In actuality, three other categories have been far more important: the citizenry are divided into "loyal," "wavering," and "hostile" classes depending on their likely loyalty to the state. A more detailed classificatory system, known as the *sŏngbun*, further divides these three groups into 51 specific grades based on family backgrounds, occupation, and past track record. For example, Korean "returnees" from Japan that were "welcomed" back to the North in the late 1950s with great fanfare were, with a few exceptions, ranked in the lowest category of the "hostile" class.[1] The loyal constitute around 30% of the total population, the wavering 40%, and the hostile 30%. Since Pyongyang's population is around 15% of the national total, which is around 22 to 23 million, its residents are indeed the privileged minority.

Even then, in Pyongyang there are wide gaps in standards between the homes of the different groups: the top officials live in large detached residences; the elite or the privileged live in spacious apartments comparable to suites in Washington, DC; and the rank and file might live six people to one room. Radios are fitted into the kitchens of most apartments, piping state propaganda and news into the households of Pyongyang – the volume can be adjusted, but it cannot be turned off. There is one TV station which broadcasts for five hours each day (although NHK, Nippon Hōsō Kyōkai, the primary Japanese public TV station, and other foreign channels can be viewed in the hotel rooms for foreigners). Revolutionary music fills the streets via loudspeakers in the mornings, urging people to wake up and fulfil their duties.

Outside of Pyongyang, impressions can change depending on region and locale. A peek inside one of the many residences of Kim Jong-Il which dot the country would transport the viewer into sybarite territory. Kim Jong-Il's menus are based on ingredients that most people in any country would enjoy – fresh fruits from Thailand, caviar from Iran, pork from Denmark, and marine products from Japan. There are Toyota sports cars for use just within some of his retreats, while a fleet of black Mercedes carry him and the "royal family" here and there. The different retreats have motorbikes, horses, jet skis, motorboats, extensive collections of movies from around the world, full-sized basketball courts, and televisions that can be tuned into numerous satellite stations.

Driving south from Pyongyang for around two hours along the straight highway (one of three in the country) takes the traveler from Pyongyang to Kaesŏng, only 8 kilometers north of the DMZ. Rather than aggressive soldiers or forests of missiles, there is instead a cluster of factories in the Kaesŏng Industrial Park, the main site of investment by South Korean firms into the North. The plan was that between 2002 and 2008, first some small and medium-scale manufacturing facilities would be established, then production and export would begin, and lastly there would be investment in heavy industry development. The plan is behind schedule, but many South Korean firms, such as the leading manufacturer of timepieces, Romanson, have established factories there. A highway connects the South through a checkpoint in the DMZ to the industrial park.

Traveling northwest from Pyongyang brings a greater sense of the current economic flux, of state control fraying at the edges. The major border checkpoint between the Chinese city of Dandong and the North Korean city of Sinŭiju has heavy traffic across the bridge over the Yalu River, trucks taking Chinese goods into North Korea, as well as North Korean traders going into China on limited travel passes. A wired fence extends along the banks of the Yalu eastward from the western coast; it can be crossed more easily further east where the wires stop and the river is shallow. Guards have been known to engage in informal trade, wading across the river with goods in areas they are supposed to be guarding. In this area, personal wealth has reportedly become as important as official *sŏngbun* status: some merchants have accumulated private wealth, emerging as a small group of nouveaux riches with better access to food, information, and other goods than most KWP cadres or KPA officers.

In the northeastern areas of the country, where most foreigners from the West have not been granted access, the legacies of the great famines of the mid-1990s are more visible than in Pyongyang. Many of the orphans lost their parents due to the famine, and are much smaller than might be expected for their ages. This area has a higher concentration of "wavering" and "hostile" classes than other regions of North Korea, and was the hardest hit during the famines, leading some observers to claim that there was a deliberate attempt to starve the area (see page 139). Hidden-camera video footage taken by members of NGOs has captured rural landscapes dotted with thatched farmhouses seemingly built decades ago, people dressed in faded clothes, with nary a Kim Il-Sung badge or monument in sight. The cities and towns in this region have markets, but also young homeless orphans dressed in adult clothing orbiting the stalls looking for food scraps and rummaging around the garbage piles for usable items – sights that might be hard to imagine walking along the concrete boulevards of Pyongyang.

A traveler to the US who visits the capitalist cathedrals of, say, Upper East Side Manhattan, then visits the poorest rural areas of Arkansas, might experience a similar sense of surreal dislocation based on geography. As we saw in Chapter 2, South Korea also is facing increasing income inequity. Even with these qualifiers, it would be difficult to say that the North Korean economy has been flourishing in relative terms. The CIA estimates North Korean per capita GDP for 2006 to be around $1,800, which is only around 8% of South Korea's $24,000. At the same time, North Korea is in the news for its nuclear weapons and missiles, its diplomatic brinkmanship. What helps explain how such an economically embattled country has managed to produce missiles and nuclear weapons? What caused the famines of the mid-1990s? Is North Korea a threat, and, if so, for whom?

The Four Economies

The first step to understanding the North Korean economy is to acknowledge that the statistics and estimates related to the North are all problematic to varying degrees. As even the mandarins of statistical surveys would readily acknowledge, all social and economic statistical surveys have a "subjective" element to them: but in North Korea, we are further handicapped by the long-extant explicit division of statistics for internal use, domestic public use, and foreign consumption. A gradual opening of North Korea's statistical profile did begin in 1989, when the United Nations Population Fund (UNFPA) helped the government conduct a full-scale census. North Korean authorities, with the assistance of the UNFPA, made public the census data for 1993 (although the census did not include soldiers in the KPA). Since the mid-1990s, there have been at least four competing sets of numerical narratives, emanating from the North Korean government, from several governmental and nongovernmental organizations in South Korea, from UN organizations such as the Food and Agriculture Organization (FAO) and the World Food Programme (WFP), and from US agencies such as the US Department of Agriculture. Predictably, estimates for several issues vary greatly: for example, estimates of deaths between 1994 and 1998 from the famine generally range from 200,000 to 3 million.

The second step is to recognize that the North Korean economy can be differentiated into four tiers. This structure makes possible the contemporaneous existences of Kim Jong-Il's epicurean lifestyle, the development of missiles and advanced game software, and massive food shortages. First, there is a "personal" economy at Kim Jong-Il's disposal; there is a "second economy" under the jurisdiction of specific units within the two "Apostles" – the KPA and the KWP; there is a public or formal economy; and there is also a black market or informal economy. The first economy essentially funds the luxurious lifestyle of Kim Jong-Il and his family. The second economy generates funds for missiles and weapons development. The famines affected the third and fourth economies the most.

The first and second economies

According to defector accounts, Kim Jong-Il himself established the first or personal economy in the 1980s.[2] Bureau 89 of the KWP is responsible for the General's personal finances, and those of the upper echelons of the KPA and the KWP. It also directly operates sixty manufacturing facilities and one school. The first and second economies help pay for the various trips, limitless toys, and the varied menu of foods enjoyed by the North Korean "royal family."

The second economy emerged in North Korea in the 1970s. From 1967 on, around 30% of the national budget was allocated to munitions, causing a strain on the budget. Between 1972 and 1974, the KPA and KWP budgets and the public budget became separate. One likely motive for this was to provide a means of accumulating and allocating funds for operations against the South. Thus, the production and revenue creation carried out in the second economy were not just for supplying luxury items to the elites but also for strategic and munitions purposes.[3]

Bureau 38 and Bureau 39 of the KWP form the core of the second economy: Bureau 38 runs the trade of *matsutake* mushrooms (the most expensive wild mushrooms in the world after truffles) and marine products. Bureau 39 manages the Taesŏng Bank, the ginseng trade, and other commercial trade; it also operated a foreign exchange transactions bank in Vienna called the Kumsŏng (Goldstar) Bank, which operated from 1982 to 2004. Bureau 39 acts as the KWP moneybox, and supervises the Kwangmyŏng Trade Group, which reportedly is in charge of economic joint ventures with the South. In the KPA, there are at least two units responsible for economic activity, the No. 2 Economic Bureau and the Military Economic Bureau, under which Unit 99 and Department 44 run trading companies that aim to generate foreign currency rather than procure parts related to munitions.[4] Some KPA units have also mobilized civilians and forced them to collect a certain quota of mushrooms or clams by a set deadline. The KPA No. 2 Economic Bureau then exported these products, mainly to Japan – until the Japanese government imposed full economic sanctions in 2006.

How large are these sectors? The information on the non-public sectors is relatively scarce, even by the standards of North Korean data. One estimate places the size of the second economy at around 150–200 agricultural plants, factories, and marine product harvesting stations, which employ roughly 500,000–600,000 people. Other estimates place the size of the second economy at around 50% to 70% of the total, based on information emanating from the KWP Central Politburo Assembly in December 1993. Other estimates, such as the one by South Korea's Defense Academy, are more conservative, placing the KWP portion of the economy at 10% and the KPA portion at 13%.

Elite luxury and mass starvation

It is true that Kim Jong-Il has been living lavishly while many died of starvation in the mid-1990s. Despite his occasional obligatory statements about caring for his people, it is unlikely that visions of the impoverished masses haunt Kim Jong-Il or invade his dreams at night. But the indifference seems to be a matter of degree rather than of kind.

In any country, grandeur and squalor often sit side by side: US presidents and the constitutional monarchs of Western Europe spend inordinate amounts of money on entertainment and dining while many people live in poverty in the very same countries. After all, in 2004, US president George W. Bush's entertainment (tax-exempt) budget was around \$4 million.[5] In the same year, according to official estimates, around 13% or 37 million Americans lived under the poverty line, and roughly 12% of the population faced constant food insecurity.[6] Federal government initiatives such as the Food Stamps program distributed benefits to some 24 million people, but this accounted for only 40% of those eligible to receive the Food Stamps.

The British monarchy's expenditures have been subjected to intense scrutiny, but like Kim Jong-Il, the royals have an array of services and properties at their disposal, among them the Royal Train. The official rationale that portrays the Royal Train as a moneysaver seems curiously reminiscent of North Korean propaganda in its logical gymnastics.

> The Royal train makes efficient use of travelling time by allowing travel overnight. This not only increases the time available for public engagements ... but by serving in effect as a mobile hotel for Members of the Royal Family and their staff, the Royal Train minimizes disruption to the general public and saves security costs.
> (http://www.royal.gov.uk/output/Page5024.asp)

Kim Jong-Il's personal economy is not part of public accounts; but it is relevant to recall that the annual budget for the British royal family was not opened to parliamentary inspection until 1998. If North Korean citizens puzzlingly worship Kim Il-Sung, many citizens in the Commonwealth equally puzzlingly follow the British monarchy with seemingly unrelenting ardor, and some countries of the Commonwealth place images of the Queen on their currencies for no discernible logical reason.

There are differences, of course: republicans in the UK are free to express their opinions without fear of being banished to years of exile and hard labor in the Falkland Islands. Even if entertainment personalities who publicly opposed the US Second Gulf War against Iraq were harassed or hounded out of work in the US, at least the Dixie Chicks and Phil Donahue were not sent to reeducation camps to dig potatoes for a year. In some Commonwealth countries, there are watchdogs, such as the Canadian Taxpayers Federation established in 1989, which monitor excessive spending of taxpayer money by politicians, while no equivalent public checks exist for Kim Jong-Il. Moreover, no constitutional monarch generated direct revenues in the 1990s on the basis of $100 million in reported sales of missiles and related technologies to Iran, Pakistan, Yemen, Libya, and Syria, as did the leader of North Korea. However, it should be noted that profits of US firms from the sales of arms in the post-First Gulf War era were reportedly in the range of $1 billion per month, and that one estimate calculated that the US accounted for around 50% of arms delivered in the world market in 1999, followed by the UK at 19%.

Third and fourth economies

The public and the informal economies have undergone long-term changes. Despite the problems with North Korean statistics, theexchange rates, and category semantics, the majority of scholars agree that the North Korean economy in 1970 was at the very least the equal of South Korea in terms of per capita GDP. In fact, Khieu Samphan, president of Democratic Kampuchea, told Cambodia's monarch Prince Norodom Sihanouk in the late 1970s after a visit that the North Koreans, "have fine houses and cars, nice cities. The people are too attached to their new life. They will never want to start or even fight in a new war."[7] Although this may say more about the Khmer Rouge than North Korea, it does indicate that, on the surface at least, the North Korean economy was seemingly flourishing.

However, the North Korean economy, which had operated under three-, five-, or seven-year economic plans since 1954, began showing signs of serious economic slowdown in the 1980s. The Second

Seven-Year Plan from 1978 to 1984 supposedly generated around 12% growth rates per year, but indications of trouble surfaced when a two-year "adjustment period" was announced for 1985–6. The Third Seven-Year Plan was launched in 1987, but ended in 1993 without realizing its goals. Thus, the North Korean economy is currently a planned economy without an economic plan.

Farmers' markets have existed in North Korea since the late 1940s; there were two officially recognized ones in Pyongyang in 1950, but after the collapse of the food distribution system in 1994, the numbers of informal markets proliferated. The July 2002 economic reforms recognized many of these markets, then placed them under central supervision under a general policy of one major market for each province.[8] Some observers estimated that 60–70% of basic foods and necessities were purchased in these markets during the disruption of the food distribution system in the mid-1990s.

Causes of the Famine

Although the tallest basketball player in the world, Lee Myong-Hun (Yi Myŏng-Hun), height 235 cm (7'9"), weight 128 kg, was a North Korean, the dominant images of North Korea in the 1990s were of emaciated children, missiles, and nuclear power plant inspections.[9] According to reports released to the UN, North Korean domestic grain output before the floods declined by nearly 50% between 1984 and 1994, from 10 million tons (likely an inflated number) to 5.7 million tons. North Korea has been constantly facing a major grain shortage since at least 1994. Although the annual grain need was estimated at 6.2 million tons, actual grain production, according to estimates by the Bank of Korea and the Ministry of Unification, ranged between 3 and 4 million tons per year between 1995 and 2004.

Not surprisingly, North Korea has been dependent on aid since 1995: some 7 million out of the 22–23 million people in the country rely on food aid. The total value of aid sent to North Korea between 1995 and 2004 was $2.19 billion. Of this amount, $1.38 billion came from the UN's Consolidated Appeals Program (CAP), of which the US donated $644 million, and South Korea $393 million. An additional $290 million in direct aid from China and Russia and $905 million from South Korea have poured into North

Korea without causing much in the way of effusive expressions of gratitude. So what caused the famine of the mid-1990s?

The North Korean official explanation

The North Korean government attributed the food shortages to a series of natural disasters, and to treason by some of its officials. In 1994, 1995, 1996, and 1997, when the North Korean government acknowledged food shortages and asked for foreign assistance, the reasons cited in each year were natural disasters. There were floods in 1994 and 1995, with the 1995 flood described as the worst in a hundred years. There were further floods in 1996, then a drought in 1997, and severe wind damage to crops in 1998. It is most likely that significant damage was caused by floods prior to 1994, but the North Korean government never publicized the data.

In addition, a human culprit for the famines was identified when the government accused former Secretary of Agriculture (Minister) Sŏ Kwan-Hŭi of collaborating with the US, failing to develop higher-yield seeds, and not distributing fertilizers to the farms. Sŏ and his wife were killed by the government in a widely publicized August 1997 public execution in Pyongyang. However, it seems unlikely that the massive famines were the result of the sabotage of one or two KWP officials.

The damage from major natural disasters was clearly the immediate cause of the food shortage. However, more fundamental factors need to be addressed to understand why grain production failed to recover dramatically even after the floods and droughts ended.

Problems of planned economies

Among the more long-term factors, first, North Korea suffered from a problem common to centrally planned socialist economies: constant shortages of consumer goods, inefficient distribution, and ideologically driven policies. Even as early as 1958, the Soviet ambassador to North Korea sent reports to Moscow detailing the shortage of consumer goods in North Korea under the *Chŏllima* Movement, a mass mobilization movement generally analogous to the Soviet Stakhanovite movement or the Chinese Great Leap Forward (mass injections of human labor and spirit without much planning for efficiency). Clothes, soap, and other everyday goods were in short supply as the government emphasized heavy industries. Koreans living in Japan who "returned" to the North in 1959 to start a new life in the "paradise on earth" were shocked by the material conditions.[10] Those that complained audibly were immediately hauled off to jail.

As Kim Il-Sung confessed to the KWP in February 1973, "The chief drawback of the present materials supply system is that it makes it impossible for the state to control and guide the work of material supply in a uniform way."[11] Encouragement of partial self-sufficiency for non-staple food items began as early as the 1960s. Further indications of the shortage in consumer goods come from the recollections of Kim Hyŏn-Hŭi, the North Korean agent convicted of the bombing of KAL flight 858 in 1987: "It was a luxury [in North Korea] ... to always have cooking oil in the house and to be able to fry food. I would later learn that cooking oil was very common in the South, and that everyone could fry food."[12] There were reports of refugees crossing the border into China in search of food as early as 1979 and 1985. The official campaign "let's eat two meals per day" which began in 1991, ostensibly as a patriotic movement, can also be seen as a reflection of food shortages.

Impact of ideological economics

This is not to suggest that North Korean bureaucrats ignored economics or planning. There were systematic attempts to incorporate the latest Soviet economic theories, such as the System of Optimally Functioning Socialist Economy (SOFE), often called "economic cybernetics," which combined mathematics with the economics of central planning and state-owned enterprises.[13] The problem, however, was that economic cybernetics and the competing political economy approach, which emphasized political ideology, excluded the behaviors of producers and consumers since both were assumed to be stable in the absence of market mechanisms. Rather than actually supplying consumer needs, fulfilling policy targets and increasing outputs became the overriding goals, encouraging a relative neglect of inter-factory linkages and of the distribution of final goods.

The North Korean economy was dictated by ideology and the on-the-spot guidance of the leaders. One example is the development of Vinalon, a synthetic fabric that was supposedly cheaper than nylon, and of higher quality. Vinalon was developed by Korean and Japanese chemists in Japan in 1939, around the time nylon was also being developed. One of the three holders of the patent, Dr Lee Sŭng-Ki (Yi Sŭng-ki), took the technology with him when he defected to the North from the South in 1950. Kim Il-Sung liked it so much that he bestowed on the material the title of "Juche fibre," and granted preferential funding. When another prominent North Korean chemist noted the numerous problems with the properties and the production costs of Vinalon, he was predictably expelled from the KWP for "ideological revisionism." The economy was further burdened by the construction costs of gargantuan commemorative memorials and monuments, especially some of the monuments built in the early 1980s for Kim Il-Sung's seventieth birthday, as well as the construction and hosting costs for the 1989 World Youth Festival. According to Hwang Jang-Yop, the mausoleum for Kim Il-Sung's mummified body cost some $890 million to build during the famine.[14]

Other examples more directly linked to agriculture abound. Motivated in equal parts by the long winters, the relative shortage of arable land, and the belief that the human will could overcome material conditions (Feuerbach again), in 1981 the North Korean government launched a mass campaign called the Four Great Nature Reformation Projects. The effects of the ten-year campaign on grain output is not clear, but it did result in an estimated 80% of the country's mountains becoming denuded of trees, which in turn made the land more vulnerable to the effects of the flooding of the mid-1990s. The Juche agricultural method, outlined by Kim Il-Sung himself after on-site inspections, was the embodiment less of long-term planning than of ideology animating agricultural policy. The Juche method decreed that all grain seeds were to be planted close together, which resulted in a planting density around twice those of Japan and South Korea. The volume of yield increased so long as large amounts of fertilizer were used. However, this method also made the grain plants vincible to disease, which in turn required greater use of pesticides. Eventually, the Juche method resulted in soil exhaustion.[15]

Lack of seed variety

The second fundamental cause of the famines was the relative lack of diversity in grain seeds. South Korean agricultural experiments have determined that North Korean rice varieties are generally resistant to cold, but less resistant to disease. Several tests concluded that North Korean rice seeds generated 86% of the yields of South Korean types when grown under the same conditions due to this vulnerability to diseases.[16] In comparison, Japanese hybrid seeds engineered to withstand cold and disease transplanted well in Chinese areas north of North Korea.[17]

Another problem was that North Korean rice types have growing times that average between 160 and 180 days. This is longer than most types used in Japan, which require 140 to 150 days. The longer growing time rendered the North Korean varieties vulnerable by creating longer windows of opportunity for floods and typhoons to damage the crops, and also effectively prevented double planting.

Fertilizer and energy shortages

The third causal factor behind the famines was a severe fertilizer and fuel shortage. North Korea in fact had a very high grain tonnage yield per hectare throughout the 1970s and actually hit a peak level in 1990 that was comparable to Japan's, according to North Korean statistics. However, output per hectare dropped by 50% over the course of the 1990s. The problem was that the original increases in per hectare output had been achieved mainly through the intensive use of chemical fertilizers for rice and corn. For example, in an agricultural cooperative in Hwanghae Province, the North Korean farmers used 150 to 180 kg per hectare during the 1980s, compared to Japan's 78 kg. In the 1990s, the fertilizer used per hectare dropped to 20–60 kg, and some fertilizer factories ceased operations due to shortages of fuel for their machinery.[18] The shortage of chemical fertilizers, especially nitrogen, caused a precipitous decline in grain output.

In addition, imports of fertilizers from China and Russia decreased after 1990. The arable land in the North had low fecundity to begin with, and the long-term use of fertilizers depleted soil fertility, making soil recovery difficult despite the widespread use of nightsoil as fertilizer since the mid-1990s. Given that large fertilizer inputs have come from aid rather than improvements in production, since 1998 North Korean scientists have concentrated on improving the seeds. North Korean scientists have also been attempting to improve the fertilizer absorption rate of the seeds to produce rice that requires relatively little fertilizer for optimal harvests.

A long-term energy shortage hindered the recovery of the domestic chemical fertilizer plants. Estimates in 1945 and 1958 placed North Korean hydroelectric capacity at three times that of South Korea. However, poor casings on electric turbines created frequent power outages: since officials were rewarded for early completion of turbines then rotated to a new post, there was little accountability for long-term problems. The shortage of electricity meant that the electrically powered irrigation systems that drew the groundwater up had to be shut down. It also became difficult to power the country's rail system, since an estimated 80% of it ran on electricity or diesel.

The shortage of electricity and oil also severely affected the mining and the distribution of coal. This in turn meant that the engineers of the coal-fueled steam locomotives (leftovers from the Japanese colonial period) used for the transport of coal from the mines faced a dilemma, since if the coal was used to operate the trains, this meant less coal to distribute. This resulted in less coal available for coal-fueled power plants, which in turn led to decreases in energy output.

In order to address this constant energy shortage, North Korea undertook several initiatives. In 1996 and 1997 the government began building a large hydroelectric plant and several smaller hydroelectric generators. The smaller hydroelectric generators were susceptible to damage from flooding, which meant that many of these were shut down any time there were floods. The situation was desperate enough that North Korea invited a team from the Nautilus Institute (a think tank in California) to install windmills or wind turbines in 1998–99.

North Korea also increased imports of used tires from Japan to burn as ersatz coal (at least 70% of all Japanese exports of non-recycled, used rubber went to North Korea during 2002–03). Starting around 2002, North Korea also began to import used bicycles from Japan to promote the use of non-fuel-burning transportation (although, technically, children under 12 and women could not ride them under a 1999 law). A Swedish firm reportedly helped upgrade the electrical grid for Pyongyang in 2003, but the small hydroelectric generators have remained prone to flooding, and none of the other measures have been able to resolve the basic problem – the absence of a stable power grid for the entire country.

Decline in imports and socialist aid

The famine was greatly exacerbated by a fourth factor, the pronounced drop in imports and aid from Russia and China after 1990. Despite the ideological rhetoric of economic self-sufficiency under Juche, the North Korean economy had been dependent on aid from China and the Soviet Union from its very inception. Even someone relatively close to North Korea, the Albanian socialist ruler Enver Hoxha, could not refrain from observing with irony the glaring disconnect between North Korean propaganda and the reality in which the country could not "live without foreign aid."[19]

Russian oil shipments at "friendly prices" ceased in 1988, and the volume dropped from around 1 million tons in 1986 to 80,000 tons in 1993, while fertilizer imports also dropped from around 20,000 tons to 7,000 tons. During the worst of the famines from 1994 to 1996, Russia exported minimal oil, ranging from 0 in 1994 to 20,000 tons in 1996. Russia sent emergency shipments of fertilizers in 1994 and 1995, but from 1996 on sent only token amounts.[20]

Chinese export prices for grains to North Korea increased to all-time highs in 1995–97 and only returned to 1994 levels in 1998. This was in consequence of increases in the price of grain on the Chicago market, and correlated increases in Chinese prices. As a result, North Korean imports of grains from China dipped from 900,000 tons in 1993 to 81,000 tons in 1995. The tonnage bounced back to 919,000 by 1997, but most of these grain imports were in corn – China basically sent 1.1 to 1.9 tons of corn for 1 ton of North Korean rice between 1985 and 1994. This was consistent with North Korea's basic grain trade policy since the mid-1960s of exporting rice at higher prices, and importing larger volumes of cheaper grains, such as corn and wheat.

Food imports from OECD member states also dropped during the famine years. From 1986 to 1992, the OECD generally exported around 200,000 tons of grains to North Korea, mainly in the form of wheat. In 1993, imports of wheat dipped to 100,000 tons, and in 1994 wheat imports stopped altogether.[21] The amount rebounded to a total of 100,000 tons of wheat over the three-year period 1995–97; all of it was in the form of aid after the North Korean government publicized the food shortages. One of the reasons for the absence of imports between 1995 and 1997 was that the international price of wheat and corn reached extremely high levels, making it difficult for North Korea, with its minimal reserves of foreign exchange, to purchase additional grain.

Even then, the fact that North Korea actually exported small amounts of rice to Russia from 1994 to 1998 without receiving any grains at all in exchange is puzzling in light of the severity of the famine. The tonnage was small, from 2,700 tons in 1994 and averaging around 500 tons from 1995 to 1998, and it is not clear whether or not these were payments for previous loans. In 1994 and 1995, North Korean rice was sold to Russia at low prices per ton, hinting at unpolished or unprocessed rice. Foreign aid rice was all polished, so this was likely stock from previous years. After 1997, however, North Korea sold the rice to Russia at higher prices, so there is some possibility that this was polished rice from foreign aid that was sold to earn foreign currency rather than feed the population.

Deliberate triage or indifferent food distribution?

The effects of entitlement or differential distribution of food based on rank and region, and Military-First Politics resulting in preferential allocation of resources to the KPA during the famine have engendered a range of interpretations despite the paucity of accurate information. At one extreme, there are accusations that Kim Jong-Il deliberately cut off food distribution to the mountainous northeastern provinces of North and South Hamgyŏng, where most of the political prisoners' camps and the "hostile" classes were located, and that he and his cronies were guilty of "crimes against humanity" or deliberate "triage."[22] According to one researcher, only 18% of World Food Programme (WFP) aid was shipped to ports on the east coast in 1997–98, despite the fact that this region had 33% of the pre-famine population.[23]

Estimates for the total number of deaths from the famine for 1994–98 have ranged from 200,000, as claimed by the North

Korean government, to 3 million, the figure repeated by some NGOs. However, defector accounts indicate that inefficient distribution and ineffectual policy responses, rather than a deliberate policy of starving whole regions, compounded the problem.[24] The Public Distribution System (PDS) was discriminatory, and, despite monitoring efforts by the WFP, it was difficult to assure that those in most need received the food aid.[25] The resultant violation of food rights should be addressed thoroughly. Moreover, defectors who have been in gulags attest that the prisoners received minimal food, which is a violation of human rights.

However, brandishing terms such as "crimes against humanity" does little to help resolve or understand the problem, since the line between sustained human rights abuses and "crimes against humanity" (deliberate triage) will have to be defined more clearly for charges to stick. The difficulties of raisings charge of "crimes against humanity" against Saudi Arabia for its long record of systematic discrimination against women, foreign expatriates, and homosexuals; its public executions involving stoning and beheading; and its torture of prisoners, indicate that the situation in North Korea might more usefully be examined as human rights violations rather than as crimes against humanity.[26]

Furthermore, the view that the North Korean government deliberately starved its citizens ignores the various attempts at agricultural reform — even if these reforms appear feckless in retrospect. The government, for example, introduced incentive measures for the whole country in 1996, allowing families to keep surplus harvests above the quota. North Korea also started cooperative projects in 1998 with the UN's International Fund for Agricultural Development (IFAD) to reform its agriculture.[27] While these initiatives could be seen as propagandistic exercises, it makes little sense to start these programs if the policy aim was to commit regional genocide.

Entitlement theory

A more plausible argument has been the application of Amartya Sen's "entitlement theory." People will starve to death, Sen argued, when their entitlement or income is insufficient to buy the food necessary to keep them alive.[28] Analysis of past famines in other socialist countries concluded that there had been a rural–urban divide in distribution of scarce food resources, which amplified the effects of the decline in food supply.[29]

In the North Korean case, it should first be noted that the KWP-run food distribution system, the Public Distribution System (PDS), had always covered only around 70% of the total population, and clearly differentiated between the ranks in terms of frequency, volume, quality, and variety of food distribution.[30] Moreover, even during the famine, food continued to be distributed to key factories, and top party officials in hard-hit regions, according to defector accounts. But the PDS was disrupted in the cities, including Pyongyang, and rumours of cannibalism spread throughout the country. During the peak of the famine from 1994 to 1998, the PDS broke down most dramatically in the rural areas in the northeast, leading to KWP and KPA elites confiscating food from the citizenry and the rank-and-file soldiers. Accounts also differ over whether cities or rural areas were more affected by the famines. Some NGOs observed that urban residents in the northeast had less access to grains and cereals than those in the rural areas due to ineligibility for food aid. Although some 60% of the total North Korean population lived in cities by the mid-1990s, regional variations in famine conditions seem to have been more significant than a rural–urban divide.

Preferential distribution of food to the KPA

Another criticism is that the Military-First policy intensified the effects of the famine. Food was distributed preferentially to the KPA, and according to this view, foreign currency earned from exports were used to purchase weapons and munitions and to feed the KPA instead of the needy.[31]

It is true that the KPA received large portions of the annual budget. Military expenditures initially spiked after the Park Chung-Hee coup in South Korea in 1961, and continued through the 1970s and the 1980s to take up around 10% of the annual GNP. Kim Il-Sung confessed to Eric Hoenecker during the East German prime minister's visit to North Korea in 1977 that maintaining military preparedness in the face of regular US and South Korean military exercises was a strain on the economy.[32] Military expenditures increased to 15–20% of North Korea's GNP after the introduction of Military-First Politics in 1998. In comparison, South Korea spent around 3% of its much larger GNP on its military during the late 1990s. The difference was that Seoul spent $38 billion more on the military between 1972 and 1990 than Pyongyang. In 1991, the South spent $7.8 billion compared to the North's $2 billion in military expenditures; by 2001, this gap had grown to $10 billion to $1.3 billion.[33]

However, a clear distinction should be made between the KPA generals, other officers, and the rank and file. The KPA is estimated to be around 1.1 million strong (army 950,000, navy 46,000, air force 86,000) with 4.7 million reserves. The generals appear to have been generally protected from the effects of the famine, but the majority of the rank and file were clearly affected by it. In the mid-1990s, emaciated soldiers and lower-ranking officers defected in increasing numbers. They provided numerous first-hand accounts of officers taking food away from lower-ranking soldiers. If a KPA internal notice printed in August 2003 warning soldiers against stealing food from farmers is any indication, the problems with the PDS distribution to the KPA continued even after the worst of the famines were over. More quantitative evidence of malnutrition was reflected in changes in the minimum standards for military service. The minimum height for military service had been 150 cm, but it was lowered to 148 cm in 1994, and the service age was also lowered from 21 to 16.[34] This was despite the fact that, starting in 1987, ordinary citizens had 10% of their rice rations withheld for use by the KPA under the glorious rubric of "Patriotic Rice."

The impact of the miliary system on agricultural output manifested itself more in its creation of labor shortages on the farms. Many men, after their three years of compulsory military service, were not sent back to their homes but to areas of labor shortage. Industrial facilities also required labor, which was drawn from the rural areas.[35] As a result, there was a vast shortage of farm labor in the rural areas.

Due to the aforementioned four-tier segmentation of the economy, the KPA continued to harvest and export mushrooms and seafood to Japan in exchange for other imports, and to export missiles to Syria and Iran for foreign currency. The funds from the first and second economies explain how North Korea managed to finance missile tests or experiment with weapons improvements even during the famine. The problem was less to do with entitlement preferences to the KPA, but more related to the segmented structure of the entire economy, and the process of agricultural decline that I explained above in the section on the causes of the famines.

The reality is that decades of far greater South Korean investment in equipment and weapons, combined with North Korean shortages in food and fuel, have eroded the threat posed by conventional North Korean ground forces. One incident that illustrated the weapons gap was the June 15, 1999 naval clash on the West Coast, in which an estimated eighty North Koreans were killed in a clash that lasted for all of twenty minutes. The South Korean navy only suffered a few men lightly wounded. Another was a June 2002 clash that resulted in the deaths of four South Korean sailors and an estimated thirty North Koreans.

Threat?

If North Korean conventional forces are becoming less of a threat, does North Korea still pose a threat, and if so, to whom? The apparent answer has been trumpeted in the mass media with monomaniacal repetitiveness – nuclear weapons. The fervor with which North Korea is portrayed as an imminent nuclear threat in some of the Western media has ironical resonances with the endless North Korean propaganda against the US. A respectable stream of articles that urge caution and rationality invariably follows the hysterical coverage.

Threat perception

Looking at the grand parade of past *bêtes noires* of the US – Joseph Stalin, Nikita Khrushchev, Fidel Castro, Moammar Qaddafi, Manuel Noriega – brings back memories of similar spikes in media coverage. In the 1970s, Qaddafi was constantly portrayed as a raving madman who posed a danger to most of humanity, but more recently Libya has been lauded for mending its ways – despite official acknowledgement in 2003 of state involvement in past terrorist acts.[36]

The problem is less whether North Korea has nuclear weapons or not, but more one of threat perception.[37] Why is it that some countries are deemed "qualified" to have nuclear weapons and others are not? Unlike North Korea, which was a signatory (at least in form) to the Nuclear Non-Proliferation Treaty (NPT) from 1985 to 2003, neither Pakistan nor India have ever been signatories to the NPT, and many of their nuclear reactors have not been subject to IAEA inspections. Pakistan has a longer history of nuclear weapons testing than North Korea (although its last test was in 1998), and a verified history of exporting nuclear weapons technology. US sanctions against Pakistan dissipated, however, after Pakistan became a strategically important "frontline" state in the "war on terrorism."

In North Korea's case, nuclear weapons first emerged as an issue in the 1980s. After starting nuclear research in the mid-1960s with initial Soviet assistance, North Korea had joined the International Atomic Energy Agency (IAEA) in 1977, and signed the NPT in December 1985. However, it refused to agree to inspections under safeguard agreements with the IAEA, which was a requirement of the NPT. In a turnabout, in December 1991 North and South Korea signed the Agreement on Reconciliation, Non-aggression, Exchanges and Cooperation and the Joint Declaration on the Denuclearization of the Korean Peninsula, in which both sides pledged not to test, manufacture, or deploy nuclear weapons. North Korea finally agreed to safeguard agreements with the IAEA in January 1992, seemingly signaling the end to tensions.

When Pyongyang refused to allow IAEA inspections of two facilities in January 1993, the media began covering North Korea as a potential nuclear threat. In March of the same year, North Korea claimed that it would leave the NPT, but it changed its mind in June 1993 after negotiations with the US. In June 1994, North Korea announced the country would exit from the IAEA, but after Jimmy Carter's visit with Kim Il-Sung in the same month, the US and North Korea concluded the Agreed Framework in October 1994.

Collapse of the Agreed Framework and the Berlin Agreement

Under the Agreed Framework, North Korea pledged to freeze its existing nuclear reactors in exchange for shipments of heavy oil totaling 500,000 tonnes per year and two operational light-water reactors (LWRs), which would produce less plutonium, to be completed by 2003. Once the LWRs were operational, the North would dismantle its reactors. The two sides also promised to work towards normalization of relations, and not to attack each other. North Korea froze its reactors but balked at receiving South Korean-designed LWRs. This issue was resolved under the 1995 Kuala Lumpur agreement, in which North Korea agreed to follow the decisions of the Korean Peninsula Energy Development Organization (KEDO), a multilateral consortium established in 1995 to facilitate the delivery of the LWRs primarily financed by South Korea (70%) and Japan (20%).

Despite a groundbreaking ceremony at the site of the first LWR in 1997, KEDO eventually lost steam, ultimately terminating the LWR project in May 2006. On its official website, KEDO states that the official decision to terminate the project was undertaken due to the "continued and extended failure of the DPRK [Democratic People's Republic of Korea] to perform steps that were required in the KEDO–DPRK Supply Agreement for the provision of the LWR project."[38] However, criticisms that North Korea failed to dismantle its nuclear reactors overlook the fact that the Agreed Framework stipulated dismantlement only after the completion of both LWRs, not upon an agreement to start building one. Moreover, inconsistent political and financial support from Japan, the US, and South Korea played a major role in undermining the project. The Republican Party-controlled US Congress constrained implementation of other components of the 1994 Agreed Framework as well, such as the lifting of economic sanctions.

The US and North Korea reached another set of agreements in September 1999, when US envoy Charles Kartman and North Korean Vice Foreign Minister Kim Gye-Gwan (Kim Kye-Kwan) hammered out an agreement in Berlin. In it North Korea agreed to refrain from future tests of long-range missiles in return for the partial lifting of economic embargoes. This agreement disintegrated amidst another round of reinterpretations, accusations, and counteraccusations. The 1999 Perry Report, commissioned by US president Bill Clinton, concluded in essence that the 1994 Agreed Framework, as unpopular as it might be, was the best basis for negotiations over the cessation of future missile tests. The historic June 2000 summit meeting between Kim Dae-Jung and Kim Jong-Il spurred Clinton to act to improve relations with North Korea – but with insufficient time. Although Madeleine Albright visited North Korea, Clinton chose to visit the Middle East rather than North Korea in the last months of his term.[39]

In October 2002, after the first substantive meetings between a US delegation led by Assistant Secretary of State James Kelly and Vice Foreign Minister Kang Sok-Ju (Kang Sŏk-Chu) of North Korea, the US claimed that North Korea had "confessed" to having a highly enriched uranium program (HEU). While North Korea denied this claim, this "confession" (in fact, several observers who speak Korean language, and the State Department translator who was present, have stated that translation difficulties were involved) served as the primary basis for a November 2002 unilateral US decision to abrogate the Agreed Framework when it ceased shipments of heavy oil to North Korea. In January 2003, North Korea announced its withdrawal from the NPT.

There were also reports that Dr A. Q. Khan of Pakistan, the controversial figure behind Pakistan's HEU program, received $75 million from North Korea in 2002, and that North Korea purchased centrifugal machines needed for HEU from Pakistan. News accounts that North Korea had exported nuclear weapons technology to Libya in 2005 remained unverified but also fueled calls within the US for more sanctions against the North. However, in March 2007, US officials sent out mixed signals regarding their confidence in the intelligence about North Korea's HEU program.

The problem lay in the distinction between weapons-grade uranium (a violation of the 1994 Agreed Framework), and lower-levels of enrichment (technically banned by the 1994 accord, but permitted for energy purposes under the NPT). Further complicating the issue was the 2004 South Korean confession that their scientists had successfully processed small amounts of near-weapons-grade uranium in 2000.

The fundamental cause of the breakdown of the agreements of 1991, 1994, and 1999 appeared to be that in each case all three countries – the US, North Korea, and South Korea – surreptitiously attempted to stretch the boundaries of the agreement, and were essentially unwilling or unable to comply with the terms because of domestic political conditions and fixed foreign policy agendas. It should be noted that the 1991, 1994, and 1999 agreements were all non-binding.

Nuclear red herring

Since the 1990s, North Korea has had the technology to produce weapons-grade plutonium, as well as to trigger tests.[40] Thus, the test of a small plutonium weapon in October 2006 should not have come as a major surprise, since it did not change the fundamental dynamics. The whole issue of North Korea's nuclear weapons program, plutonium or uranium, is a bit of a red herring so long as the US, Japan, and/or South Korea remain committed to a retaliatory attack after any North Korean first strike. If the US makes it clear that any attacks on South Korea or Japan would trigger a retaliatory strike, the North Korean leadership would risk being killed, and also losing access to its main sources of energy and capital.

Thus, Kim Jong-Il or the KPA need missiles and nuclear weapons for domestic political positioning, but in international relations these are essentially the only negotiating cards it possesses. Actually to use them would be to deal out of this game of high-stakes poker. Moreover, although Kim Jong-Il's personal bank account in Switzerland may be safe, these funds are unlikely to be allocated to the public economy; thus, there are no domestic sources of capital that can help resurrect the economy and help Kim Jong-Il maintain power. Having nuclear weapons or being perceived as having them has in essence allowed North Korea to demand more investments and aid from South Korea, the US, and Japan in exchange for freezing its nuclear weapons programs.

In Kim Jong-Il's mind, weapons also served as deterrents to pre-emptive strikes by the US. In 1989, Kim told his Japanese sushi chef, "If we don't have nuclear weapons, other countries will attack us."[41] In August 2000 Kim reportedly acknowledged to South Korean visitors that the missiles did not pose a direct threat to the US, but having them allowed him to negotiate with Washington.[42] For the North Korean government, regime survival has far outweighed other objectives, including conventional definitions of national security: thus, attacking their potential sources of funds and energy or risking retaliation seems counter-productive. At the very least, the nuclear and the missile cards have been somewhat effective in bringing the US to the negotiating table through the 1990s and the 2000s.

Human rights

In fact, North Korea poses a bigger threat to its own citizens in terms of its restrictions on freedom of speech and its mistreatment of prisoners. While the US in the mid-2000s also has problems with manipulations of information, with its judiciary system, and with mistreatment of prisoners, at least in the US there are more avenues for expression and debate than in North Korea. Several prison camps have been identified through independent, collaborating testimony by defectors who were confined to the same camps at different times; most of the camps appear to be located in the northeast border areas far from prying eyes. The amount of food distributed to the prisoners tends to be minimal, and the physical labor assigned to them arduous. The UN Committee on Human Rights has been pressuring North Korea to improve its human rights situation since 2000.[43]

Unfortunately, the protection of human rights of North Korean citizens have also been used to advance the cause of coerced regime change by neoconservatives in the US, South Korea, and Japan. We thus end up with the irony of some organizations in Japan using human rights abuses in North Korea as the basis for attacks against North Korea-affiliated Korean residents of Japan (*Zainichi Chōsenjin Sōrengōkai* – hereafter, Sōren), or conservatives in South Korea using human rights to push for regime change in North Korea. It is important to clarify that North Korean prison camps have harsh conditions, and that the human rights standards in North Korea generally do not meet OECD standards. However, most of the information comes from defectors who left North Korea after being released from their stints in prison.[44] In other words, although there have been public executions (several videotaped by NGOs), and prisoners' rights to food and shelter seem neglected or violated, these gulags were not necessarily designed to exterminate prisoners.

Further complicating matters is the proliferation of fabricated or exaggerated allegations by some North Korean defectors. For example, a group of defectors testified before the British Parliament in spring 2004 that North Korea conducted chemical and biological weapons experiments on political prisoners. They brought with them a pamphlet allegedly documenting orders to conduct such tests. However, a scholar highly critical of North

Korea's human rights record looked at the pamphlet and concluded on the basis of the quality of the paper, print, stamps, and characters, that this was a fake produced in China.[45]

The plight of the North Korean "food refugees," who flee North Korea as a result of continuing food shortages, is another area of genuine concern. An estimated 200,000 North Korean refugees live in China: of these, some 90% live in the Yŏnbyŏn (in Chinese, Yanbian) region that borders northwestern North Korea. Ethnic Koreans form some 40% of Yŏnbyŏn's total population, which helps explain why the refugees are concentrated in this area. NGOs and ethnic Korean brokers help some of these North Koreans reach South Korea (the brokers usually ask for most of any money the defector receives from the South Korean government on arrival). South Korean activists, along with Japanese and North American NGOs, also attempt to help the refugees move from China to any other country, as China's policy has been to repatriate the refugees back to North Korea, claiming they are illegal migrants. Moreover, many of the female refugees become victims of human trafficking, "sold" as picture brides in China or South Korea.[46] Some North Korean women end up working in bars and clubs that cater to South Korean businessmen visiting Yŏnbyŏn.[47]

If we return to the original question, is North Korea a threat, the answer would be yes, but first and foremost against its own citizens. North Korea's nuclear weapons program seems to be a combination of sincere and misguided belief and shrewd negotiating tactic, but is little immediate threat. The priority should be placed on looking for ways to improve human rights conditions rather than assuming that regime change is a necessary condition for reforming this area, especially given that there is little indication of an imminent regime collapse from internal pressures.

Reforms

Although it would be a mistake naïvely to assume that Kim Jong-Il is simply a victim of American imperialism, some recent changes indicate the possibility of gradual, albeit limited, reform through negotiation. The fact that North Korea has signed up to some international conventions and initiated several largely unsuccessful economic reforms does not mean that the country is ready to abandon its political system, but it does indicate that Kim Jong-Il is willing to make changes to ensure long-term regime survival.

International conventions

The North Korean government has promised that it will improve human rights conditions. In 2003, it enacted a Handicapped Persons Protection Law, and in 2004 it amended its Constitution and Criminal Procedure Law to ensure strict adherence to law in terms of arrest procedures, interrogations, and detentions. The problem is that for criminal cases, these procedures have been followed, but for cases of political crime, these legal provisions have usually been ignored. North Korea is a signatory to the UN Convention on the Elimination of All Forms of Discrimination against Women, but not to the UN Convention against Torture and other Cruel, Inhuman or Degrading Treatment or Punishment.

Economic reforms

North Korean attempts at economic reforms since 1989 have been gradual and sustained, if similarly ambiguous in their results. A joint Investment Law had been promulgated in 1984, some seven years after Vietnam and five years after China had adopted similar measures, but this has resulted in little inflow of foreign funds other than Sōren investments into textile production facilities. After the dissolution of the Soviet Union, the North Korean government was forced to consider more serious methods to diversify its trade relations and solicit investment. In 1992, a new Foreign Investment Law was enacted which lowered taxes and allowed for joint ventures as well as joint investments.

New economic zones and projects were also initiated, although the results were mixed at best. The Tumen River dam project, begun with China, Russia, and the UNDP in 1990, began with high hopes but has now utterly stagnated. The Rajin–Sŏnbong Free Economic and Trade Zone in the northeast was started in 1991. The Rajin project resulted in the opening of several hotels, including a large casino–hotel complex called the Emperor Hotel constructed by a Hong Kong group. However, because of incidents involving at least two high Chinese officials who lost large sums of public funds there gambling, the casino was closed in 2004. In 2002, North Korea announced the establishment of the Sinŭiju special economic zone, but this initiative also collapsed, this time over the Chinese government's opposition to the appointment of Yang Bin, a Chinese businessman with Dutch citizenship, to the position of governor of the zone.

Trade diversification has been another strategy. For example, in 2004, North Korea's trade with Thailand overtook its trade with Japan. In 2005, North Korea imported $207 million worth of goods from Thailand, while exports to Thailand totaled $121 million.

Attempts to develop computer-related industries have also emerged. Communications infrastructure had been slowly expanding since the mid-1980s. The number of international telephone lines doubled between 1984 and 1994, and in 1990, Pyongyang established the Chosŏn Computer Center with donations from Sōren. Silver Star 2006, a Go or Paduk computer game software that won a world tournament for game software in 1998, began commercial sales distribution in South Korea in fall 2006.[48] A fiber optic line was connected between Seoul, Pyongyang, Sinŭiju, Dandong, and Beijing, although it is not connected to the Internet. Some Internet cafés have sprung up in Pyongyang, although the ones for the use of North Koreans are connected only to an Intranet, with firewalls put up so that users can only use North Korean websites. The ones for use by foreigners cost $10 per hour, and in 2002 one journalist reported that he read articles on the kidnappings of Japanese nationals by North Korea in the 1970s and 1980s and sent e-mails without any difficulty.[49]

Efforts to address the constant food shortages have concentrated on piecemeal reforms that sometimes verge on the surreal. These included raising 200 ostriches as stock for meat and for eggs, and importing giant rabbits from a German farmer. The North has also invited agricultural specialists, including Professor Kim Sun-Kwŏn, a South Korean corn specialist at Kyŏngbuk University who developed "super corn," and Dr Higa Teruo of Ryukyu University in Okinawa, Japan, who has patented effective microorganisms (EM) technology that uses combinations of microorganisms to foster long-term soil sustainability, to help revive the agricultural sector. None of these experiments have yet provided a solution to the North Korean economy's doldrums.

The most significant reforms were the so-called July 2002 reforms. These consisted of: microeconomic policy changes to increase incentives; macroeconomic policy measures to decentralize decision-making; the establishment of special economic zones; and an aid-seeking strategy.[50] As a result, wages increased, along with commodity prices. The full effects of these reforms are difficult to gauge, especially with some of the ambivalent signals emanating from Pyongyang. However, as has been the case with former Southeast Asian command economies such as Vietnam and Laos, significant economic reform is unlikely to trigger parallel sprouts of political reform, especially as the July 2002 reforms were not intended to dismantle the existing economic system but to revitalize and resuscitate the current regime.

Economic futures

Kim Jong-Il may appear to be the last of the socialist/nationalist dictators howling against the ineluctable darkness of capitalist/ imperialist world domination, but all indications are that he is aware that the North Korean economy must be revived, one way or another. The pace and scope of the measures to resuscitate the economy are still being contested.

There are several possible future scenarios for the North Korean economy: maintaining the present path of limited reforms; systematic reform, which would eventually result in absorption by the South; heading towards economic collapse; or collapse from an endogenous shock such as a coup or foreign intervention. The first option, of piecemeal reforms and maintaining a limited hybrid economy, seems to be the choice that Pyongyang has made, especially in light of the fact that there have been no sustained efforts to dismantle the four-tiered structure of the economy.

Conclusion

Undoubtedly North Korea's own behavior, such as the unannounced test launches of missiles into the Pacific in August 1998 and July 2006, or promises made during negotiations then reneged on within days, have provided fuel for strident reactions overseas, particularly among neoconservatives in Japan, South Korea, and the US. Media images of Kim Jong-Il as a ruthless mad-man who deliberately starves his own citizens and brandishes nuclear weapons proliferate. On the basis of these images, Kim Jong-Il seems to give credence to Albert Camus's assertion that "every intelligent man ... dreams of being a gangster and of ruling over society by force alone."[51]

However, the North Korean system has to some extent always recognized the importance of material resources in controlling the state. The four discrete tiers of the economic system explain how a country can contain both starving masses and a missiles program. At the same, this economic system and the indifference of Kim Jong-Il and his high officials to the sufferings of the regular people fostered long-term problems that in turn exacerbated the effects of the famine. Human rights violations make the North Korean government a bigger threat to its own people than to foreign countries. However, indifference, incompetence, and ruthlessness should not be mistaken for madness or a suicidal death wish. The overriding desire to ensure long-term regime survival has led to limited attempts at reform; and it is this very desire that might be used to negotiate for improvements in human rights.

5 | Decussation Effects?
North–South Relations since 1989

As we have seen, the two Koreas are in many ways more polarized than ever. South Korea has become a sustainable democracy, while North Korea has an apparently sustainable political dynasty. Social and economic change in the South contrasts starkly with the relative stagnancy of the North. As of 2006, the South–North difference in per capita gross national income (GNI) was roughly 15 to 1, and North Korea still has 27% of its working population in primary industries compared to just 4% for South Korea.

Nonetheless, there have been several indications of improving inter-Korean relations in the 2000s. According to a fall 2004 survey of Seoul residents, 67% of those in their twenties had positive feelings towards North Korea, as opposed to 45% for those in their fifties. In contrast, the popularity of the US appeared to be falling – another poll indicated that among those in their twenties, 76% disliked the US, while only 26% in their fifties disliked the US.[1] Although more an Internet ripple than a *bona fide* hit in the music charts, the South Korean underground song "Fucking USA" asks, "Threatening war against North Korea, Cold War meddling in South Korea, country of hoodlums, Fucking USA; Is America the beautiful and is North Korea the enemy we must kill?"

This chapter explores how this apparent contradiction of increased income and democratization in South Korea engendered an apparent decline in relations with the US and an improvement in relations with North Korea. Rather than a linear causal linkage, what we apparently see is what I would call a "decussation effect," where the apparent opposite of the expected result emerges from a correlation. The term "decussation" comes from anatomy, and refers to an X-shaped crossing, especially of nerves or bands of nerve fibers, connecting corresponding parts on opposite sides of the brain or spinal cord. We shall first look at the alleged rise of "anti-American" sentiment in South Korea, and then at the apparent improvements in inter-Korean relations. Third, we will turn to the experiences of the North Korean defectors in South Korea to highlight the fact that, ultimately, the bipolar order still remain.

"Anti-Americanism"

Why have I placed quotations marks around "anti-Americanism"? Although some media outlets depict "anti-Americanism" in South Korea as a rampant rage that billows and spreads throughout society, and although perhaps some demonstrators actually despise everything about the US, the label itself is misleading. For the most part, demonstrators have been protesting specific incidents, policies, individuals, statements, and places. If objecting to the war in Iraq is "anti-American," presumably, the US itself is riddled with "anti-American sentiments." Seen in this light, the fact that participants in the large "anti-American" demonstrations during the winter of 2002–03 wore for the most part Western styles of clothing and running shoes emblazoned with American corporate logos is not really a contradiction. Considering that the vast majority of South Koreans have come into indelible contact with innumerable American cultural commodities and influences, study in the US, and immigrate there, it seems unlikely that there are many people who advocate the total obliteration of all American influences on South Korea.

The apparently sudden surge of "anti-American" sentiment is based in part on the long-term presence of US soldiers and bases in South Korea. The immediate cause of the demonstrations in 2002–03 was the deaths of two middle-school girls who were killed when hit by a US armored vehicle in June 2002. The deaths sparked massive demonstrations, which became even larger in November 2002 when in two separate trials a US military court found both soldiers in the armored vehicle not guilty of negligent homicide. The South Korean government asked that the soldiers be tried in Korean courts, but the US refused, invoking the US–Korea Status of Forces Agreement (SOFA) that provides for the US to exercise jurisdiction over most types of criminal cases involving US military personnel in South Korea. While this incident involved US soldiers on duty, there is a much longer history of violent crimes involving off-duty US soldiers, with some cases in the 1960s of US soldiers serving time in South Korean prisons for rape.[2] Although there was a storm of media coverage around the tragic deaths of the two girls in 2002, the rape and murder of camptown prostitutes by US soldiers also received media coverage throughout the 1990s.[3]

The legacies of Kwangju

Incidents such as the short-track ice-skating competition in the Salt Lake City Winter Olympics in 2002, when the American Apolo Ohno received the gold medal after the South Korean Kim Tong-Sŏng was judged to have fouled him, garnered massive media attention at the time, but these ultimately ephemeral reactions were less important than longer-term historical resonances, such as the legacies of the Kwangju Massacre, and structural changes including demographic shifts. The residues of resentment and distrust over what exactly US officials knew or did (or did not) do during the Kwangju Massacre of 1980 propelled the rise of radical student movements in the 1980s, resulting in several dramatic incidents. In 1982, the American Cultural Center in Pusan was bombed by a group of Catholic student activists, and in 1985, the American Cultural Center in Seoul was occupied May 23–26 by members of the National Student Association who demanded an apology from the US government for allowing Chun Doo-Hwan to move troops into Kwangju in 1980. As explained in Chapter 1, more mainstream NGOs have displaced radical student organizations since 1987, but the suspicions stemming from the Kwangju Massacre remained into the twenty-first century.

The generational gap

Structural changes and generational shifts in the South also enabled criticisms of specific US policies. Democratization, the end of the Cold War in the post-1987 period, and generational gaps provided for greater freedom of expression and broadened the political spectrum. For example, a 2004 survey indicated that 64% of those in their twenties and thirties opposed the despatch of South Korean troops to Iraq, while only 38% of those in their fifties and sixties felt the same. In the same survey, 30% of the 20–30 cohort responded that US was South Korea's closest ally, while 53% of the 50–60 generation espoused the same sentiment.[4] Another indication of the generational change among politicians is that the leader of the 1985 occupation of the American Cultural Center, Kim Min-Sŏk, was elected to the National Assembly in 1996, and was returned for a second term in 2000.

Anti-Bush or Anti-US?

However, these changes and the advent of Kim Dae-Jung's Sunshine Policy, the policy of separating political and economic issues and working towards gradual unification, did not by themselves trigger "anti-American" sentiments. For example, the combination of the Sunshine Policy with the 1999 disclosure of the No Gun Ri (Nogŭn-ri) massacre of South Korean civilians during the Korean War by a US battalion did not result in an outburst of hatred against the US.[5]

Opposition to George W. Bush's foreign policies, especially towards North Korea, seems to have been the primary fuel that combined with other factors to diffuse discontentment toward US foreign policy in South Korea. With some afterglow from the 2000 summit meeting between Kim Dae-Jung and Kim Jong-Il still palpable, around 65% of those polled for one South Korean survey deemed the label "Axis of Evil" as applied to North Korea "inappropriate."

Given the combination of opposition to US foreign policy, the cumulative tensions from the Kwangju Massacre, crimes involving US soldiers, the structural shift towards a more open and diverse political culture, and improvements in relations with the North, we can foresee that continued criticisms of US policies will emanate from South Korea. These, however, should be parsed for the specific substance of the protests, internal contradictions, and other substantive points, rather than simply stuffed under the rubric of "anti-Americanism."

Inter-Korean Relations

Much like the development of democracy in South Korea, improvements in inter-Korean relations were the result of previous cycles of rapprochement and conflict. The chronology of inter-

Korean relations can be divided into five periods, 1953–72; 1972–84; 1984–88; 1988–98; and 1998 to the present.

First period

The first period from 1953 to 1972 was marked by increased tensions after Park Chung-Hee's coup in 1961. There was some diplomatic dialogue, but incidents such as the North's assassination attempt on Park Chung-Hee at the Blue House and the North–US standoff over the capture of the US ship *Pueblo* in 1968 led to increased tensions.[6] In fact, a special South Korean unit was established to infiltrate North Korea and assassinate Kim Il-Sung, but the mission was aborted after a shift in policy in 1972.[7]

Second period

The second period, 1972–1984, started on a promising note. Richard Nixon's visit to China in February 1972 set the stage for surface improvements in inter-Korean relations. North Korea revised its constitution to formally recognize Pyongyang as its capital – its previous constitution had named Seoul as its official capital. On July 4, 1972, North and South released the Joint Declaration, which stated that unification would be peaceful, transcend ideological differences, and be conducted without foreign interference. The very first meeting of the respective Red Cross organizations followed in August 1972. There were obvious parallels to German moves toward reconciliation in 1971–72 under West German chancellor Willy Brandt's *Ostpolitik* (Eastern Policy), and the East–West Basis of Relations Treaty of 1972; however, Park Chung-Hee's *Nordpolitik* (Northern Policy) and the July Joint Declaration did not result in sustained improvements in relations.

Relations took a downturn starting in 1974. The assassination attempt on Park Chung-Hee in that year triggered a period of intense internal clampdowns and human rights violations. The brutal killings of two US soldiers in 1976, the so-called Axe Murders (see page 17) also symbolized the extent to which hatred still permeated relations. The October 1983 assassination attempt on Chun Doo-Hwan in Rangoon resulted in the deaths of 17 South Korean and 3 Burmese officials.[8] During the early 1980s, North

Korea also began digging several tunnels in preparation for either future attacks or infiltration: some of these tunnels are now part of the tour of the DMZ.

Third period

The third period, from 1984 to 1988, was also launched on a conciliatory note. In August 1984, South Korea announced that it would not pursue the Rangoon incident investigations any further. In September 1984, Pyongyang offered aid to Seoul after severe flooding in the South. To Kim Il-Sung's surprise, Chun Doo-Hwan accepted the offer, and the North Korean Red Cross sent rice, cement, and textiles. This was followed by the first inter-Korean economic summit of cabinet ministers in November 1984, with both sides agreeing to promote inter-Korean trade in the future, and the first official reunions of divided families in September 1985.

But the defection of a Soviet diplomat across the DMZ in November 1984 and the subsequent shootout dampened relations. In 1985, Chun Doo-Hwan suggested holding a summit meeting, fielding a joint team for the Olympics (something that was first suggested by North Korea in 1958), and reopening the Kyŏnggi railway line that connected the peninsula in the pre-1945 period, but he received no response from the North. Tensions mounted over the large-scale Team Spirit military exercises held by South Korea and the US; these tensions led to the suspension of all meetings and talks in 1986 by North Korea. After the 1987 bombing of KAL flight 858 by two North Korean agents, relations deteriorated further, resulting in North Korea's absence from the 1988 Seoul Olympics.

Fourth period

The fourth period, 1988 to 1998, marked the beginning of a more sustained shift in relations due mainly to South Korea's democratization, Seoul's "Olympic diplomacy," and the collapse of the Soviet bloc. On July 7, 1988, Roh Tae-Woo announced a new *Nordpolitik* that involved increasing North—South exchanges; reuniting separated families; increasing trade; cross-recognition by the neighbouring four countries; and joint UN entry.

After July 1988, South Korea also phased out its "Anti-communist" education and gradually replaced it with "Unification Education," which stressed the common ethnic roots of the two countries. Throughout the 1960s and 1970s cartoons and school pamphlets had depicted communists as red devils: many adults in their forties and fifties can recall thinking as children that North Koreans were literally red-skinned with horns. A popular TV cartoon of the 1960s depicted Kim Il-Sung as a pig that received a beating from the hero on a weekly basis. Under Unification Education, North Koreans were now depicted as humans from the same race of Koreans. Protestant churches had also publicly promoted anti-communism but renounced this worldview in 1988.[9] Public renouncement of anti-communism was a major shift in epistemology for the South, since the history of domestic opposition to communism stretched back to the 1920s – for example, Syngman Rhee's anti-communism originated from the colonial period.[10] After July 1988, however, most of the posters urging citizens to be alert for Northern spies were taken off the walls of subway trains, or their sizes were greatly reduced.

Other indicators of apparent improvements in relations mushroomed. Indirect trade between the two Koreas began in 1988, followed by limited direct trade starting in 1990. Inter-Korean soccer games were held in 1990. Several interministerial meetings were held in 1990, and in September 1991 North and South Korea entered the UN at the same time. In December 1991 the two sides signed the Agreement on Reconciliation, Non-Aggression, and Exchanges and Cooperation (Basic Agreement), and the Joint Declaration on the Denuclearization of the Korean Peninsula, apparently signaling a new era in North–South relations.

There were limits however. When South Korean student activist Im Su-Kyŏng went to North Korea without her government's permission to participate in the World Youth Festival in July 1989, then attempted to return via Panmunjom, she was arrested. Moreover, while North Korea's sense of its precarious position amidst the crumbling of the Soviet bloc prompted this reconciliation, these developments were, however, coeval with the emergence of the nuclear card. The nuclear standoff with the US in 1993–94 was resolved via the Agreed Framework, which should have led to incremental improvements in relations.

The unexpected death of Kim Il-Sung in 1994, and South

Korean president Kim Young-Sam's failure to extend condolences to North Korea resulted in severely strained relations between 1995 and 1998. Several defectors have recounted that Kim Jong-Il was enraged by Kim Young-Sam's inaction. In fall 1996, there was a dramatic incursion by a North Korean submarine, which ran aground on the eastern coast of South Korea's Kangwŏn province, that resulted in shootouts in the forest and collateral deaths of South Korean civilians.

Fifth period

The fifth period, from 1998 to the present, has been characterized mainly by the North's attempt to retain autonomy and control the inflow of capitalism under the South's Sunshine Policy. In June 1998, the chairman and founder of the Hyundai Group, Chung Ju-Yung (Chŏng Chu-Yŏng), donated 500 cows to North Korea, and met with Kim Jong-Il. The Diamond Mountains (Kŭmgang-san), a series of jagged mountains that have long been renowned for their spectacular hikes and vistas, were opened to South Korean tourists in December of the same year. About 150,000 South Korean tourists visited the Diamond Mountains in the first year of operations. In fact, there were 3,300 South Korean visitors to the North in 1998 alone (not counting tourists to the Diamond Mountains), when there had been a total of 2,400 between the years 1989 and 1997.

After Kim Dae-Jung's inauguration in 1998, relations steadily improved, culminating in the historic summit meeting between Kim Dae-Jung and Kim Jong-Il in June 2000. During this meeting, the first between the heads of these states, Korean and international media coverage reached frenzied heights. The more substantive negotiations were difficult, but Kim Dae-Jung and Kim Jong-Il agreed a number of matters: unification was a Korean issue – it should be determined by North and South Korea rather than by foreign powers; Kim Jong-Il would visit Seoul at an appropriate time; separated families should be reunited; the Kyŏnggi railway would be reopened; there would be a joint entrance of both teams at the Sydney Olympics opening ceremony; and inter-Korean defence ministers' meetings would be held.

While Kim Dae-Jung won the Nobel Peace Prize for this summit, Kim Jong-Il made the bigger splash in South Korea – his image in the South had been so caricatured that it could only improve. The extent of the "Kim Jong-Il shock" was reflected in the fact that nearly 100% of those surveyed in the South directly following the summit responded that their perception of Kim Jong-Il had improved dramatically over the three days of the summit. The wave of positive sentiment towards Kim Jong-Il in South Korea drowned out the reminders that he had most likely personally ordered military incursions into parts of the South.

Another indication of the improvement in relations was the subtle changes in the North's propaganda. For decades, official North Korean sources had tirelessly reiterated that South Korea was a colony of the American imperialists. However, the official North Korean annual review (*Chosŏn chungang nyŏnban*) began toning down this rhetoric after the 2000 summit. The 1999 version had condemned South Korea as an incorrigibly corrupt society with prohibitive education fees, rampant crime rates, proliferating AIDS, rising juvenile crimes, exorbitant hospital fees, all of which drove slaves of capitalism to suicide. In the 2000 version, the section heading titled "American Imperialist Colony South Korea" disappeared, and the criticisms of the corruption of South Korean society were shortened.[11]

The number of meetings and exchange programs, the amount of investments, and the volume of trade between North and South increased dramatically as well after 2000. One indication of this improvement in relations is the fact that of the total of 6,175 South Koreans who visited North Korea to do humanitarian aid work from 1991 to 2003, 5,621 of them went under the Kim Dae-Jung administration. South Korean NGOs were initially more constrained than other international NGOs, as Pyongyang feared that the inflow of food items, fertilizers, and rice from South Korea would bring in undesirable information about South Korea's relative prosperity that might corrode support for the regime.[12] However, even this stance softened gradually.

Indications of the changes were reflected in popular representations as well. The 1990 South Korean film *Nambugun* by director Chŏng Chi-Yŏng, about partisan leftist armies in the South fighting against the South Korean army, portrayed leftist partisans sympathetic to North Korea as humans rather than as evil caricatures as had been the previous practice in movies. A

1992 North Korea–Japan joint production, director Im Chan-Bong's *Bird*, was a dramatization about an actual bird scholar and his daughter that depicted the tragedy of separated families. This film, which debuted at the 5th Tokyo International Film Festival, was notable for what it did not contain: maledictions against the South and demonization of the Japanese. In the 1999 South Korean action romance blockbuster *Shiri*, the heroine, a North Korean agent planted in South Korea, ultimately could not overcome her training. But her genuine love for her South Korean intelligence agent husband provided the character with a redeeming quality. The 2000 hit *JSA* was even more sympathetic in its portrayal of North Korean soldiers, as the film revolved around the friendship between two North Korean and two South Korean soldiers patrolling the JSA.

Reading too much into shifts in popular representations and consumer reactions can be misleading or downright pointless, but an indication of the sensitivity of the issue of the portrayals of North Koreans in the South was an incident that followed the release of *JSA*: several veterans of the Korean War physically attacked the Seoul office of Myŏng Films, the production company that made the movie, protesting that the depiction of Northern soldiers in the movie was unrealistic and misleading, and an insult to the memories of those who died in the war.

However, as with previous cases of improvements in relations, a downturn followed what had seemed to be a major breakthrough. In 2003, a special prosecutor concluded that the Hyundai Group had paid North Korea around $100 million (out of an official total $500 million paid out by Hyundai to North Korea ostensibly as fees to operate the Diamond Mountains Tours and other business activities) to facilitate the summit meeting of 2000. Chung Mong-Hun (Chŏng Mong-Hŏn), the fifth son of the founder and chairman of Hyundai Asan, the company within the Hyundai Group that spearheaded inter-Korean business, committed suicide in August 2003. Even though North Korea's annual overviews diluted their rhetoric, the North continued to publish pamphlets that condemned South Korea's attempts at "peaceful coexistence" as a mere disguise of South Korea's "puppet" status under American imperialism. North Korea also roundly denounced the South Korean dispatch of troops to Iraq to support the US "war on terror," and the ineffectualness of the South Korean government's reactions to the deaths of the two girls hit by a US armored vehicle in June 2002.

There were other hints that the fundamental distrust between the two sides remained. While public opinion surveys can be unreliable weathervanes of inter-Korean relations, the testing of missiles and nuclear weapons in 2006 triggered a round of public opinion surveys expressing concern about the military threat that North Korea posed to the South.[13] Northern spies continued to be arrested throughout the period of reconciliation, with dramatic arrests in the summer of 2006. South Korea was not a signatory to UN statements criticizing human rights conditions in North Korea, but the awareness of military threat was revived rather easily, which in turn resurrects doubts regarding the real extent of improvements in inter-Korean relations.

Defectors

The experiences of North Korean defectors in adjusting to life in South Korea further reflect the wide gap in values and lifestyles that still exists between the two countries. Some defectors have gone from the South to the North, or from Japan or the US to the North, especially during the 1950s, but the majority of defectors have gone from North to South, or to China. The long-term trend, especially since the 1990s, has seen more defections for material reasons, an increasing range of occupations and classes represented by defectors, and an acceleration in flows and numbers.[14] The statistics reflect this trend: in 1995, there were 561 North Korean defectors living in South Korea, and by 2004 this number had risen to 6,304. By February 2007, the total reached 10,000. According to South Korean government statistics, in 1990, only 9 North Korean defectors entered South Korea; in 2000 this number had risen to 312, and in 2006 there were 2,019 such entries.[15]

Receiving defectors in the South

The gradual decrease in benefits provided by South Korea to defectors reflects the increase in overall numbers and in the proportion of unskilled workers. South Korea first passed a formal law in April 1962 to provide defectors with resettlement allowances, arrange for vocational training, and work. A December 1978

Special Law to Compensate Brave Defectors to the South created more systematic benefits, such as preferential housing, work, and education opportunities, the same benefits as were provided to officially recognized "patriots." These benefits were in part designed to impress upon the defectors the superiority of the South.[16] The 1993 Law to Protect North Korean Defectors reduced the material benefits provided to defectors, because they were no longer prized acquisitions for propaganda, but additional burdens on the social welfare system. The terms were further amended in 1997 via the Law on the Protection and Resettlement of North Korean Defectors.

Until 1996, defectors were first interrogated to confirm their identity, motives, information, method of defection, and achievements. After the debriefing, they were sent to a resettlement facility run by the Ministry of Defense, where they were reeducated in the rituals and beliefs of capitalism, and began the paperwork to obtain South Korean citizenship. Many of these defectors were then protected or supervised by police for the following two years, as some defectors were discovered to have been double agents. After 1997, the periods of initial assessment, training, and supervision were reduced. In 1999, the Ministry of Unification took over jurisdiction over defectors from the Ministry of Defence, housing around five hundred people at any one time in an integration and debriefing facility called the Hanawŏn. The rapid increases in defector numbers strained the Hanawŏn's resources in the 2000s: the social adaptation training was reduced from ten to six and then to three months. The basic adjustment training was still followed by six to eight months of vocational education, but job placements were no longer guaranteed.

Adjusting to life in the South

Several voluntary organizations help defectors in their adjustment to South Korea. There are two large defector associations, and one anti-North Korea radio station (Free Korea) is run by defectors. Nonetheless, the vast majority of defectors agree that the three-month education for adjustment to capitalism is insufficient. A 2003 survey indicated that some 60% of them were satisfied with life in South Korea overall, with only 7% dissatisfied.[17] However, another 2003 survey indicated that 66%

felt that they had not adjusted to the South, with only 5% expressing confidence that they had integrated into the capitalist society. According to the same surveys, an estimated 53% developed clinical depression, 43% suffered health issues, and 60% concluded that their incomes were insufficient for life in the South. Around 50–60% had difficulty obtaining regular employment or skilled jobs.[18] Prejudice against defectors in everyday life has been listed as a difficulty by many defectors to the South. Although North Korea and South Korea both use the Korean language, several differences in vocabulary and loan words, as well as in pronunciation, together were another factor that made the initial adjustment periods difficult.[19]

Finding jobs, earning an income, and getting married have been challenges for any South Korean, but they have been even more challenging for defectors, especially in the first five or six years after arrival. Cultural differences make marriages between South and North Koreans difficult, partially because of the expectations that there would be no difference because of the supposed bonds of language and history. There are agencies that arrange marriages solely between defectors, and for North Korean women to marry South Korean males (over 500 North Korean women are currently registered). In general, the trend has been towards more women defecting than men per year.

North Korean men find adjusting to capitalist life in South Korea more difficult than women, and some North Korean women's images of South Korean men have been distorted by the portrayals of the male protagonists of South Korean soap operas that they watched in China before arrival, compounding the difficulties for male defectors seeking marriage partners.[20] The plight of North Korean men is symbolized by the fact that there are marriage agencies that promise to match Southern men with Northern women, but there are at present none that attempt to match Northern men with Southern women.

The profound sense of alienation, a paucity of social connections, and encounters with everyday forms of prejudice – these difficulties are common to most immigrants, but the fundamentally different values underlying the two Korean societies make the transition more difficult for defectors. Their credentials are usually rendered meaningless in the South, resulting in a loss of social status. Like other types of asylum seekers, defectors find that their attempts at liberation often result in an exchange of yokes. Kim Hyŏng-Dŏk, who had arrived in the South in 1994 after two spells in prison in North Korea, found life under capitalism even more miserable. He attempted to flee back to North Korea through China in 1996, but was arrested and sent to prison. The system was changed in 2000 so that former North Koreans could travel more freely after obtaining South Korean citizenship, and Kim himself was released, eventually realizing that there was no heaven on earth, even in the South.[21]

South Koreans are constantly reminded that North Koreans are of the same blood, but in fact many South Koreans see North Korea as a foreign country and the defectors as poor immigrants from a "backward" and "strange" place. As indicated in surveys, defectors themselves sense that many South Koreans view them as second-class citizens or refugees, not as long-lost family who have returned to the fold. The injustices are exacerbated in the eyes of many defectors who can observe that the defectors who were highest-ranking in the hierarchy of the North are the most handsomely rewarded in the South – in other words, the elites who cooperated most closely with Kim Jong-Il and who thus, from the perspective of ordinary defectors, share the most responsibility for North Korea's current woes, are the most prized by South Korea. There is some hope that new approaches that emphasize the need to acknowledge not just political and economic but also social differences between North and South as the first step towards developing policies to prepare for unification, may provide long-term solutions for the current gap in norms and systems.[22] However, the celerity of diffusion and the depth of impact of such policy suggestions remain to be seen.

Decussation Effects?

After the unifications of Yemen and Germany in 1990, Korea remains the only divided nation left other than Ireland, or so the common rhetoric goes. The magnetic power of the slogan "One People, One Nation" is curious when viewed in the light of the reality that, quite often, people do not get along with each other precisely because they can apparently understand what the other side is saying. Whether it is irredentist claims over populations and territory, or visions of "reunification" *à la* Germany, the message of unity under ethno-nationalism, as embodied in West German chancellor Willy Brandt's statement that there were "two German states, but only one German nation," has resonances that seems to appeal to many as an aspiration even if the reality turns out to be far more arduous.[23]

In the 1990s, a proliferation of comparative studies were undertaken in South Korea on the German and Yemen precedents. North Yemen was wealthier than South Yemen, at least in part because the commercial class had migrated to the North. After 1989, with South Yemen shorn of Soviet aid and advisors and its economy floundering, its officials attempted to implement economic reforms, but these failed to produce results, which eventually led to a politically negotiated unification.[24] Subsequent tensions, and the 1994 civil war in Yemen served as warnings to the more optimistic of the unification-scenario-builders in Korea. Some comparative studies characterized unification in Germany as a process from "below" and the Yemen process as one from "above."[25] However, despite grassroots support and institutional integration prior to legal unification, Germany has had difficulties with integration, and these have helped consolidate a spectrum of South Korean views around gradual, incremental unification. The awareness of the difficulties in German integration was heightened by the fact that the current economic gap between South and North Korea is larger than the economic gaps of divided Germany or Yemen. Concerns about the economic capacity of South Korea to integrate the North revolve around the projected short-term effects of unification: sky-rocketing inflation, rising unemployment, possible mass migration, and ballooning budget deficits.[26]

However, the various comparisons and scenarios seem almost desperate to skirt a simple fact – that both the North and the South have been comfortable proposing some form of long-term confederation in lieu of absolute unification. In 1960, 1973, and 1980, Kim Il-Sung proposed slightly varying versions of the Democratic Confederal Republic of Korea (DCRK): under this plan, both Koreas would have one seat in the UN, and they would unify their currency and foreign policies, but maintain two separate socio-economic systems. On some levels, however, South

Korean governments have been reluctant to officially endorse confederation, at least as the ultimate terminus.[27]

Nonetheless, since the 1960s, South Korean utterances and policies have been consistent on the point that unification would be peaceful, and gradual, and would require long periods where confederation would be the *modus vivendi*. In January 1966, Park Chung-Hee announced that economic strength would be needed before any form of unification, a statement to which Kim Il-Sung essentially responded in kind. In August 1970, Park reinforced his earlier statement by proposing that the two Koreas should compete to see which one could make its citizens happier rather than focus on military capacity.

This rhetoric gave birth to more explicit proposals for unification that essentially acknowledged the vast gap between the two Koreas. In 1971, the then opposition leader Kim Dae-Jung proposed a three-stage model to unification – confederation (peaceful coexistence); federation (peaceful exchange); and unification (peaceful unification). Confederation would involve increased exchanges and cooperation, and peaceful coexistence between the two political and economic systems. In the second stage, a federal government would handle foreign affairs, while two autonomous regional governments would retain all jurisdiction over domestic affairs. The third stage, unification, would result in one market economy, ruled by one central government. In 1988, Roh Tae-Woo announced a three-stage unification policy, reiterated in 1994 by Kim Young-Sam: both plans envisaged a three-stage process of reconciliation and cooperation; alliance; and unification. In 1991, Kim Il-Sung proposed a three-stage alliance of the two nations that sounded very much like Kim Dae-Jung's 1971 suggestion.

On the surface, all these plans (other than North Korea's confederation proposals) result in unification. The key, however, is that each stage would take decades, resulting in a situation where there would be two systems for two ethnicities, North and South Korea. For example, following his election in 1998, Kim Dae-Jung reiterated the same principles he had first used in 1971 – no armed provocation, no absorption of the North by the South, positive and peaceful reunification. This Sunshine Policy recognized from the outset the need for at least ten years for each of the first two stages. After the 2000 summit meeting, Kim Dae-

Jung conceded that the first stage would require much longer than ten years, in a sense acknowledging that any realistic unification policy had to recognize that two systems would be required for one race for the next several decades – in other words, confederation as a stable bipolar order.

In fact, the Sunshine Policy was made possible by the economic and political polarization between the North and the South. South Korea can afford reconciliation: this reality rankles the North Korean government, which views the policy as patronizing and ultimately corrosive to its hold on power. The result is the seemingly paradoxical formulation that polarization or increasing divergence has at the same time resulted in some convergence: in other words, the apparent decussation effect is the result of the bipolar order.

It is useful to remember that despite the state propaganda about the need for unification, roughly 85% of South Koreans were born after 1945, making the state of division the "natural" condition for them. A 2000 survey of high school students indicated that 82% hardly discussed unification.[28] In fact, only 27% of those surveyed responded that unification was "necessary." Another survey in 2001 showed that 73% thought that Unification Education was inadequate, and 80% thought that divergent values made North Korea a heterogenous country.[29]

Conclusion

Greater freedom of speech and social changes in South Korea have led to more vocal protests against specific issues related to the US, and some improvements in relations with North Korea. However, the use of the label "anti-Americanism" can lead to simplistic reactions to criticisms that may not be directed at the entirety of the US. Moreover, celebrations of (or protests against) the improvements in relations between the North and South need to be tempered by the realization that there have been previous cycles of improvement and deterioration. The difficult experiences of the defectors indicate that there are indeed two very different cultures on the Korean peninsula, and that some acknowledgement of these differences, whether defined as cultures or as ethnicities, is required before further improvements in inter-Korean relations are possible.

Most important, in addition to the potential economic costs of unification, it is important to interrogate the ideal of one homogenous race housed in one state, and call for deeper reflection on the impact of fifty years of division. After all, some nation-states such as Italy have long contained within them apparently perpetual political and economic divisions.[30] In other cases, such as Cameroon, the political efficacy of "unification" of Anglophone and Francophone areas in 1961 was questioned over thirty years later.[31]

These examples signal that unification is hardly a magic potion that would erase the scars of contemporary history; similarly the division of the peninsula cannot be dismissed as a mere interregnum. The longevity of the division calls for further analyses that do not treat the current situation as some ossified fossil from the Cold War, a "bipolar disorder," but as a state of affairs that has survived for some sixty-plus years, a "bipolar order."

6 | Conclusion
Two Koreas in the Present

History inhabits all our presents in multifarious ways. However, the flow is not unidirectional. Our perceptions of the present and our desires for different futures also permeate our perspectives on the past. We ransack histories for a key to unlock a contemporary puzzle, or perhaps for materials with which to weave narratives to resurrect departed collective pride. Knowledge of the past can help form knowledge in and for the present, or so it is often said. For some, the analysis of history may involve teasing out secret algorithms that hover nebulously and elusively out of reach, equations that would allow us to predict the future with a certainty that would make Cassandra weep in self-recognition.

There remains considerable debate within the confines of the academic discipline of history about the relationship between the past and the present. Some historians are content to leave anything within the last ten or twenty years to social scientists, while other historians loathe calling anything within the last hundred years "history." More recently, there has been widespread acknowledgement that most studies of history are borne on present-day obsessions, or at least infused with current concerns. This emergent agreement notwithstanding, the issue of whether increasing power or affecting change in the "present" (however it might be defined) should be the primary goal of history or a secondary one remains unresolved. Some scholars argue that all histories are in essence products of their times and little else, while others respond that "presentist" agendas and assumptions distort attempts to comprehend the past.

The problem is compounded by the fact that the present itself is a perpetually moving target. If a North Korean nuclear weapons test is portrayed as the harbinger of Armageddon one day, the media might present a pop star changing his or her hairstyle as a seismic shift in our epistemological world on the next. While the mission of historicizing the present is laden with the danger of anachronistically projecting our current preoccupations onto the past, these concerns themselves may become anachronisms after one development or another. In short, our notion of what constitute significant history is often provisional and fleeting. Furthermore, the portrayal of the division of the Korean peninsula as an abnormal condition, for example, reflects in many ways a sense of what ought to be rather than what is – in other words, assumptions about a desirable future.

Consequently, the act of writing, reading, and thinking about history might be better conceived as the construction of a contingent Moebius loop (the twist being the attempt to understand history in the moving present) that fuses together the horizons of the past, the present, and the future, rather than merely the tracing of a linear progression of events with a clear teleology. If we think in these terms, the gutted husks of formerly authoritative predictions of collapse or dramatic change that litter the contemporary study of North Korea make for interesting history in the sense that they captured the assumptions and projections of the time they were written. Another application of the Moebius loop metaphor might be to reflect – when people were brandishing as a breakthrough North Korea's wave of normalizations in 2000 with countries such as Italy, Canada, Australia, the Philippines, and the UK – that in 1972, North Korea normalized relations with eight countries (including Pakistan, Malaysia, and India), and in 1973 it did the same with twelve countries (Sweden, Norway, Denmark, Finland, Iran, and Afghanistan, among others) following the South–North Joint Declaration of 1972. The flurry of imports into plants up to 1975 from Japan (cement), Australia (chemicals), France and the UK (petrochemicals) also seemed to promise North Korea's participation in the world economy. But due in large part to the First Oil Shock, North Korean exports of metals and other primary goods plummeted in value, while interest rates increased. Also, the plants were intended for import substitution rather than export, which meant that there was no increase in foreign currency earnings as a result of the capital investment: this resulted in North Korea defaulting on its international loans in the late 1970s.

All this is not to suggest that North Korea's economic reforms of

2002 must end at the same terminus, since domestic and international conditions have changed since the early 1970s. Nevertheless, it is always important to note that the trajectories of the past might appear obvious from the present, but the various twists and turns are in many respects given their meaning within the context of retrospect. The wide spectrum of outcomes in the past should warn us from monomaniacal searches for singular narratives or from overestimating the effects of the latest fibrillations on possible future developments.

More specifically, North Korea's July 2002 reforms, the latest round of the Six Party Talks for denuclearization in spring 2007, or the accession of South Korean diplomat Ban Ki-Moon (Pan Ki-Mun) as the Secretary General of the UN in December 2006, will undoubtedly have some effects on particular issues such as North Korea's economic growth rates, the likelihood of North Korea exporting nuclear weapons technology, or the degree to which proposals related to the Korean peninsula gain traction within the UN. However, these smaller developments, touted as major fluctuations in the media, are unlikely to shatter the bipolar order of the two Koreas.

It might be useful to consider, even heuristically, that the division is not just an anomalous vestige from the Cold War, but a functioning system, a bipolar order, which has maintained its general outline for sixty-plus years. Polarization between North and South has led to the fortification of two very distinct nation-state identities whose very divisions lead paradoxically to apparently improving relations. Claims that a united Korea is incontrovertibly "normal" or "natural" need to be assessed with an eye to the contingent nature of most historical interpretations.

In terms of parallels, cascades of comparative work flowed from pens in the aftermath of the German and Yemen unifications, but in thinking further about the post-1989 histories of North and South Korea, we might also consider the need to distend the comparisons beyond the usual, such as the aforementioned cases, or the often-used comparisons of South Korea's economic development with Japan's. The complex imbrications of foreign influences, malleable collective identities, ideological frictions, and socio-economic gaps might more fruitfully be compared to the tangled territorial and cultural skein linking countries such as

Greece, Turkey, Albania, Serbia, Bulgaria, and the Republic of Macedonia. The abortive experiment with unification of Singapore and Malaysia from 1963 to 1965 is rarely mentioned as a point of comparison for South Korea, perhaps with good reason given the vast differences in contexts and social structure: nonetheless, the example is not utterly irrelevant since it represents at least one possible outcome of unification.

The most intriguing avenue of comparative history might be to examine, for example, how South Korea applies its own experiences in contemporary history in its relations with other countries. More specifically, it will be worth monitoring domestic South Korean reactions to protectionist policies in parts of Southeast Asia against its cultural products, particularly as the developments are akin to some of the protectionist policies used to foster the growth of the South Korean movie industry in decades before. Other issues such as: the common denominators between the Status of Forces Agreement between the US and South Korea, and South Korea and Kazakhstan; or comparisons between the treatment of foreign migrant workers and refugee applicants in Japan and similar responses in South Korea; and whether questions and policies that do not assume unification as the ultimate terminus of contemporary history proliferate or not, are significant issues that bear further research.

In terms of connections, even though domestic events in both Koreas have been the major engines of change, the Korean peninsula has undoubtedly been influenced greatly by global developments, in particular, the actions of the US, Japan, and China. Space restrictions do not permit an extended discussion of the foreign relations of the two countries. Nonetheless, it should be pointed out that it would be difficult to imagine any attempts at unification that were not supported by Washington. Regime changes within the US have generally had significant impact on inter-Korean relations. While the bilateral relations between South Korea and the US have not been immutable, especially as the post-1989 international environment has created spaces for greater South Korean autonomy, ultimately both South and North acknowledge the primacy of the US as either major ally or primary negotiating counterpart.

If the bipolar order between North and South has remained

176 | Bipolar Orders

extant for the past few decades, more recently, polarization within each of the two countries has created a sense of plurality in the bipolarity. In North Korea, Kim Jong-Il dined on caviar and champagne while many of his citizens starved; the number of tourists coming to the North increased in the Diamond Mountains on the east coast, while military clashes with the South occurred on the west coast. In South Korea, the wealthy consumed brand-name products at increasing volumes while unemployment increased in many sectors of the economy; conservative politicians called for regime change in North Korea, while the proponents of the Sunshine Policy were disinclined to alienate the North. The multiple polarities and divergences that intersect on the Korean peninsula (decussated or not) serve as the basis for the metaphoric title of this book, *Bipolar Orders*.

However, there are no magical incantations or one talismanic theory that can transport the historian into a realm of eternal truths and immutable pasts, and certainly one book will not cause the past, the present, and the future of the two Koreas to become fused into an incontrovertibly perfect whole. Nonetheless, in exploring the polarization, decussation, and bipolar order of the contemporary histories of the two Koreas, this book serves as a reminder that the constant streams of "up-to-date" information flowing through the newswires can often mean very little without an understanding of the more long-term historical dynamics at work in our fleeting present.

Notes

Introduction

1 Richard Rorty, *Contingency, Irony, and Solidarity* (Cambridge: Cambridge University Press, 1989), p. 165.

2 The Northern village is an essentially uninhabited propaganda outpost. The Southern village is a farming village restricted to residents who were born in the village or immediate family members and descendants of such villagers.

3 The term "turbo-capitalism" is associated with Edward Luttwak, *Turbo-Capitalism: Winners and Losers in the Global Economy* (New York: Harper Collins, 1999). Luttwak points to Japan and France as exceptions to this pattern of accelerated capitalism resulting in extreme income polarization. I use it here not as an application of Luttwak's ideas, but as shorthand for the accelerated changes brought on by compressed economic development in South Korea.

4 International Monetary Fund, *World Economic Outlook Database*, April 2006. Viewed at <http://www.imf.org/external/pubs/ft/weo/2006/01/data/index.htm>

5 Hong Yŏng-Lim, "Yŏron chosa – Han'guk anbo wihyŏp kukga, Miguk il-wi ro," *Chosŏn Ilbo* (January 11, 2004). Viewed at <http://www.chosun.com/editorials/ news/200401/200401110271.htp>

6 Lee Kwang-Gil, "Kungmin 44% – 'Puk haek poyu, t'ongil tui kungnyŏk toum,'" *T'ongil News* (April 12, 2005). Viewed at <http://www.tongilnews.com/article.asp?mainflag=Y&menuid=101000&articleid=53722>

7 Rosemary Foot, *A Substitute for Victory: the Politics of Peacemaking at the Korean Armistice Talks* (Ithaca: Cornell University Press, 1990), pp. 184–9; and Park Tae-Gyun, *Han'guk chŏnjaeng* (Seoul: Ch'aek gwa hamkke, 2005), pp. 343–56.

8 "President Roh spoke at the 50th meeting of the Standing Committee of National Unification Advisory Council" (December 21, 2006). <http://www.korea.net/ news/news/ newsView.asp?serial_no=20061226007&part=101>

9 For details, see for example Jonathan Ritchie and Don Markwell, "Australian and Commonwealth Republicanism," *Round Table*, Vol. 95, No. 5 (October 2006): 727–37; also, David E. Smith, *The Republican Option in Canada, Past and Present* (Toronto: University of Toronto Press, 1999).

10 For more on the epistemological underpinnings to this issue, see

for example Pierre Bourdieu's conceptualization of "doxa" – what might be summarized as the naturalization of arbitrariness in framing and producing knowledge that makes it look like the assumptions are somehow "self-evident" or commonsensical. Pierre Bourdieu, *Outline of a Theory of Practice* (Cambridge: Cambridge University Press, 1977), pp. 164–70; and John F. Myles, "From Doxa to Experience: Issues in Bourdieu's Adoption of Husserlian Phenomenology," *Theory, Culture and Society*, Vol. 21, No. 2 (April 2004): 91–107.

11 James A. Foley, "'Ten Million Families': Statistic or Metaphor?" *Korean Studies*, Vol. 25, No. 1 (January 2001): 108.

12 As described in several South Korean works, but most prominently in Kang Man-Gil, *Pundan sidae ŭi yŏksa insik* (Seoul: Changjak kwa pip'yŏng, 1978).

13 Roh has made this statement on several occasions. This particular speech was given to Korean residents of Mongolia on May 9, 2006.

14 For more on "ethnicity," see, for example, J. Milton Yinger, *Ethnicity* (Albany: State University of New York Press, 1994), pp. 10–26; Rogers Brubaker and Frederick C. Cooper, "Beyond 'Identity'," *Theory and Society*, Vol. 29, No. 1 (February 2000): 1–47; and Joane Nagel, *Race, Ethnicity, and Sexuality: Intimate Intersections, Forbidden Frontiers* (New York: Oxford University Press, 2003), p. 6.

15 The accumulated discussion on the "end of history," globalization, and of globalization theory is voluminous. For an overview that provides samples of some the major issues and positions related to globalization see, for example, Frank Lechner and John Boli, eds., *The Globalization Reader* (Malden: Blackwell, 2004).

16 I have deliberately limited the number of notes for each chapter to around fifty or under, although far more sources were used in writing each chapter.

17 A more detailed overview of Korea's pre-modern history can be found in other works, for example, Carter J. Eckert, Ki-baik Lee, Young Ick Lew, Michael Robinson, and Edward W. Wagner, *Korea Old and New: A History* (Seoul: Ichokak, 1990), pp. 9–230.

18 North Korea's land area is roughly 120,000 square kilometers and South Korea's is roughly 100,000 square kilometers for a total of 220,000 square kilometers. The land area of the United Kingdom is roughly 240,000 square kilometers.

19 See, for details, Carter Eckert, *Offspring of Empire: the Koch'ang Kims and the Colonial Origins of Korean Capitalism, 1876–1945* (Seattle, University of Washington Press, 1991).

20 See, for details, Kim Chin-Song, *Hyŏndaesŏng ŭi hyŏngsŏng-Seoul ae dancehall ŭl hŏhara* (Seoul: Hyŏnsil munhwa yŏn'gu, 1999); and Hyung Gu Lynn, "Fashioning Modernity: Changing Meanings of Clothing in Colonial Korea," *Journal of International and Area Studies*, Vol. 11, No. 3 (Spring 2005): 75–93.

21 See, for details, Michael Robinson, *Cultural Nationalism in Colonial Korea* (Seattle: University of Washington, 1988).

22 See, for details, Bruce Cumings, *The Origins of the Korean War,* Vol. 1 (Princeton: Princeton University Press, 1981).

23 See, for details, Pak Myŏng-Lim, *Han'guk chŏnjaeng ŭi kiwŏn gwa palbal,* 2 vols. (Seoul: Nanam, 1994).

Chapter 1

1 Padraic Kenney, *The Burdens of Freedom: Eastern Europe since 1989* (London: Zed Books, 2006), p. 4.

2 The 2006 World Audit Democracy listed Finland at 1, the United Kingdom at 9, Germany at 10, Canada at 10, the United States at 14, Taiwan at 22, Italy at 30, and Poland at 31. World Audit Democracy <http://www.worldaudit.org/democracy.htm>

3 Francis Fukuyama, *The End of History and the Last Man* (New York: Free Press, 1992).

4 Mark Granovetter, "Threshold Models of Collective Behavior," *American Journal of Sociology,* Vol. 83, No. 6 (May 1978): 1423–5.

5 Reinhold Niebuhr, *Irony of American History* (New York: Charles Scribner's Sons, 1952), p. 63.

6 Gregory Henderson, *Korea: The Politics of the Vortex* (Cambridge, MA: Harvard University Press, 1968), p. 174.

7 Sung-Joo Han, *Failure of Democracy in Korea* (Berkeley: University of California Press, 1974), p. 30.

8 John Kie-Chiang Oh, *Democracy on Trial* (Ithaca: Cornell University Press, 1968), pp. 104–5.

9 Lee Kyun-Sŏk, "Ijhyŏjin 'Masan ŭi adŭl'-Kim Chu-Yŏl yŏlsa 46 chugi," *Taejabo,* March 15, 2006. Viewed at <http://www.jabo.co.kr/sub_read.html?uid=14725&section=section3>

10 Sung-Chick Hong, "The Students' Values," in C.I. Eugene Kim, ed., *A Pattern of Political Development: Korea* (Kalamazoo: Korea Research and Publication, 1964), p. 65.

11 Chŏng Yŏng-Guk, "Yusin ch'eje sŏngnip chŏnhu ŭi kungnae chŏngch'i," in Han'guk chŏngsin munhwa yŏn'guwŏn, ed., *1970 nyŏndae chŏnbangi ŭi chŏngch'i sahoe pyŏndong* (Seoul: Paeksan sŏdang, 1999), pp. 205–37.

12 See, for details, Kim Dae-Jung sŏnsaeng napch'i sakgŏn ŭi chinsang kyumyŏng ŭl wihan simin ŭi moim, ed., *Kim Dae-Jung napch'i sakgŏn ŭi chinsang* (Seoul: P'urŭn namu, 1995),

13 Ko Sŭng-Hyŏn, *Han'guk ŭi First Lady* (Seoul: Milal, 1996), pp. 168–70.

14 Ma In-Sŏp, "1970-nyŏndae hubanki ŭi minjuhwa undong gwa Yusin ch'eje ŭi pungoe," Han'guk chŏngsin munhwa yŏn'guwŏn, ed., *1970-nyŏndae hubanki ŭi chŏngch'i sahoe pyŏndong* (Seoul: Paeksan sŏdang, 1999), pp. 264–5.

15 For some of these accounts, see Chung Sangyong, Rhyu Simin, et al., *Memories of May 1980: A Documentary History of the Kwangju Uprising in Korea* (Seoul: Korea Democracy Foundation, 2003), pp. 210–21.

16 Kim Min-Hwan, *Han'guk ŏllonsa* (Seoul: Sahoe pip'yŏngsa, 1996),

180 | Notes

pp. 522–23.

17 Jung-kwan Cho, "The Kwangju Uprising as a Vehicle of Democratization: A Comparative Perspective," in Gi-Wook Shin and Kyung Moon Hwang, eds., *Contentious Kwangju: The May 18 Uprising in Korea's Past and Present* (Lanham: Rowman & Littlefield, 2003), pp. 70–7.

18 Lee Hŭi-Yŏng, "Ch'ehŏm toen p'ungnyŏk kwa sedaekan ŭi sot'ong," *Kyŏngje wa sahoe*, No. 68 (Winter 2005): 107–32.

19 Yun Sang-Ch'ŏl, "Chiguch'on 'che-3 ŭi mulgyŏl' minjuhwa wa Han'guk ŭi minjuhwa," *Kyŏngje wa sahoe*, No. 51 (Fall 2001): 20.

20 See, for example, William H. Gleysteen Jr., *Massive Entanglement, Marginal Influence: Carter and Korea in Crisis* (Washington: Brookings Institute, 1999), pp. 134–43.

21 Im Hyŏk-Baek, *Sijang, kukka, minjujuŭi: Han'guk minjuhwa wa chŏngch'i kyŏngje iron* (Seoul: Nanam, 1994), pp. 269–70.

22 The political scientist Samuel Huntington posits that liberalization without democratization is inherently unstable over the long haul, Samuel Huntington, *The Third Wave: Democratization in the Late Twentieth Century* (Norman: University of Oklahoma Press, 1991), pp. 136–7.

23 Hong Nack Kim and Sunki Choe, "Urbanization and Changing Voting Patterns in South Korean Parliamentary Elections," in Ilpyong J. Kim and Young Whan Kihl, eds., *Political Change in South Korea* (Seoul: Paragon House, 1988), pp. 153–5.

24 John Kie-Chiang Oh, *Korea Politics: The Quest for Democratization and Economic Development* (Ithaca: Cornell University Press, 1999), pp. 66–70.

25 Roh Tae Woo, *Korea in the Pacific Century: Selected Speeches, 1990–1992* (Lanham: University Press of America, 1992), pp. 396–7.

26 Hagen Koo, "Middle Classes, Democratization, and Class Formation: The Case of South Korea," *Theory and Society*, Vol. 20, No. 4 (August 1991): 493–94.

27 The original plan to bid for the Olympics had been formulated by Park Chung-Hee in October 1979, but had been put on hold until Chun revived the project.

28 James F. Larson, and Heung-Soo Park, *Global Television and the Politics of the Seoul Olympics* (Boulder: Westview Press, 1993), p. 162.

29 Junhan Lee, "Primary Causes of Democratization in Asia: Dispelling Conventional Myths," *Asian Survey*, Vol. 42, No. 6 (November–December 2002): 835.

30 Don Oberdorfer, *The Two Koreas: A Contemporary History* (Reading: Addison-Wesley, 1997), pp. 171–2.

31 Kim Sŏng-Ik, *Chun Doo-Hwan yuksŏng chŭngŏn* (Seoul: Chosŏn ilbosa, 1992), pp. 337, 375–6, 388, 425.

32 Wonmo Dong, "Domestic Politics in 1990: A Year of Crisis," in Donald Clark, ed., *Korea Briefing, 1991* (Boulder: Westview, 1991), p. 9.

33 Sunhyuk Kim, "Civil Society and Democratization," in Charles Armstrong, ed., *Korean Society: Civil Society, Democracy and the State*

(New York: Routledge, 2002), p. 99.

34 Carl Saxer, "Generals and Presidents: Establishing Civilian and Democratic Control in South Korea," *Armed Forces and Society*, Vol. 30, No. 3 (Spring 2004): 393–5.

35 Lim Hy-Sop, "Historical Development of Civil Social Movements in Korea: Trajectories and Issues," *Korea Journal*, Vol. 40, No. 3 (2001), pp. 11–14.

36 Kenneth Wells, ed., *South Korea's Minjung Movement: The Culture and Politics of Dissidence* (Honolulu: University of Hawai'i Press, 1995), p. 14.

37 Cho Hŭi-Yŏn, "Minjung undong gwa simin sahoe, simin undong," *Silch'ŏn munhak*, No. 32 (Winter 1993): 232–70.

38 Yee Jaeyol, "Network Analysis of Solidarity Ties among Social Movement Organizations," *Korea Journal*, Vol. 40, No. 3 (Autumn 2000): 89–90.

39 For details on the Ukrainian case, see for example, Michael McFaul, "Transitions from Postcommunism," *Journal of Democracy*, Vol. 16, No. 3 (July 2005): 13–14; and Andrew Wilson, "Ukraine's Orange Revolution, NGOs and the Role of the West," *Cambridge Review of International Affairs*, Vol. 19, No. 1 (March 2006): 21–32.

40 See, for details, Amy Gurowitz, "Migrant Rights and Activism in Malaysia: Opportunities and Constraints," *Journal of Asian Studies*, Vol. 59, No. 4 (November 2000): 880–3. There has at least been one case of a domestic NGO allying with INGOs. In February 1998, the Korean Federation for Environmental Movement initiated a campaign to oppose the construction of a dam in the northeastern province of Kangwŏn, which eventually drew support from INGOs such as the Worldwatch Institute, Greenpeace International, and the Sierra Club. After an extensive government study, Kim Dae-Jung announced the cancellation of the Kangwŏn dam project in June 2000.

41 Jessica T. Mathews, "Power Shift," *Foreign Affairs*, Vol. 76, No. 1 (January/ February 1997): 50–66.

42 The Taiwanese government canceled this plan in December 1997 due in large part to the KFEM's activities. South Korea's economic growth had come at a high cost to the environment, but the problems had remained relatively localized until a major chemical spill into the Naktong River in 1991. Norman Eder, *Poisoned Prosperity: Development, Modernization, and the Environment in South Korea* (Armonk: M.E. Sharpe, 1996), pp. 108–9.

43 Yun Su-Chong, "Sosuja undong ŭi t'ŭksŏng gwa sahoe undong ŭi panghyang," *Sahoe wa kyŏngje*, No. 67 (Fall 2005): 12–38.

44 After the 2000 election, the courts ruled that CAGE was unconstitutional.

45 Elizabeth Theiss-Morse and John R. Hibbing, "Citizenship and Civic Engagement," *Annual Review of Political Science*, Vol. 8 (2005): 227–49.

46 Yun Sang-Ch'ŏl, "1990-nyŏndae Han'guk sahoe undong," *Kyŏngje*

182 | Notes

wa sahoe, No. 66 (Summer 2005): 70.

47 Song Ho-Keun, "Analysis of Participants in the New Social Movements in Korea: Mobilization and Network," *Korea Journal*, Vol. 40, No. 3 (2000): 106–8.

48 Kim Dae-Jung appointed Roh to his cabinet as the Maritime Affairs and Fisheries Minister in August 2000.

49 See, for details, O Yŏn-Ho, *Taehan minguk t'ŭksanp'um-OhmyNews* (Seoul: Humanist, 2004).

50 The Internet was first introduced into Korea in 1982 on SDN, Seoul National University and Korea Institute of Electronic Technology (KIET), and became available on a commercial basis in 1994 through Konet. Internet World Stats viewed at <http://www.internetworldstats.com/top25.htm>. See also, Kyu-Ho Youm, "The Internet and Democracy in South Korea," in Indrajit Banerjee, ed., *Rhetoric and Reality: The Internet Challenge for Democracy in Asia* (Singapore: Eastern Universities Press, 2003), pp. 144–8.

51 See Woojin Moon, "Decomposition of Regional Voting in South Korea: Ideological Conflicts and Regional Interests," *Party Politics*, Vol. 11, No. 5 (2005): 579–99.

52 Eui-Hang Shin, "Political Demography of Korea: Political Effects of Changes in Population Composition and Distribution," *East Asia: An International Quarterly*, Vol. 19, No. 1 (Spring–Summer 2001): 175–8.

53 *Hangyoreh 21*, No. 536 (November 25, 2004) <http://h21.hani.co.kr/section-021067000/2004/11/ 021067000200411250536033.html>

54 See, for example, Choi Jang Jip, *Minjuhwa ihu ŭi minjujuŭi* (Seoul: Humanitas, 2003).

55 See Doh-Chull Shin and Byong-Kuen Jhee, "How Does Democratic Regime Change Affect Mass Political Ideology? A Case Study of South Korea in Comparative Perspective," *International Political Science Review*, Vol. 26, No. 4 (October 2005): 393–4.

Chapter 2

1 See for example, Pyong Choon Hahm, "Korea's 'Mendicant Mentality'?" *Foreign Affairs*, Vol. 43, No. 1 (October 1964): 165–74.

2 For an overview of the "developmental state" model, see for example Meredith Woo-Cumings, ed., *Developmental State* (Ithaca: Cornell University Press, 1999). For details of the "flying geese model," see for example Kiyoshi Kojima, "The 'Flying Geese' Model of Asian Economic Development: Origin, Theoretical Extensions, and Regional Policy Implications," *Journal of Asian Economics*, Vol. 11, No. 4 (Fall 2000): 375–401.

3 Atul Kohli, *State-Directed Development: Political Power and Industrialization in the Global Periphery* (Cambridge: Cambridge University Press, 2004), pp. 385–6.

4 US aid averaged around 13% of Korean GNP for the period 1953–59. Han'guk ŭnhaeng, *Han'guk ŭi kungmin chŏch'uk* (Seoul: Han'guk ŭnhaeng, 1961), p. 9.

5 See Jung-en Woo, *Race to the Swift: the State and Finance in Korean Industrialization* (New York: Columbia University Press, 1991), pp. 43–72.

6 Yu Kwang-ho, "Chang Myŏn chŏnggwŏn'gi ŭi kyŏngje chŏngch'aek," in Han'guk Chŏngsin Munhwa Yŏn'guwŏn, ed., *Han'guk hyŏndaesa ŭi chaeinsik 5: 1960 nyŏndae ŭi chŏnhwanjŏk sanghwang kwa Chang Myŏn chŏnggwŏn* (Seoul: Orŭm, 1998), pp. 119–91; and David C. Kang, *Crony Capitalism: Corruption and Development in South Korea and the Philippines* (Cambridge: Cambridge University Press, 2002), pp. 65–74, 182–3.

7 Alexander Gerschenkron, *Economic Backwardness in Historical Perspective* (Harvard University Press, Boston, 1966), p. 7.

8 Alice Amsden, *Asia's Next Giant: South Korea and Late Industrialization* (New York: Oxford University Press, 1989), pp. 139–40.

9 For details on all the implications of the 1965 treaty, see Hyung Gu Lynn, "Systemic Lock: The Institutionalization of History in Post-1965 South Korea–Japan Relations," *Journal of American East Asian Relations*, Vol. 9, No. 1–2 (Spring/Summer 2000): 55–84.

10 See, for details, Pak Kŭn-Ho, *Kankoku keizai hatten to Betonamu sensō* (Tokyo: Ochanomizu shobō, 1993).

11 Eun Mee Kim, *Big Business, Strong State: Collusion and Conflict in South Korean Development, 1960–1990* (Albany: State University of New York Press, 1997), pp. 51–211.

12 Some scholars label these values "Confucian." See Kyong-Dong Kim, "Confucianism and Capitalist Development in East Asia," in Leslie Sklair, ed., *Capitalism and Development* (London: Routledge, 1994), p. 99.

13 Yu Ch'ŏl-Kyu, "80-nyŏndae huban ihu kyŏngje kujo pyŏnhwa ŭi ŭimi," *Ch'angjak kwa pip'yŏng*, No. 130 (Fall 2005): 75–6.

14 Suk Bum Yoon, "Regional Income Distribution in South Korea," *Journal of the Asia Pacific Economy*, Vol. 5, No. 1–2 (February 2000): 57–72.

15 Samuel S. Kim, "Korea and Globalization (Segyehwa): A Framework for Analysis," in Samuel S. Kim, ed., *Korea's Globalization* (Cambridge: Cambridge University Press, 2000), pp. 1–28.

16 The debt-to-equity ratio is generated by dividing total liabilities by shareholder equity. It does not reflect a firm's growth potential, but is often used to gauge financial durability.

17 Hong Tŏk-Ryul, "Chaebŏl kwŏnryŏk, ŏje onŭl kurigo naeil," *Yŏksa pip'yŏng*, No. 77 (Fall 2006): 98–101.

18 Linda M. Weiss, "Guiding Globalisation in East Asia: New Roles for Old Developmental States," in Linda M. Weiss, ed., *States in the Global Economy: Bringing Domestic Institutions Back In* (Cambridge: Cambridge University Press, 2003), pp. 245–70.

19 Iain Pirie, "Better by Design: Korea's Neoliberal Economy," *Pacific Review*, Vol. 18, No. 3 (September 2005): 355–74.

20 James Crotty and Lee Kang-kook, "The Effects of Neoliberal 'Reforms' on the Post-Crisis Korean Economy," *Review Of Radical Political Economics*, Vol. 38, No. 4 (December 2006): 669–75.

21 Judith Cherry, "Killing Five Birds with One Stone: Inward Foreign Direct Investment in Post-Crisis Korea," *Pacific Affairs*, Vol. 79, No. 1 (Spring 2006): 17.

22 The politics of IMF decision-making has tended to favour pro-US countries. Strom C. Thacker, "High Politics of IMF Lending," *World Politics*, Vol. 52, No. 1 (October 1999): 38–75.

23 Jiho Jang, "Economic Crisis and Its Consequences," *Social Indicators Research*, Vol. 62, No. 1 (April 2003): 56.

24 Hyun-Chin Lim, and Jin-Ho Jang, "Neo-liberalism in Post-Crisis South Korea: Social Conditions and Outcomes," *Journal of Contemporary Asia*, Vol. 36, No. 4 (Winter 2006): 455.

25 Edward S. Mason et al., *The Economic and Social Modernization of the Republic of Korea* (Cambridge, MA: Harvard University Press, 1980), p. 408.

26 Paul Kuznets, *Economic Growth and Structure in the Republic of Korea* (New Haven: Yale University Press, 1977), pp. 106–7.

27 There are still debates about what types of Gini coefficients best reflect inequality and facilitate international comparisons. Although the theoretical range is 0 to 1, the effective range usually falls between 0.2 and 0.6.

28 David Rueda and Jonas Pontusson, "Wage Inequality and Varieties of Capitalism," *World Politics*, Vol. 52, No. 3 (April 2000): 350–83.

29 Yun To-Hyŏn, Kim Sŏng-Hŭi, and Kim Chŏng-Hun, *Han'guk ŭi pin'gon kwa pulp'yŏngdŭng* (Seoul: Minjuhwa undong kinyŏm saŏphoe, 2004), pp. 82–3.

30 Lee Joung-Woo, "Financial Crisis and Economic Inequality in Korea," *Korea Journal*, Vol. 42, No. 1 (Spring 2002): 192–9.

31 Kim Kyŏng-Ok, *Blockbuster ŭi hwansang, Han'guk yŏnghwa ŭi narcissism* (Seoul: Ch'aek sesang, 2002), pp. 59–72.

32 The number of admissions for 2006 was the third highest in South Korean history, after 1969 (173 million) and 1968 (171 million).

33 Kim Hyun Mee, "Korean TV Dramas in Taiwan: With an Emphasis on the Localization Process," *Korea Journal*, Vol. 45, No. 4 (Winter 2005): 202.

34 Hirata Yukie, *Han'guk ŭl sobihanŭn Ilbon-Hallyu, yŏsŏng, durama* (Seoul: Ch'aek sesang, 2005), p. 46.

35 In its heyday from the 1960s into the mid-1970s, before television sets were common in households, domestic films had been the main form of entertainment. From the late 1960s into the early 1970s, over 200 movies were made per year, although many were of questionable quality.

36 Lee Dong-Hoo, "Cultural Contact with Japanese TV Dramas: Modes of Reception and Narrative Transparency," in Koichi Iwabuchi, ed., *Feeling Asian Modernities* (Hong Kong: Hong Kong University Press, 2004), pp. 270–1.

37 In May 1996, the government allowed local governments up to 40 days of discretionary screening: this meant that local governments could allow theaters to play Korean films for 126 days in larger cities and 106

days in smaller cities.

38 Doobo Shim, "Hybridity and the Rise of Korean Popular Culture in Asia," *Media, Culture and Society*, Vol. 28, No. 1 (2005): 32–3.

39 Pak Chi-Yŏn, "Pak Chŏng-Hŭi kŭndaehwa ch'egye ŭi yŏnghwa chŏngch'aek," in Chu Yu-Sin et al., *Han'guk yŏnghwa wa kŭndaesŏng* (Seoul: Pantagram, 2005), pp. 209–10.

40 Jim Dator and Yongseok Seo, " Korea as the Wave of a Future: The Emerging Dream Society of Icons and Aesthetic Experience," *Journal of Futures Studies*, Vol. 9, No. 1 (August 2004): 31–44.

41 Paek Wŏn-Dam, *Tong Asea ŭi munhwa sŏnt'aek – Hallyu* (Seoul: Pantagram, 2005), p. 288.

42 Pak Kwang-Ju, "Asea kongdongch'e, hyŏnsil inga sinho inga" in Sejong yŏn'guso, ed., *Asea wa segyehwa* (Seoul: Sejong yŏn'guso, 1998), pp. 126–236.

43 This comic book was a rant about outstanding historical issues between Japan and South Korea, with only some perfunctory references to the Korean Wave itself. For a critique of the various problems with the Ken-Kanryū series, see Tanaka Hiroshi and Itagaki Ryūta, eds., *Nikkan aratana hajimari no tame ni* (Tokyo: Iwanami shoten, 2007).

44 Suzuki Yūko, *Jūgun ianfu, naisen kekkon* (Tokyo: Miraisha, 1992), pp. 76, 83, 106.

45 Kim Ŭng-Ryŏl, "Chae-Han Ilboninch'ŏ ŭi saenghwalsa," *Han'guk yŏn'gu*, No. 8 (2000): 463, 469.

46 Kamisaka Fuyuko, *Kyŏngju Nazare-en: wasurerareta Nihonjintsuma tachi* (Seoul: Chūō kōronsha, 1982), pp. 23–4, 243–4.

47 Kasetani Tomoo, "Seoul ŭi 'Chinatown': paeje wa tonghwa sokŭi chae-Han Hwagyo essunsity," *Han'guk yŏn'gu*, No. 9 (2001): 337.

48 Chang Su-Hyŏn, "Han-Hwa, ku paeje ŭi yŏksa," *Tangdae pip'yŏng*, No. 4 (2001): 107–58.

49 Some 197,000 South Korean children were sent abroad for adoption between 1955 and 1998. Eleana Kim, "Wedding Citizenship and Culture: Korean Adoptees and the Global Family of Korea," *Social Text*, Vol. 21, No. 1 (Spring 2003): 63.

50 See Kwŏn K'oe-Hyŏn, "Lai Daihan dŭl, ch'inja sosong sŭngsoe naengdamhan panŭng," *Hangyoreh*, February 28, 2002.

51 Katharine Moon, "Strangers in the Midst of Globalization: Migrant Workers and Korean Nationalism," in Samuel S. Kim, ed., *Korea's Globalization* (Cambridge: Cambridge University Press, 2000), pp. 147, 165–6.

52 Timothy C. Lim, "Race *from* the Bottom in South Korea: The Nexus between Civil Society and Transnational Migrants," *Asian Survey*, Vol. 43, No. 3 (May/June 2003): 440–1.

53 Minwon Lee, "Filipino Village in South Korea," *Community, Work and Family*, Vol. 9, No. 4 (November 2006): 429–40.

54 Tai-Hwan Kwon, "Demographic Trends and Their Social Implications," *Social Indicators Research*, Vol. 62, No. 1 (April 2003): 19–38.

55 Andrew Eungi Kim, "The Social Perils of the Korean Financial

Crisis," *Journal of Contemporary Asia*, Vol. 34, No. 2 (2004): 221–37.

56 Baochang Gu and Krishna Roy, "Sex Ratio at Birth in China, with Reference to Other Areas in East Asia: What We Know," *Asia-Pacific Population Journal*, Vol. 10, No. 3 (September 1995): 17–42.

57 Chai Bin Park and Chai Bin Park, "Consequences of Son Preference in a Low-Fertility Society: Imbalance of the Sex Ratio at Birth in Korea," *Population and Development Review*, Vol. 21, No. 1 (March 1995): 59–84.

Chapter 3

1 This poem is from the website for a documentary on Kim Jong-Chol produced by Jinnet Productions, "Kita Chŏsen no ŏji – shirazareru sugao ni semaru," originally aired June 21, 2006. Viewed at http://www.jinnet.co.jp/sakuhin15.htm

2 Ludwig Feurbach, *The Essence of Christianity*, trans. George Eliot (New York: Harper & Row, 1957), p. 82.

3 Furuta Hiroshi, *Chōsen minzoku o yomi toku: Kita to Minami ni kyōtsō suru mono* (Tokyo: Chikuma shobō, 2005), pp. 56–8. See also, Karl Marx and Frederick Engels, *The German Ideology: Part One* (London: Lawrence & Wishart, 1970), p. 25.

4 For more details, see for example Robert C. Taylor, ed., *Stalinism: Essays in Historical Interpretation* (London: Transaction Publishers, 1999).

5 Bruce Cumings, "The Corporate State in North Korea," in Hagen Koo, ed., *State and Society in Contemporary Korea* (New York: Cornell University Press, 1993), pp. 197–230.

6 Kyo-Duk Lee, *The Successor Theory of North Korea* (Seoul: Korea Institute for National Unification, 2004), pp. 4–9, 21.

7 Lee Chong-sŏk, *Hyŏndae Puk-Han ŭi ihae* (Seoul: Yŏksa pip'yŏngsa, 2000), pp. 216-220.

8 Wada Haruki, *Kita Chōsen yūgekitai kokka no genzai* (Tokyo: Iwanami shoten, 1998), p. 131.

9 Suzuki Masayuki, *Kita Chōsen: shakaishugi to dentō no kyōmei* (Tokyo: Tokyo daigaku shuppankai, 1992), pp. 119–25.

10 Lin Jinshu, *Chaoxian jingji* (Changchun: Jilin renmin chubanshe, 2000), pp. 229–30.

11 Han S. Park, *North Korea: The Politics of Unconventional Wisdom* (New York: Lynne Rienner, 2002), pp. 41–50.

12 H. Gordon Skilling, "Interest Groups and Communist Politics Revisited," *World Politics*, Vol. 36, No. 1 (October 1983): 21–3.

13 See Dae-Sook Suh, *Kim Il Sung: The North Korean Leader* (New York: Columbia University Press, 1988), pp. 10–11; and Wada Haruki, *Kim Il-Sung to Manshū kō-Nichi sensō* (Tokyo: Heibonsha, 1992), p. 140.

14 Charles Armstrong, *The North Korean Revolution, 1945–1950* (Ithaca: Cornell University Press, 2003), pp. 116–19.

15 Andrei Lankov, *Crisis in North Korea: The Failure of De-Stalinization* (Honolulu: University of Hawai'i Press, 2005), pp. 3–4, 121–35.

16 Hagiwara Ryō, *Rachi to kaku to gashi no kuni Kita Chōsen* (Tokyo:

Bungei shunju, 2003), p. 64.

17 Suzuki Masayuki, "Chōsen jinmingun ni okeru yuiitsu shisō taikei no kakuritsu," in Izumi Hajime and Chang Dal-Joong, eds., *Kim Chŏng-Il taisei no Kita Chōsen: seiji, gaikō, keizai, shisō* (Tokyo: Keio gijuku daigaku shuppankai, 2004), pp. 159–64.

18 For other examples of the artwork of the Kim Il-Sung cult, see Jane Portal, *Art Under Control in North Korea* (London: Reaktion Books, 2005), pp. 81–104.

19 Catalan Augustin Stoica, "Once Upon a Time There Was a Big Party: The Social Basis of the Romanian Communist Party (Part I)," *East European Politics and Societies*, Vol. 19, No. 4 (November 2005): 700.

20 There have been numerous fakes produced in China that have been sold abroad since the late 1980s. One of the telltale signs is that back pinholder clasps are welded together from two separate "arms" in the genuine one: the fake ones generally use u-rings welded onto the back.

21 Ch'oe Chin-Uk, "Chipkwŏn kwajŏng," in T'ongil yŏn'guwŏn, ed., *Kim Chŏng-Il yŏn'gu: lidŏship kwa kwajŏng (I)* (Seoul: T'ongil yŏn'guwŏn, 2001), pp. 29–36.

22 Kim Il-Sung was revived by Soviet doctors that Kim Jong-Il brought in. Alexandre Y. Mansourov, "Emergence of the Second Republic: The Kim Regime Adapts to the Challenges of Modernity," in Young Whan Kihl and Hong Nack Kim, eds., *North Korea: The Politics of Regime Survival* (Armonk: M.E. Sharpe, 2006), p. 43.

23 On the Holy Spirit as eschatology, see for example, C.F.D. Moule, "The Holy Spirit in the Scriptures," *Forgiveness and Reconciliation: Biblical and Theological Essays* (London: SPCK, 1998), p. 124.

24 Kim Jong-Il, *Wagatō no Juche shisō ni tsuite* (Pyongyang: Oegungmun ch'ulp'ansa, 1985), pp. 13–14.

25 In his 1902 pamphlet, *What is to be done?* Lenin argued that a successful revolution required a highly centralized, loyal, and secretive core of "professional revolutionaries" that would act as the vanguard of the working classes. Such a group was necessary as the workers were chained to their jobs for most of the day and therefore could not digest Marxist theory or comprehend systemic problems.

26 On details of the reforms, see for example Tim Cheek, *Living With Reform: China Since 1989* (London: Zed Books, 2006), pp. 62–73.

27 Chŏng Yŏng-Ch'ŏl, *Kim Chŏng-Il lidŏsip yŏn'gu* (Seoul: Sŏn'in, 2005), pp. 327–8.

28 Kim Jong-Il, "Sahoejuŭi nŭn kwahak ida," *Rodong sinmun*, November 1, 1994.

29 Kim Jong-Il, *On the Juche Idea* (Pyongyang: Foreign Languages Publishing House, 1982), p. 32.

30 For details on the recent rise of Chinese nationalism, see Richard Baum, "Present Nationalism and Communist Power," in David Arase, ed., *The Challenge of Change: East Asia in the New Millennium* (Berkeley: Institute of East Asian Studies, 2003), pp. 19–23.

31 Chŏng Yŏng-Ch'ŏl, *Puk-Han ŭi kaehyŏk, kaebang: ijung chŏllyak*

kwa silli sahoejuŭi (Seoul: Sŏn'in, 2004), pp. 52–6.

32 Kongdan Oh and Ralph C. Hassig, *North Korea: Through the Looking Glass* (Washington: Brookings Institution Press, 2000), p. 27.

33 For details, see for example, Samuel Decalo, "African Personalist Dictatorships," *Journal of Modern African Studies*, Vol. 23, No. 2 (June 1985): 222–6; and Robert H. Jackson and Carl G. Rosberg, "Personalist Rule: Theory and Practice in Africa," *Comparative Politics*, Vol. 16, No. 4 (July 1984): 430–36.

34 Chae-Jin Lee and Stephanie Hsieh, "China's Two-Korea Policy at Trial: The Hwang Chang Yop Crisis," *Pacific Affairs*, Vol. 74, No. 3 (Fall 2001): 325–6.

35 Sin Sang-Ok and his wife, Ch'oe Ŭn-Hŭi, were kidnapped and brought to North Korea in 1978. They defected in 1985. The North Korean position is that the couple had originally defected to the North to escape the oppressive policies of Park Chung-Hee. Ch'oe Ŭn-Hŭi, and Sin Sang-Ok, *Kim Chŏng-Il wangguk*, Vol. 2 (Seoul: Tonga ilbosa, 1988), p. 72.

36 The cause of death of the Mother is not mentioned in her official biography. *Kim Chŏng-Suk chŏn* (Pyongyang: Oegungmun ch'ulp'ansa, 2002), pp. 440–41. Some defectors asserted that she died of complications from a miscarriage, while others claimed that having learnt of Kim Il-Sung's infidelities, she refused treatment after the difficult birth of her daughter.

37 P'yŏng-Il's birth year varies by source from either 1953 or 1954. Yŏng-Il's year of birth is cited as either 1955 or 1956. There are also conflicting defector accounts of a marriage before Kim Chŏng-Suk, and of another illegitimate son born in 1951. Kim Yŏng-Il completed a PhD in Electric Engineering at Humboldt University in 1984. His name was transliterated as "Kim Jong-Il," possibly leading to the rumours of Kim Jong-Il having studied at the Air Force Academy in East Germany. Kim P'yŏng-Il, some defectors claim, was the one who learnt to fly civilian aircraft at an East German airport.

38 Fujimoto Kenji, *Kim Chŏng-Il no ryōrinin* (Tokyo: Fusōsha, 2004), p. 144.

39 Madeleine Albright, *Madame Secretary* (New York: Miramax, 2003), pp. 464–6.

40 Lee Chong-Sŏk and Paek Hak-Sun, *Kim Chŏng-Il sidae ŭi tang gwa kukga kigu* (Seoul: Sejong Yŏn'guso, 2000), pp. 16–19.

41 Kim Yŏng-Ryong, who had been made a general by Kim Il-Sung in 1992, reportedly committed suicide by drinking poison after his purge.

42 "Internet Cafes Popular Among North Korean Youths," *Korea Times*, November 14, 2004.

43 Yamamoto Kōichi, *Kita, mita, totta: Kita Chōsen* (Tokyo: Shūeisha, 2003), p. 46.

44 An Yong-Kyun, "Kim Chŏng-Il 4-bŏn puinsŏl," *Wŏlgan Chosŏn*, July 24, 2006.

45 The story, initially broken by a conservative Japanese newspaper, asserts that a "Northeast Asian" country's intelligence service succeeded

in tapping the calls. "Bei-kinyū seisai – aegu Kita," *Sankei Shinbun*, May 1, 2006.

46 See also Bradley Martin, *Under the Loving Care of the Fatherly Leader: North Korea and the Kim Dynasty* (New York: St Martin's Press, 2004), p. 702.

47 See, for example, Lee Kyo-Kwan, "'Kim Chŏng-Ch'ŏl badge' ga tŭngjang haetta," *Chugan Chosŏn*, March 5, 2006 <http://www.chosun.com/magazine/news/ 200603/200603040096.html>

48 Suzuki Takuma, *Kim Chŏng-Il to Ko Yŏng-Hŭi* (Tokyo: Easto puresu 2005), pp. 195–209, 224, 289–90.

49 Ha Sin-Gi, *Kim Chŏng-Il no kōkeisha wa 'Zai-Nichi' no musuko* (Tokyo: Kōdansha, 2004), pp. 104–5.

50 Fujimoto Kenji, *Kim Chŏng-Il no ryōrinin*, pp. 125, 130.

51 Moreover, according to Fujimoto, Ko and Kim Ok were close, and Kim Ok had agreed to look after Ko's children after her death. Another defector with less direct contact with the "royal family" has claimed that the two had less than cordial relations.

52 Passage from the book by Emmanuel Goldstein/O'Brien in George Orwell, *1984* (New York: Signet, 1984 edition), p. 173.

Chapter 4

1 Lee U-Hong, *Angu na kyōwakoku: Kita Chōsen kōgyō no kikai* (Tokyo: Aki shobō, 1990), pp. 21–3.

2 Yang Mun-Su, *Kita Chōsen keizairon-keizai teimei no mekanizumu* (Tokyo: Shinzansha, 2000), pp. 167–8.

3 Vasily Mikheev, "Reforms of the North Korean Economy: Requirements, Plans and Hopes," *Korean Journal of Defense Analysis*, Vol. 5, No. 1 (1993): 52–66.

4 Chŏng Kwang-Min, "Kita Chōsen no seiji keizai sisutemu to shokuryō entitorumento," *Hikaku keizai taisei gakkai nenpō*, Vol. 42, No. 1 (January 2005): 25–34, 27.

5 Vice President Richard Cheney's annual salary directly from his office for 2004 was $203,000, and his annual travel and entertainment budget (non-taxable) was $90,000. These figures do not include income from other sources.

6 Mark Nord, Margaret Andrews, and Steven Carlson, *Household Food Security in the United States, 2004* (Washington DC: United States Department of Agriculture, 2005), pp. 12, 36.

7 Norodom Sihanouk, *War and Hope: The Case for Cambodia* (New York: Pantheon Books, 1980), p. 86.

8 Young-Chul Chung, "North Korean Reform and Opening: Dual Strategy and 'Silli (Practical) Socialism'," *Pacific Affairs*, Vol. 77, No. 2 (Summer 2004): 283–304.

9 Although he came close to playing in the National Basketball Association (NBA) in the US, due to international tensions Lee only played in North Korea. Yao Ming, originally from China, is the tallest player in the NBA at 226 cm, weighing 134 kg. See Michael Murphy, "Big

Disappointment," *Houston Chronicle*, June 22, 2002. <http://www.chron.
com/disp/story.mpl/special/yao/1465758.html>

10 Some 93,000 Koreans living in Japan, most of whom were originally from the southern half of Korea but with North Korean affiliations, "returned" to the North from 1959 on. Expecting the country to look like the propaganda images, most of them suffered from discrimination. For details see, for example, Aoki Atsuko, "Kioku jigyō ni okeru 'Nihonjin tsuma' o megutte," in Takasagi Sōji and Pak Chŏng-jun, eds., *Kikoku undō towa nanndattanoka* (Tokyo: Heibonsha, 2005), pp. 121–44.

11 Kim Il Sung, *Kim Il Sung – Works*, Vol. 28 (Pyongyang: Foreign Languages Publishing House, 1986), pp. 102, 110.

12 Kim Hyun-Hee, *The Tears of My Soul* (New York: William Morrow, 1993), p. 14.

13 For details on SOFE, see for example, Stanley L. Bruce and Craig R. MacPhee, "From Marx to Markets: Reform of the University Economics Curriculum in Russia," *Journal of Economic Education*, Vol. 26, No. 2 (Spring 1995): 183–4.

14 Hwang Chang-Yŏp, *Kaein ŭi saengmyŏng poda kwijunghan minjok ŭi saengmyŏng* (Seoul: Sidae chŏngsin, 1999), p. 21.

15 See Nam Sŏng-Uk, *Hyŏndae Puk-Han ŭi singnyangnan gwa hyŏpdong nongjang kaehyŏk* (Seoul: Han'ul, 2004).

16 Chŏng Ŭng-Ki, et al., "Puk-Han pyŏ p'umjong ŭi nae'naengsŏng kwallyŏn hyŏngjil bunsŏk," *Hanyukji*, Vol. 32, No. 1 (Spring 2000): 45–50.

17 The Japanese developer of this strain of rice, Ishimoto Seiichi, became the first foreigner given a municipal honor by the city of Dalian. Better irrigation also helps explain the greater success in China.

18 Amano Takahisa, "Kita Chōsen no ine no shūryō teika ni tsuite kangaeru," *Sekai heiwa kenkyū*, Vol. 31, No. 1 (Winter 2005): 29–33.

19 Enver Hoxha, *The Artful Albanian: Memoirs of Enver Hoxha* (London: Chatto & Windus, 1986), p. 316.

20 Gotō Fujio, "Kita Chōsen no shokuryō yunyū: 1985–1999," *Chūō daigaku keizai kenkyūjo nenpō*, No. 31 (2000): 112–13.

21 Marcus Noland, *Avoiding the Apocalypse: The Future of the Two Koreas* (Washington DC: Institute for International Economics, 2000), pp. 173–4.

22 See the report produced by the law firm DLA Piper, and US Committee for Human Rights in North Korea, *Failure to Protect: A Call for the UN Security Council to Act in North Korea* (DLA Piper, and US Committee for Human Rights in North Korea, October 2006), pp. 83–93.

23 Andrew S. Natsios, *The Great North Korean Famine: Famine, Politics, and Foreign Policy* (Washington: United States Institute of Peace, 2001), p. 108.

24 Bradley Martin, *Under the Loving Care of the Fatherly Leader: North Korea and the Kim Dynasty* (New York: St Martin's Press, 2004), pp. 555–61, 577.

25 Hazel Smith, *Hungry for Peace: International Security, Humani-*

tarian Assistance, and Social Change in North Korea (Washington DC: United States Institute for Peace, 2005), pp. 118–23.

26 This is not to suggest that there is an absence of domestic laws that protect rights – in theory at least. See, for example, Mashood A. Baderin, "A Comparative Analysis of the Right to a Fair Trial and Due Process under International Human Rights Law and Saudi Arabian Domestic Law," *International Journal of Human Rights*, Vol. 10, No. 3 (September 2006): 241–84.

27 Ch'oe Su-Yŏng, *Puk-Han ŭi kangsŏng taeguk kŏnsŏl: kyŏngje pumun chungsim ŭro* (Seoul: T'ongil yŏn'guwŏn, 1999), pp. 71–3.

28 Amartya Sen, *Poverty and Famines: An Essay on Entitlement and Deprivation* (Oxford: Clarendon Press, 1981).

29 See, for example, Michael Ellman, "The 1947 Soviet Famine and the Entitlement Approach to Famines," *Cambridge Journal of Economics*, Vol. 24, No. 5 (September 2000): 603–30; and Justin Y. Lin and Dennis T. Yang, "Food Availability, Entitlements and the Chinese Famine of 1959–61," *Economic Journal*, Vol. 110, No. 460 (January 2000): 136–58.

30 Kim Yŏng-hun and Kim Un-Gŏn, "Puk-Han ŭi singnyang sugŭp," *Nongch'on kyŏngje*, Vol. 16, No. 3 (September 1993): 90–2; also Sŏ Tong-Ik, *Inmin ŭi sanŭn mosŭp*, Vol. 2 (Seoul: Charyowŏn, 1995), pp. 203–49.

31 Kimura Mitsuhiko, *Kita Chōsen no keizai-kigen, keisei, hōkai* (Tokyo: Sōbunsha, 1994), p. 194.

32 Don Oberdorfer, *The Two Koreas*, pp. 96–9.

33 Jae-Jung Suh, "Assessing the Military Balance in Korea," *Asian Perspective*, Vol. 28, No. 4 (Winter 2004): 67–8.

34 Miyatsuka Toshio, *Gambaruzo! Kita Chōsen* (Tokyo: Shōgakkan, 2004), pp. 48–9.

35 Nicholas Eberstadt and Judith Bannister, *The Population of North Korea* (Berkeley: Institute of East Asian Studies, Center for Korean Studies, 1992), pp. 29, 64.

36 See Hussein Solomon and Gerrie Swart, "Libya's Foreign Policy in Flux," *African Affairs*, Vol. 104, No. 416 (July 2005): 469–2.

37 Roland Bleiker, *Divided Korea: Towards a Culture of Reconciliation* (Minneapolis: University of Minnesota Press, 2005).

38 KEDO <http://www.kedo.org/>

39 Bill Clinton, *My Life* (New York: Knopf, 2004), p. 938

40 Larry A. Niksch, "North Korea's Weapons of Mass Destruction," in Young Whan Kihl and Hong Nack Kim, eds., *North Korea: The Politics of Regime Survival*, p. 100.

41 Fujimoto Kenji, *Kim Chŏng-Il no ryōrinin*, p. 142.

42 Paul French, *North Korea: The Paranoid Peninsula* (London: Zed Books, 2005), p. 207.

43 Korean Institute for National Unification, *White Paper on Human Rights in North Korea, 2006* (Seoul: Korean Institute for National Unification, 2006), pp. 11–12.

44 See for example, Kang Chol-Hwan, *Aquariums of Pyongyang: Ten Years in the North Korean Gulag* (New York: Basic Books, 2001), pp.

184–95.

45 Lee Yŏng-Hwa, "Kita Chōsen baburu no hateni nokosareta 'gohō' to 'kyohō' no zangai," *Sapio,* May 12, 2004.

46 Kyungja Jung and Bronwen Dalton, "Rhetoric Versus Reality for the Women of North Korea: Mothers of the Revolution," *Asian Survey,* Vol. 46, No. 5 (September/ October 2006): 756–7.

47 Kathleen Davis, "Brides, Bruises and the Border: The Trafficking of North Korean Women into China," *SAIS Review,* Vol. 26, No. 1 (Winter–Spring 2006): 131–41.

48 "North Korean Computer Game Goes on Sale in South Korea," *Sydney Morning Herald,* September 7, 2006. <http://www.smh.com.au/news/Technology/North-Korean-computer-game-goes-on-sale-in-South-Korea/2006/09/07/1157222264848.html>

49 Yamamoto Kōichi, *Kita, mita, totta – Kita Chōsen* (Tokyo: Shūeisha, 2003), p. 26. For details on the abductions issue and subsequent reaction, see for example, Patricia Steinhoff, "Kidnapped Japanese in North Korea: the New Left Connection," *Journal of Japanese Studies,* Vol. 30, No. 1 (Winter 2004): 123–42; and Hyung Gu Lynn, "Vicarious Traumas: Television and Public Opinion in Japan's North Korea Policy," *Pacific Affairs,* Vol. 79, No. 3 (Fall 2006): 482–508.

50 For details, see, Ruediger Frank, "Economic Reforms in North Korea (1998-2004): Systemic Restrictions, Quantitative Analysis, Ideological Background," *Journal of the Asia Pacific Economy,* Vol. 10, No. 3 (August 2005): 278–311.

51 Albert Camus, *The Fall* (New York: Vintage, 1991), p. 55.

Chapter 5

1 Kohari Susumu, *Kankokujin wa, kō kangaeteiru* (Tokyo: Shinchō shinsho, 2004), pp. 96–7.

2 See also the novel by Ahn Junghyo, *Silver Stallion: a Novel of Korea* (New York: Soho Press, 1990) for a depiction of rapes and their long-term aftermaths during the Korean War.

3 Katharine Moon, "Resurrecting Prostitutes and Overturning Treaties: Gender Politics in the "Anti-American" Movement in South Korea," *Journal of Asian Studies,* Vol. 66, No. 1 (February 2007): 129–57.

4 Chungang Ilbo and Hyŏndae kyŏngje yŏn'guwŏn, eds., *Sedae kaldŭng e kwanhan kungmin yŏron chosa* (Seoul: Hyŏndae kyŏngje yŏn'guwŏn, 2004), p. 15.

5 Meredith Woo-Cumings, "Unilateralism and Its Discontents: The Passing of the Cold War Alliance and Changing Public Opinion in the Republic of Korea," in David I. Steinberg, ed., *Korean Attitudes towards the United States: Changing Dynamics* (Armonk: M.E. Sharpe, 2005), pp. 67–8.

6 Mitchell B. Lerner, *The Pueblo Incident: A Spy Ship and the Failure of American Foreign Policy* (Lawrence: University Press of Kansas, 2002), pp. 236–7.

7 The story of the secret unit was the basis of the 2003 South Korean

film dramatization, *Silmido*.

8 The Burmese government captured two North Korean soldiers, and killed another during the manhunt for the culprits. The two captured agents received the death sentence, but one was released and eventually applied for residency in South Korea, obtaining permission to live there in 2006.

9 Kang In-Ch'ŏl, "Han'guk kaesingyo pangongjuŭi ŭi hyŏngsŏng gwa chaesaengsan," *Yoksa pip'yŏng*, No. 70 (Spring 2005): 56–7.

10 Lew Young-Ick, *Yi Sŭng-Man ŭi salm gwa kkum* (Seoul: Chungang ilbosa, 1996), pp. 221-223.

11 *Chosŏn chungang yŏngam 1999* (Pyongyang: Chosŏn chungang t'ongsinsa, 1999); and *Chosŏn chungang yŏngam 2000* (Pyongyang: Chosŏn chungang t'ongsinsa, 2000).

12 Chung Ok-Nim, "The Role of South Korea's NGOs: The Political Context," in Gordon Flake and Scott Snyder, eds., *Paved with Good Intentions: The NGO Experience in North Korea* (Westport: Praeger, 2003), p. 106.

13 Kim T'ae-Hyŏn, "Puk-Han haebŏp," *Han'guk ilbo*, December 17, 2006.

14 Suh Jae-Jean, et al., *White Paper on Human Rights in North Korea 2003* (Seoul: Korean Institute for National Unification, 2003), pp. 208–9.

15 Pak Min-Hŭi, "'Saet'ŏmin ilmanmyŏng sidae': kŭdŭl to iot ida," *Hangyoreh*, February 13, 2007.

16 Pak Yŏng-Ho, et al., *T'ongil sinario wa t'ongil kwanjŏng ŭi chŏngch'aek pangan: ironjŏk model gwa chŏnmunga insik chosa* (Seoul: T'ongil yŏn'guwŏn, 2002), pp. 8–10.

17 Lee Kŭm-Sun et al., *Pukhan it'al chumin chŏgŭng silt'ae yŏn'gu* (Seoul: T'ongil yon'guwŏn, 2003), pp. 158–67.

18 Kang Kwŏn-Ch'an, "Puk-Han it'al chumin chiwŏn chŏngch'aek punsŏk," *Minjok yŏn'gu*, Vol. 14 (March 2005): 39–40.

19 Cho Min-Yŏng, *Puk-Han sahoe ŭi saeinsik* (Seoul: Namp'ung, 1988), pp. 232–8.

20 Kim Tong-Uk, "Saet'ŏmin yŏsŏng sillanggam cheiljokkŏn ŭn 'ch'egyŏk'," *Tonga ilbo*, November 27, 2006.

21 Lee Hyŏn-Jŏng, "Simch'ung intŏbyu – Saet'ŏmin Kim Hyŏng-Dŏk ssi," *Polinews*, March 11, 2007 <http://www.polinews.co.kr/interview/deep?interview?view.php?listmode=interview&no=293>

22 Im Hyŏn-Jin and Chŏng Yŏng-Ch'ŏl, *21 segi t'ongil Han'guk ŭl hyanghan mosaek* (Seoul: Seoul taehak ch'ulpanbu, 2005), pp. 279–315.

23 A. James McAdams, *Germany Divided: From the Wall to Reunification* (Princeton: Princeton University Press, 2003), pp. 77, 167.

24 Paul Dresch, *A History of Modern Yemen* (Cambridge: Cambridge University Press. 2000), pp. 120–3, 149–50.

25 Hwang In-Kwan, "Korean Reunification from a Comparative Perspective," in Young Whan Kihl, ed., *Korea and the World: Beyond the Cold War* (Boulder: Westview, 1994), pp. 291–2.

26 Selig S. Harrison, *Korean Endgame: A Strategy for Reunification*

and US Disengagement (Princeton: Princeton University Press, 2002), pp. 97–8.

27 Roy Grinker, *Korea and Its Futures: Unification and the Unfinished War* (New York: St Martin's Press, 1998), p. 23.

28 Ham Pyŏng-Su et al., *NGO rŭl t'onghan Nam-Puk-Han ch'ŏngsonyŏn kyoryu hyŏmnyŏk pangan yŏn'gu* (Seoul: T'ongil yŏn'guwŏn, 2000), pp. 30–40.

29 Kil Ŭn-Pae et al., *Nam-Puk-Han p'yŏnghwa kongjon ŭl wihan ch'ŏngsonyŏn ŭi sahoe munhwajŏk tongjilsŏng chŭngjin pangan yŏn'gu* (Seoul: T'ongil yŏn'guwŏn, 2001), p. 46.

30 John A. Agnew, *Place and Politics in Modern Italy* (Chicago: University of Chicago Press, 2002), pp. 14–15.

31 Nicodemus Fru Awasom, "The Reunification Question in Cameroon History: Was the Bride an Enthusiastic or a Reluctant One?" *Africa Today*, Vol. 47, No. 2 (Spring 2000): 91–119.

Suggestions for Further Reading

Aside from the works listed in the notes, there are many other books and articles in English on various aspects of the modern history of Korea and the contemporary histories of North and South Korea. The following is a limited sample of some works that deal with post-1940 themes and issues.

Textbooks

Cumings, Bruce. *Korea's Place in the Sun: A Modern History*. New York: W.W. Norton, 1997; 2005.

Eckert, Carter, Ki-baik Lee, Young Ick Lew, Michael Robinson, and Edward W. Wagner. *Korea Old and New: A History*. Seoul: Ilchogak, 1990.

Modern History Background

Cumings, Bruce. *The Origins of the Korean War*. 2 vols. Princeton: Princeton University Press, 1981; 1990.

Eckert, Carter. *Offspring of Empire: The Koch'ang Kims and the Colonial Origins of Korean Capitalism, 1876–1945*. Seattle, University of Washington Press, 1991.

Henderson, Gregory. *Korea: The Politics of the Vortex*. Cambridge: Harvard University Press, 1968.

Lee, Sang-Dawn. *Big Brother, Little Brother: The American Influence on Korean Culture in the Lyndon B. Johnson Years*. Lanham: Lexington Books, 2002.

Lee, Stephen H. *The Korean War*. London: Longman, 2001.

Matray, James I. *The Reluctant Crusade: American Foreign Policy in Korea, 1941–1950*. Honolulu: University of Hawai'i Press, 1985.

Myers, Ramon H., and Mark R. Peattie, eds. *The Japanese Colonial Empire, 1895–1945*. Princeton: Princeton University Press, 1984.

Shin, Gi-Wook, and Michael Robinson, eds. *Colonial Modernity in Korea*. Cambridge: Harvard University Asia Center, 1999.

South Korean Politics

Armstrong, Charles, ed. *Korean Society: Civil Society, Democracy and the State*. New York: Routledge, 2002.

Kim, Sunhyuk. The *Politics of Democratization in Korea: The Role of Civil Society*. Pittsburgh: University of Pittsburgh Press, 2000.

Larson, James F., and Heung-Soo Park. *Global Television and the Politics of the Seoul Olympics*. Boulder: Westview Press, 1993.

Lewis, Linda B. *Laying Claim to the Memory of May: A Look Back at the 1980 Kwangju Uprising*. Honolulu: University of Hawai'i, Center for Korean Studies, 2002.

Oberdorfer, Don. *The Two Koreas: A Contemporary History*. Reading: Addison-Wesley, 1997.

Oh, John Kie-chiang. *Korean Politics: The Quest for Democratization and Economic Development*. Ithaca: Cornell University Press, 1999.

Shin, Doh C. *Mass Politics and Culture in Democratizing Korea*. Cambridge: Cambridge University Press, 1999.

Shin, Gi-Wook, and Kyung Moon Hwang, eds. *Contentious Kwangju: The May 18 Uprising in Korea's Past and Present*. Lanham: Rowman & Littlefield, 2003.

Wells, Kenneth, ed. *South Korea's Minjung Movement: The Culture and Politics of Dissidence*. Honolulu: University of Hawaii Press, 1995.

South Korean Economy and Society

Amsden, Alice H. *Asia's Next Giant: South Korea and Late Industrialization*. New York: Oxford University Press, 1989.

Chang, Se-jin. *Financial Crisis and Transformation of Korean Business Groups: The Rise and Fall of Chaebols*. Cambridge: Cambridge University Press, 2003.

Eder, Norman. *Poisoned Prosperity: Development, Modernization, and the Environment in South Korea*. Armonk: M.E. Sharpe, 1996.

Haggard, Stephan. *Pathways from the Periphery: The Politics of Growth in the Newly Industrializing Countries*. Ithaca: Cornell University Press, 1990.

James, David E. and Kyung Hyun Kim, eds. *Im Kwon-Taek: The Making of a Korean National Cinema*. Detroit: Wayne State University Press, 2002.

Kang, David C. *Crony Capitalism: Corruption and Development in South Korea and the Philippines*. Cambridge: Cambridge University Press, 2002.

Kendall, Laurel. *Getting Married in Korea: Of Gender, Morality, and Modernity*. Berkeley: University of California Press, 1996.

Kim, Eun Mee. *Big Business, Strong State*. Albany: State University of New York Press, 1997.

Kim, Samuel S. *Korea's Globalization*. Cambridge: Cambridge University Press, 2000.

Koo, Hagen. *Korean Workers: The Culture and Politics of Class Formation*. Ithaca: Cornell University Press, 2001.

McHugh, Kathleen and Nancy Abelmann, eds. *South Korean Golden Age Melodrama: Gender, Genre, and National Cinema*. Detroit: Wayne State University Press, 2005.

Manzenreiter, Wolfram, and John Horne, eds. *Japan, Korea, and the 2002 World Cup*. London: Routledge, 2002.

Moon, Katharine H.S. *Sex Among Allies: Military Prostitution in US–Korea Relations*. New York: Columbia University Press, 1997.

Moon, Seungsook. *Militarized Modernity and Gendered Citizenship in South Korea*. Durham: Duke University Press, 2005.

Nelson, Laura. *Measured Excess: Status, Gender, and Consumer Nationalism in South Korea*. New York: Columbia University Press, 2000.

Ogle, George. *South Korea: Dissent within the Economic Miracle*. London: Zed Books, 1990.

Sorensen, Clark W. *Over the Mountains Are Mountains: Korean Peasant Households and Their Adaptations to Rapid Industrialization*. Seattle: University of Washington Press, 1988.

North Korea

Armstrong, Charles. *The North Korean Revolution, 1945–1950*. Ithaca: Cornell University Press, 2002.

Bleiker, Roland. *Divided Korea: Toward a Culture of Reconciliation*. Minneapolis: University of Minnesota Press, 2005.

Cha, Victor D. and David C. Kang. *Nuclear North Korea: A Debate on Engagement Strategies*. New York: Columbia University Press, 2003.

Cumings, Bruce. *North Korea: Another Country*. New York: New Press, 2004.

Eberstadt, Nicholas, and Judith Bannister. *The Population of North Korea*. Berkeley: Institute of East Asian Studies, Center for Korean Studies, 1992.

Kim, Samuel S., ed. *North Korean Foreign Relations in the Post-Cold War Era*. New York: Oxford University Press, 1998.

Lankov, Andrei. *From Stalin to Kim Il Song: the Formation of North Korea, 1945–1960*. London: C. Hurst & Company, 2002.

McCormack, Gavan. *Target North Korea: Pushing North Korea to the Brink of Nuclear Catastrophe*. New York: Nation Books, 2004.

Martin, Bradley. *Under the Loving Care of the Fatherly Leader: North Korea and the Kim Dynasty*. New York: St Martin's Press, 2004.

Noland, Marcus. *Korea After Kim Jong-Il*. Washington, DC: Institute for International Economics, 2004.

Oh, Kongdan, and Ralph C. Hassig. *North Korea: Through the Looking Glass*. Washington, DC: Brookings Institution Press, 2000.

Park, Han S. *North Korea: the Politics of Unconventional Wisdom*.

Boulder: Lynne Rienner Publishers, 2002.

Park, Kyung-Ae and Dalchoong Kim, eds. *Korean Security Dynamics in Transition*. New York: Palgrave, 2001.

Porter, Jane. *Art under Control in North Korea*. London: Reaktion Books, 2005.

Suh, Dae-Sook. *Kim Il Sung: The North Korean Leader*. New York: Columbia University Press, 1988.

Yang, Sung Chul. *Korea and Two Regimes: Kim Il Sung and Park Chung Hee*. Cambridge: Schenkman, 1981.

South Korea and North Korea — Foreign and Inter-Korean Relations

Cha, Victor D. *Alignment despite Antagonism: the United States–Korea–Japan Security Triangle*. Stanford: Stanford University Press, 1999.

Chung, Jae Ho. *Between Ally and Partner: Korea–China Relations and the United States*. New York: Columbia University Press, 2006.

Cotton, James, ed. *Korea Under Roh Tae-woo: Democratisation, Northern Policy, and Inter-Korean Relations*. Canberra: Allen & Unwin, 1993.

Foley, James A. *Korea's Divided Families: Fifty Years of Separation*. New York: Routledge, 2003.

Grinker, Roy. *Korea and Its Futures: Unification and the Unfinished War*. New York: St Martin's Press, 1998.

Harrison, Selig. *Korean Endgame: A Strategy for Reunification and US Disengagement*. Princeton: Princeton University Press, 2002.

Kim, Samuel. *The Two Koreas and the Great Powers*. Cambridge: Cambridge University Press, 2006.

Steinberg, David I., ed. *Korean Attitudes towards the United States: Changing Dynamics*. Armonk: M.E. Sharpe, 2005.

Web Sources (URLs of English versions)

South Korea–related sources
The English-language versions of South Korean websites usually contain less information than the Korean-language versions; however, these sites provide additional information on current Korean news and developments.

NEWSPAPERS

Chosun Ilbo	http://english.chosun.com/
Donga Ilbo	http://english.donga.com/
JoongAng Ilbo	http://joongangdaily.joins.com/
Hangyoreh	http://english.hani.co.kr/
Ohmynews	http://english.ohmynews.com/
Korea Focus	http://www.koreafocus.or.kr/html/main.asp

POLITICAL PARTIES
OOP   http://www.uparty.or.kr/g_english/index.html
GNP   http://www.hannara.or.kr/vhannara/english/

NGOS
CCEJ   http://www.ccej.or.kr/English
CUBS   http://www.cubs.or.kr/about/about_1.asp
KEFM   http://english.kfem.or.kr/
KTU   http://english.eduhope.net/about.htm
KWAU   http://www.women21.or.kr/news/W_English/default.asp
PNAN   http://www.pnan.org
PSPD   http://eng.peoplepower21.org

North Korean and North Korea–related sources

Websites run by North Korea, its detractors, and its sympathizers are not difficult to find on the Internet. In general, the quality of information on North Korea in Korean and Japanese is much better; but there is no shortage of English-language articles, data, and posturing that reflect the entire range of the political spectrum. Approaching most sources with a healthy scepticism would be advisable when reading anything related to North Korea. Authentic North Korean propaganda and goods are also available in stores in South Korea, China, and Japan, and on eBay. Below is a limited listing of sites that provide additional information (the first few are run by North Korea or by its supporters).

DPRK Official Webpage   http://www.korea-dpr.com/
Korean Central News
  Agency   http://www.kcna.co.jp/index-e.htm
People's Korea   http://www.korea-np.co.jp/sinboj/Default.htm
Naenara   http://www.kcckp.net/ja/
North Korea Times   http://www.northkoreatimes.com/
International Institute
  of Juche Idea   http://www.cnetta.ne.jp/juche/DEFAULTE.htm
CanKor   http://www.cankor.ca/
Daily NK   http://www.dailynk.com/english/
Asia Times   http://www.atimes.com/atimes/Korea.html
Nautilus Institute   http://www.nautilus.org/fora/index.html

Index

162; state evolution, 92;
Supreme People's Assembly,
113; –Thai trade, 150; tourists,
125, 161, 163; TVs and radios
police registered, 102;
unannounced missile launches,
152; –US relations, 114, 144-6,
160; USSR subsidy loss, 5
"Democratization Declaration",
ROK June 29 1987, 24
democratization ROK,
domestically fought for, 5, 54
demography, ROK, 5; multiethnic
trend, 58; changes, 35, 53, 90;
structure, 55
demonstrations 1987, 35
Deng Xiaoping, 106
Denmark, –Norway tie, 9
developmental state, 61
Diamond Mountains, DPRK, 176;
tourism, 161; Tours, 163
DiCaprio, Leonardo, 77
divide-and-rule, Japanese colonial
strategy, 16
divorce: high ROK rates, 87, 89
Dixie Chicks, 131
domestic films, comparative
market shares, 71
Domestic Group, DPRK, purged,
100
Donahue, Phil, 131

East Asia: financial crisis 1997, 65;
ROK culture fans, 71-2; satellite
TV stations, 75
Eastern Europe: ROK normalized
relations with, 36; voter
turnout, 52
economic nationalism, 30, 60, 63,
86
effective microorganisms (EM)
technology, 151
Egypt, ROK entertainments, 79-80
elections, 1948 separate, 20
elections, ROK presidential: 1987,
38; 1992, 38; 1997, 43; 2002,
39; Park Chung-Hee period, 29;

regional voting patterns, 40;
voter turnout, 50-2
elite(s), DPRK, 97, 109, 115, 141
elitism: defector experience, 167;
revolutionary, 106
energy shortage, DPRK, 137
Equal Wage Law, ROK 1987, 47
"ethnicity", 11
export-led development, 61

famine(s), DPRK, 5, 7, 126-8;
causes, 132-8; death estimates,
139; regional variations, 141
farmers' markets, DPRK, 132
Federation of Korean Trade
Unions (FKTU), corporatist, 63
Feuerbach, Ludwig, 92, 135
financial crisis, ROK 1997, 6, 64, 65
financial markets opening, OECD
demand, 66
Fincher, David, 81
Finland, –Sweden tie, 9
floods, DPRK, 7, 133
"Flunkeyism", 105
foreign brides, ROK, 89
Fujimoto Kenji, 94, 112, 121-2
Fukuoka, 73

GATT (General Agreement on
Tariffs and Trade), Uruguay
Round, 65
gender, defector experience
differences, 166
Germany, unification example,
168, 174
Gerschenkron, Alexander, 60
"GI babies", 84
Gini coefficients, 70; ROK rise in,
69
grain: DPRK shortages, 132, 136;
seed diversity lack, 135;
"super-corn" development, 151;
world price, 138-9
Grand National Party, ROK, 50
"guerrilla state" analysis, 96

Hamgyŏng provinces, DPRK, 139

204 | Index

Paekdusan mountain, 96, 109
Pak Chong-ch'ŏl, police killing of,
35
Pak Kum-Chŏl, 100
Pakistan: NPRK arms purchases
131; NPT non-signatory, 143;
nuclear program, 146; US
sanctions dissipation, 144
Panmunjom: see, Joint Security
Area
Park Chan-Wook (Pak Ch'an-Uk),
70; Cannes Festival success, 71
Park, Chung-Hee (Pak Chŏng-Hŭi),
27, 29, 32-3, 40, 53, 63, 65, 77,
84, 169; assassination attempts,
31, 100; assassination of, 29
coup of, 141, 158; development
state, 61; Japanese military
education, 60; State of
Emergency 1971, 30
Pearl S. Buck International, 82, 89
"people's committees", US
extinguished, 18-19
People's Solidarity for
Participatory Democracy, 47
Perry Report, 145
personality cult, DPRK, 95, 100;
1967 emergence, 98
Philippines, 6, 66; migrant labor,
85; "people's power" revolution
1986, 37; voter turnout, 52;
wives from, 89
plagiarism, TV, 76
plastic surgery, ROK, 6
Poland, "South Korean" faction,
25
political parties ROK, turnover of,
39
post-authoritarian states, NGO
proiliferation, 45
Potsdam Conference, 17
poverty, 130; ROK rates of, 70
prison camps, DPRK, 148
pro-democracy demonstrations
1987: see democracy movement
"Protect the System" Declaration
1988, 3ϛ

Puch'ŏn Fantastic Film Festival,
78
Pueblo, US–DPRK standoff, 158
Pusan, ROK, 21, 31, 50, 74, 84;
American Cultural Center, 156;
International Film Festival, 78
Pyongyang, DPRK, 1, 4, 158;
Academy of Juche Sciences,
108; electrical grid, 137;
Internet cafés, 151; Juche
Tower, 104; Ryukyŏng Hotel,
124; 2000 Summit, 6, 145, 161;
USSR army in, 18

Quebec, sovereignty issue, 10

"race", 11
Rajin-Sŏnbong Free Economic and
Trade Zone, 150
Reagan, Ronald, 37
Red Cross organizations, Korean,
158-9
Refuge PNAN (ROK NGO), 48
regional economic growth rates,
East Asia, 64
Reiner, Rob, 77
Republic of Korea (ROK) (South
Korea): broadband penetration
rate, 50; Chinese communities,
84; cinema films, 71, 75-6;
construction worker export, 85;
cultural export earnings, 72;
curfew imposed, 18; Defense
Academy, 129; development
explanations, 58; DPRK aid,
132; –DPRK per capita GNI
ratio, 154; DPRK policy, 53, 55,
see also, Sunshine Policy;
DPRK submarine incursion,
161; entertainment industry, 2,
58, 70, 72, 74, 78-80; ex-Soviet
bloc rapprochement, 107; film
production subsidies, 78;
financial crisis 1997, 57-8;
foreign-owned assets, 68;
foreign threat perceptions, 8;
global GDP standing, 6; grain